Courtesy

Keith and Jennifer met as undergraduates at the University of Reading in the early 1960s. In 2017 they celebrated their fifty-second wedding anniversary; just before that they were awarded Honorary Life Membership of both Surrey County Cricket Club and the Association of County Cricket Scorers in recognition of services to county and international scoring. Between them they have scored over 150 international cricket matches.

Their substantive careers were, in Keith's case, university administration at home and overseas, and in Jennifer's, archives management, the bulk of it in the Tate Gallery. Her professional expertise has been invaluable in sourcing information for Keith's series of books which have become a canon of Surrey biography, the last two of which she has been credited as co-author. Keith and Jennifer's books have been regular nominees for the Cricket Society/MCC Book of the Year award. Including books in joint authorship, Keith's current scorecard reads seven longlisted titles, three on the shortlist and one winner.

Also by Keith Booth:
Atherton's Progress: From Kensington Oval to Kennington Oval
Knowing the Score: The Past, Present and Future of Cricket Scoring
His Own Enemy: The Rise and Fall of Edward Pooley
The Father of Modern Sport: The Life and Times of Charles W Alcock
George Lohmann: Pioneer Professional
Ernest Hayes: Brass in the Golden Age
Walter Read: A Class Act
Tom Richardson: A Bowler Pure and Simple
Rebel with a Cause: The Life and Times of Jack Crawford

THE HAYWARDS

THE BIOGRAPHY OF A CRICKET DYNASTY

KEITH AND JENNIFER BOOTH

Chequered Flag PUBLISHING

First published in the UK by Chequered Flag Publishing 2018
PO Box 4669, Sheffield, S6 9ET
www.chequeredflagpublishing.co.uk

Copyright © Keith and Jennifer Booth 2018
The moral right of the authors has been asserted

A CIP record for this book is available from the British Library

Printed in the EU by Print Group Sp. z o.o.

ISBN 978-1-9997774-2-5

Image credits
Courtesy of Roger Mann Collection: pp.26, 102, 137, 244, 248, 307.
Mitcham Cricket Green Community & Heritage: p.10.

CONTENTS

Part Three: Tom

FOREWORD

by Alec Stewart OBE

It was at Surrey's Christmas lunch that Boothy asked me to write the foreword to his and Jennifer's book on the Hayward family. The venue was appropriately the Hundred Hundreds Bar at The Oval. A few metres away from where we were sitting was a list of Tom Hayward's 104 first-class centuries, alongside those of other Surrey luminaries, Sir Jack Hobbs, Andrew Sandham, John Edrich and Mark Ramprakash.

Sporting talent often runs in families, sometimes crossing several sports – football and tennis in the case of the Matthews, cricket and rugby in that of the Bothams, while for the Nevilles it was football and netball. How far this is the result of heredity or environment I will leave to the geneticists and psychologists – probably a bit of both, as some is doubtless passed on in the genes, but stimulated by meal-table talk of sport and days out at sporting events.

Cricket certainly has its share of cricketing families, beginning with the Graces, Hearnes and Lillywhites in the nineteenth century. Surrey has had a few. Boothy has already written about the Crawfords and Richardsons who generated several future first-class cricketers. Nearer our own time, it has been my pleasure to play alongside the Bicknell brothers and the Hollioakes, and at the present time to be Director of Cricket at a club with Tom and Sam Curran, sons of a distinguished father, on its books. Alan and Mark Butcher and Graham and Richard Clinton are fathers and sons who have opened the county's innings and of course I am proud to have followed my father Micky as club captain.

The Haywards are an outstanding example of a cricketing family who have made a major contribution to the development of the game. Tom's grandfather, father and uncle all played first-class cricket – or the equivalent at the time – the latter being one of the country's leading batsmen in the far off days when Cambridgeshire was a first-class county. Tom's three brothers were also talented club and minor counties cricketers and may well have made it in the first-class game if the business of earning a living had not got in the way. There was not as much money in the game in those days.

I have a bit of a connection with Tom Hayward. One of the many records he still holds is that of Surrey's highest individual innings against Yorkshire – 273 in a bore draw in 1899. Ninety-eight years later, I came within two of that, thanks in part to an unlikely last-wicket partnership with Joey Benjamin. That was my highest first-class score: Tom had one higher, 315 not out against Lancashire the previous season.

Statistical comparisons across the years are of limited use. Different pitches, different bowlers, different playing conditions and heavier bats see to that; but some of Tom's achievements are unlikely to be beaten, if only because there is not as much first-class cricket these days as the four-day version has to live alongside limited overs and the increasingly popular hit-and-giggle Twenty20 version of the game. Nevertheless Tom's hundred hundreds, thousand runs before the end of May, four centuries in a week and record at the time of 3,518 runs in a season stand out as beacons in a past age.

The history of the Hayward family is the history of English cricket in the nineteenth and early twentieth centuries. In Tom's grandfather's day it was virtually impossible to make a living from the game, then the advent of the touring elevens and county cricket advanced the professional game, albeit with the players at times dependent on the crumbs which fell from the tables of the gentlemen amateurs. If Tom Hayward had done nothing else for Surrey, the club would be in his debt for the introduction of fellow Cambridge man Jack

Hobbs. Tom spanned the nineteenth and twentieth centuries and was one of a number of cricketers like Hobbs, like George Lohmann, Bobby Abel and Tom Richardson, who were aware of their own talent and pulling power and who brought respectability to the game and made it possible to earn a living from it.

Nowadays, although the earnings from cricket do not begin to compare with those of golf, tennis or football, today's pros, thanks to better pay and sponsorship, are able to manage a pretty decent lifestyle with sponsored cars and accommodation in five-star hotels, compared with that of their predecessors. Many, if not most, live for the present and have little or no interest in the history of the game. But their debt to Tom Hayward, his predecessors and his contemporaries is greater than they realise.

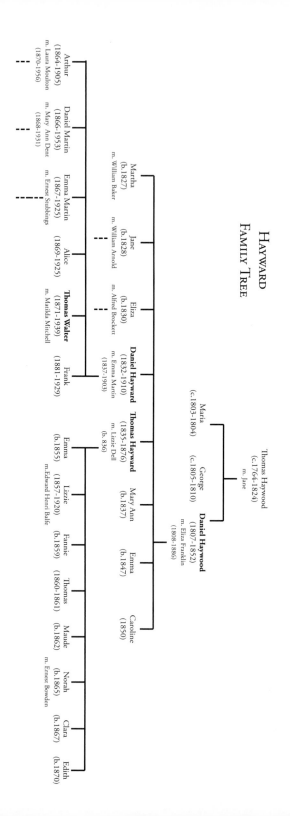

HAYWARD
FAMILY TREE

Thomas Haywood
(c.1764-1824)
m. Jane

Maria (c.1803-1804)

George (c.1805-1810)

Daniel Haywood (1807-1852)
m. Eliza Franklin (1808-1886)

Martha (b.1827)
m. William Baker

Jane (b.1828)
m. William Arnold

Eliza (b.1830)
m. Alfred Brockett

Daniel Hayward (1832-1910)
m. Emma Martin (1837-1903)

Thomas Hayward (1835-1876)
m. Lizzie Dell (b. 836)

Mary Ann (b.1837)

Emma (b.1847)

Caroline (1850)

Arthur (1864-1905)
m. Laura Moulton (1870-1956)

Daniel Martin (1866-1953)
m. Mary Ann Dent (1868-1931)

Emma Martin (1867-1925)
m. Ernest Stubbings

Alice (1869-1925)

Thomas Walter (1871-1939)
m. Matilda Mitchell

Frank (1881-1929)

Emma (b.1855)
m.Edward Henri Bailé

Lizzie (1857-1920)

Fannie (b.1859)

Thomas (1860-1861)

Maude (b.1862)
m. Ernest Bowden

Norah (b.1865)

Clara (b.1867)

Edith (b.1870)

PREFACE

A review of my biography of Tom Richardson, published under the banner of the Association of Cricket Statisticians' Lives in Cricket series on the centenary of his death in 2012, suggested that one of the omissions in my 'canon of Surrey biography' was Tom Hayward. There was no particular reason, except perhaps that, compared with other subjects Ted Pooley, Charles Alcock, George Lohmann, Walter Read, Richardson himself, Ernie Hayes, Jack Crawford and Younis Ahmed (a ghosted autobiography), all of whom in one way or another had interesting and colourful lives off the field as well as on it, the Hayward story seemed to contain little outside his cricketing career – albeit a brilliant and outstanding one. That, however, was far from being the case. While his achievements at the crease (a hundred centuries, a thousand runs before the end of May, record aggregate for a season, four centuries in a week) have been drooled over by statistically orientated anoraks both within Surrey and beyond, Hayward – while a consummate and committed professional – had a far from uninteresting life off the field. Moreover, his father, uncle and grandfather formed a pedigree of distinguished cricket professionals and his father in particular was a successful businessman and entrepreneur, rescuing the rather more unsuccessful ventures of Daniel the Elder, Tom's grandfather, and helping alleviate the financial difficulties of his sister-in-law after his brother's death.

The story of the Haywards is the epitome of nineteenth and early twentieth century professional cricket. When Daniel the Elder was

born, the country was in the midst of the Napoleonic Wars, bowling was underarm and the game was beginning to emerge from the
era when professional cricketers were few, unable to make a living
from the game and largely the playthings of the aristocracy. When
his grandson retired, the country was on the brink of the First World
War, when he died on the brink of the Second World War, and although the amateurs (and shamateurs) were dominant in Cardus's
Golden Age and the game was still run by aristocratic and autocratic
committees, bowling was almost entirely overarm and professional
cricket was established as a respectable career.

As in *Wuthering Heights* and indeed many families, forenames
are confusingly repeated from generation to generation and, for the
Haywards, Daniel and Thomas dominate. In most cases it is clear
from the context which Hayward is meant, but where there is potential for confusion, the dramatis personae have followed the Willie
Sugg practice and been distinguished from one another in the following way:

Generation 1: Daniel the Elder
Generation 2: Daniel the Younger, Thomas
Generation 3: Tom

Trans-generational statistical comparisons are to be treated with
caution, given different standards of pitches and quality of batting,
bowling and fielding. It is similar with trans-generational financial
comparisons because of inflation and market economics. There are
means of getting fairly close, however, and in general the purchasing
power of £1 in 1900 was about the equivalent of £100 in 2018. In
terms of pay, however, in cricket and elsewhere the increased negotiating power of organised labour means the factor is about four
times higher than that. After the players' strike of 1896, the fee for
playing in a Test match was increased from £10 to £20. In 2017
it was £15,000, almost twice as high as the £8,000 produced by a
straight extrapolation based on wage inflation. For those centrally
contracted for international cricket, to those fees can be added an

annual retainer of £750,000 or so. Kerry Packer, Sky Sports and the IPL have all had their impact. In the nineteenth and early twentieth centuries it was all very different and, while the occasional earnings of the top players participating in single wicket tournaments and matches for substantial prize money might begin to compare with the regular earnings of their current day counterparts, the majority struggled to stay much above the breadline.

Part One

DANIEL THE ELDER

(1807-1852)

1

SURREY ROOTS

The cover drive scorched the uneven turf and the batsmen turned to complete a second run as the labouring and overweight outfielder abandoned his cigar and strove to retrieve the ball. The small gathering of spectators on Mitcham's Cricket Green, the cradle of Surrey cricket (or one of them), stood and applauded to acknowledge a talented seventeen year old. What none of them knew was that eighty or so years later, their grandchildren and great-grandchildren would in greater numbers be similarly applauding – and some of them hero-worshipping – the grandson of this young man, who was to distinguish himself on the game's world stage.

Mitcham Cricket Club claims to be one of the oldest in the country. The date of its origin is contested and there is always likely to be debate about when a group of people playing cricket can be designated a club, but there was certainly activity on the Green well before the beginning of the nineteenth century. Mitcham itself, now part of the London Borough of Merton and absorbed into south London's suburban sprawl, was in pre-industrial days an agricultural community with a population of just over 4,000 specialising in the growing of lavender and various medicinal plants – a local bus terminus still being Lavender Fields. A contemporary report records, 'The soil is rich; about 250 acres are employed in the cultivation of lavender, wormwood, camomile, aniseed, rhubarb and other medicinal plants, but chiefly peppermint of which there are about 100 acres. Fifty years ago, only a few acres were employed in this way.'[1] It was part of the Agrarian Revolution and there was thus plenty of opportunity for gardeners, the occupation of the first of the Hayward quartet – and later, for 'gardener' read 'groundsman'.

Daniel Hayward was born on 21 August 1808 in Mitcham, so says that infallible source, Arthur Haygarth's *Scores and Biographies*. It is a date consistent with the earlier records of William Denison and repeated by later sources directly or indirectly based on those, notably the various Lillywhite publications, *Wisden* and, more recently, ESPNcricinfo, Cricket Archive and Google.[2] Except he wasn't. Although Mitcham is certainly correct, there is no entry for him in the Baptismal Register of the parish of St Peter and St Paul Mitcham for 1808. However, there is an entry for the baptism of 'Daniel Haywood, son of Thomas and Jane Haywood' on 18 October 1807.

No one can be baptised before they are born and, while it is conceivable but highly unlikely that there was another Daniel Hayward (or Haywood) born in Mitcham in the first decade of the nineteenth century, subsequent census entries and his death certificate point to a date of 1807. On the 1841 and 1851 Censuses, Daniel's age is recorded as respectively thirty-three and forty-three and, as the census took place in April, this is consistent with the earlier date. His mother was certainly called Jane: she was a witness at his wedding and lived with him in Cambridgeshire.[3]

Haygarth sent out forms for completion and it is likely that the family did not know the year of Daniel's birth. The date of birth of 21 August is probably correct as his sons would have known when his birthday was celebrated, but may have been less clear about the year. Nowadays genealogical evidence is freely available and people are more willing to admit to their true ages, but that was not always the case and there was a tendency in the nineteenth century and much of the twentieth for various reasons to be reticent about admitting one's age and to deduct – or occasionally add – a few years. Spelling of names in the nineteenth century could also be erratic and inconsistent and at the beginning of the century and in the 1841 Census the family name is recorded as 'Haywood'.

Daniel's father, Thomas (Daniel and Thomas seem to be the default names for every generation) was not born in Mitcham, but as he was a gardener probably moved there for employment. He died in 1824, aged sixty according to the burial register, which puts his birth in 1763 or 1764. Thomas's wife, Jane, Daniel's mother, was about the same age. She is seventy-eight years old on the 1841 Census, so born in 1762 or 1763.

The family are first mentioned in the parish registers when their three children are born; Maria was baptised on Christmas Day 1803, George on 2 June 1805 and, as already mentioned, Daniel on 18 October 1807. Jane was thus over forty when the children were born. There may have been earlier ones, born before the move to Mitcham, but with no knowledge of her maiden name or residence, it is difficult to extract any firm evidence.

Maria died as a baby and was buried on 25 March 1804. George followed her on 22 July 1810, the cause of death recorded by the vicar as 'killed by a carriage on the iron railway'. Therefore, in the probable absence of elder siblings (or half-siblings if Jane had an earlier marriage), Daniel, not yet three years old, was left an only child.

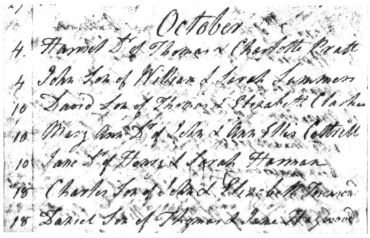

Baptism register for the parish of St Peter and St Paul in Mitcham, with Daniel's recorded on 18 October 1807.

He was seventeen when his father died and from that time seems to have taken responsibility for looking after his mother.

On 17 September 1826 Daniel married Eliza Franklin at St James, Piccadilly. Eliza was a Mitcham girl, baptised on 24 July 1808, so eighteen at the time, the daughter of John Franklin (born 1785), a gardener, and his wife, Mary. Marriages normally took place in the bride's parish, so it is likely that she was in service in central London. Witnesses were Jane Haywood, Daniel's mother, and a Mr Young, possibly Eliza's employer.

Eliza was at least three months pregnant on the wedding day since the first child of the marriage, Martha, was baptised in March 1827, six months afterwards. There were seven other children, about the norm for the period. Jane was baptised in Mitcham in 1828. Then, after the move to Cambridgeshire (of which more later), Eliza, Daniel, Thomas and Mary Ann were all baptised in Chatteris in 1830, 1832, 1835 and 1837 respectively. Finally, after a ten year gap (again, more about the reasons later), Emma and Caroline were baptised in the parish of St Paul, Cambridge in 1847 and 1851.

Daniel appears to have been playing cricket for Mitcham as early as 1825 at the age of seventeen, away to Brighton and a week later, the day after his eighteenth birthday (though most sources would say his seventeenth), in the return match on Mitcham Green, when he featured as wicketkeeper and opening batsman. Standing only 5 feet 6 inches, he gravitated naturally towards wicketkeeping, had one stumping and made 5 out of a total of 47. Scores were much lower in those days and, to put his innings in context, he was the fourth highest scorer.[4] More prolific innings lay ahead. The team included John and James Sherman, John Bowyer and Andrew Schabner, all of whom played for Surrey – or at least teams which called themselves Surrey, twenty years before the formal establishment of the county club in 1845.

In 1828, Daniel played against Kennington at Harry Hampton's Cricket Ground in Camberwell for 22 guineas a side.[5] Kennington scored 153 and 26 (including seven ducks!); Mitcham 115. Daniel had 10 and three stumpings; the Mitcham team included several well-known cricketers. The match was 'unfinished', but *Bell's Life* says 'it was decidedly the best match played in Surrey for the last seven years on both sides'.

Local historian Tom Higgs reports on the return match against the same opponents on Mitcham Green, prefacing his comments by mentioning the strength of Mitcham at the time:

> Mitcham had an especially strong side throughout the early part of the nineteenth century. In addition to Bowyer, Tom Sherman, William Caffyn and Thomas Sewell were playing regularly for Surrey; whilst Dan Hayward (born in the village in 1808 [sic]) was a celebrity in the Mitcham team long before he went to Cambridge.
>
> During the 1828 season Mitcham played Kennington on the Green and scored 110 runs in their first innings. The opposition replied with just 25 runs. In their second innings, the home side were bowled out for 38, leaving the visitors a target of 124 to win. Kennington proceeded to lose their first 5 wickets for 1 run and then 'gave up in despair'. It was in reporting this match that *Bell's Life* announced 'Mitcham were prepared to play any parish within 20 miles of London'.

The Ruff Stone on Mitcham Green commemorating outstanding cricketers from the area, including Daniel Hayward.

Daniel made 13 and 12, the top score in the second innings, and had two catches and two stumpings in the match. *Scores and Biographies* reports the second innings score as being 1 for six, rather than five, but, no matter: there was no doubt about the result

At the west corner of Mitcham Cricket Green stands the Ruff Memorial Stone which records the names of sixteen Mitcham cricketers. Among them is Daniel Hayward, of whom a publication giving more information about those players says *inter alia*:

> Daniel Hayward made 24 known appearances in first class matches as wicket keeper and middle order batsman. He played mainly for the Cambridge Town club but also represented the Marylebone Cricket Club, Surrey (3 times) and England, as well as the Players against Gentlemen and North of England against the South...
>
> Daniel Hayward's 2 sons and 4 grandsons all played first class cricket. His son Thomas played for Cambridgeshire and England, his grandson Tom Hayward played nearly 600 games as an opener for Surrey and 35 Test Matches for England.[6]

2

SETTING THE SCENE

It was not until 1894 that the game's ruling body, MCC, came up with a definition of what constituted first-class cricket – namely a contest of sufficient quality over three days between two teams of eleven players with provision for two innings each. The ICC was even slower out of the blocks and it was as recently as 1947 that the body overseeing international cricket adopted a similar definition for overseas domestic cricket. The County Championship had been established in 1890, so any matches in that competition were clearly first-class, as were the handful of Test matches played since what is generally considered to be the inaugural one in 1878.

Before that, however, the term first-class was used loosely along with 'great', 'important' and 'major' to distinguish those matches deemed to be of a higher standard. North v South and Gentlemen v Players obviously qualify, as do most MCC matches against stronger opposition, as well as the Varsity match (perversely it still does), but beyond that it is largely a question of subjective judgment. The Association of Cricket Statisticians and Historians have made an attempt at rationalisation, using as yardsticks the quality of the players, prize money, press coverage and spectator numbers.

Furthermore, the MCC definition was not retrospective and there is no agreement among statisticians and historians as to when first-class cricket actually started. Some would say it was with the legalisation of overarm bowling in 1864, others with the authorisation of roundarm bowling from 1828 (before that the Laws required that the hand be kept below the elbow) and some even earlier than that. In general, the major websites Cricket Archive and ESPNcricinfo have taken their cue from the ACS and decided that the inaugural first-class match was a Hampshire XI v an England XI on Broad Halfpenny Down in June 1772.

So to use the term first-class in relation to the time Daniel the Elder plied his trade in the 1830s and 1840s is an anachronism, but there is a consensus that inter-village and inter-town cricket was not first-class, while much of that played by Cambridge Town and its various incarnations (it was *de facto* the county side) generally was. Cricket Archive follows the lead of ACS in recognising its pseudo-first-class status and, although some matches against inferior opposition have been categorised as 'miscellaneous', refers to the team simply as the 'Cambridge Town Club' even for those years from 1844 to 1847 when it was formally constituted as 'Cambridge Town and County'. Representative matches were judged to be first-class, for example for the Players, the North and also the few matches Daniel played for his native county. Furthermore, Lord's being generally regarded as the Mecca of the game and an appearance there the criterion for inclusion in *Scores and Biographies*, matches played on that ground were generally regarded as being first-class although in some cases (for example Sixteen Gentlemen against Eleven Players) that judgment is at least questionable.

The bowling Dan faced and to which he kept wicket, and bowled on the few occasions when he did, would be largely roundarm. The Laws had been modified in 1828 and finally amended in 1835 to allow this new method, pioneered allegedly by John Willes, a Kent farmer who supposedly picked up the idea from his sister whose voluminous hooped skirts prevented her bowling underarm, although John Major maintains this was unlikely as such garments were not fashionable during the Napoleonic Wars. It is more likely that it was developed in the late eighteenth century to generate more bounce and pace to counteract what was perceived as the increasing domination of batsmen. Be that as it may, roundarm bowling was now largely superseding underarm.

The 1840s were a time of great social, industrial and political change. The repeal of the Corn Laws in 1846 and the consequent facilitating of free trade, the extension of the franchise, the penny post, the Industrial Revolution with its resulting migration from rural to urban environments, and the development of the railways all had their effect on national life. For cricket, particularly its professionals, it was the latter that was most significant, enabling the arrangement of fixtures hitherto undreamed of when a day's travelling by stage coach covered about five miles per hour. Journeys previously measured in days could now be undertaken in hours.

Gambling on matches had continued from the nineteenth century, pitches were largely unprepared, though twenty-two yards – the length of the agricultural chain – is one of the few aspects that has remained constant about the game. Protective equipment, when used at all, was basic. Tubular gloves were introduced in the 1820s in response to the new roundarm bowling and pads were rudimentary. There was also presumably some form of 'box' or abdominal protector, though nineteenth-century publications modestly say nothing about that. Wicketkeeping gauntlets appeared in 1850, too late for Daniel senior's career; bats were heavier (about four pounds) and unsprung.

Trousers had begun to replace the traditional eighteenth century breeches and tall 'beaver' hats became the norm. Shirts were no longer frilled and had high collars. Bow ties were usual, sometimes singlets were worn instead of shirts and the professionals often wore wide braces. Black shoes were worn, as were belts with metal clasps.

Professionalism was beginning to emerge from the feudalism of the previous century when professional cricketers were the playthings of their aristocratic overlords but, with rare exceptions, it was virtually impossible to make a living from the game until a form of organisation began to appear in 1846 in the shape of William Clarke's All-England Eleven, the progenitor of a number of similar touring sides.

Fixtures were arranged on a home and away basis, usually a week apart, and the numbers on each side could vary. Strengthening a side by the use of 'given men' was not unusual, but one area where it was possible to make money was in the very popular (for both players and spectators) single wicket matches where substantial prize money was often available and players were prepared to back their own ability.

Single wicket now seems as archaic as early nineteenth century costume, but it continued for a long time and its specific Laws were included in *Wisden* until just after the end of the Second World War. In the eighteenth century, this version of the game was more popular than that which over time was to become the more orthodox one and was a vehicle for gambling purposes, the resultant bed-fellow of match-fixing being not unknown. In their heyday, matches between the leading players drew huge attendances and, while they could be over fairly quickly, some were prolonged. With no time limits imposed, they could extend to a second or even a third or fourth day. The length of the pitch remained the traditional twenty-two yards but, as the name suggests, bowling was all from the same end and batsmen batted one at a time without partners. Laws differed from competition to competition and from place to place, but matches were usually one versus one, although sometimes doubles were played and there were other variations, including not always the same number of players on each side. In many ways it was the very antithesis of the limited overs and Twenty20 versions which were to characterise the game two centuries later. There were not many wickets to lose (typically no more than two) so they were zealously guarded and runs – which could be scored only in front of the wicket – were accumulated not slogged. Non-bowling fielders were allowed, but the concept of overs did not apply; and it was quite possible and not unusual for one of the participants to do all the bowling. In one-v-one matches, of course, there was no alternative.

3

MINOR MATCHES

Between 1828 and 1830, Daniel moved with his wife, two daughters and widowed mother to Cambridgeshire to take a position as gardener to Mr Thomas Skeels Fryer and to play in Fryer's cricket team at Chatteris. The move seems a strange one but may be explained by family connections. Thomas and Sarah Franklin, probably relations of Dan's wife, had raised a family in Chatteris in the early years of the nineteenth century. By 1841 they had returned to Mitcham where Thomas kept an alehouse. Living with them and presumably employed by them was Martha, Daniel's eldest child, then aged fifteen. In 1847, Martha married William Baker, who was also related to the Franklins. Thomas and Sarah had lived in Chatteris for several years and would have known that Mr Fryer, an influential local figure – brewer, magistrate and High Sheriff of Cambridgeshire and Huntingdonshire – could provide employment as a gardener, especially one who was a talented young cricketer. Recruited simultaneously were Robert Glasscock and Francis Fenner, promising cricketers both, the name of the latter living on in the name of the Cambridge University cricket ground.

Chatteris is a small market town with a current population of about 10,000 lying in the Fens in North Cambridgeshire, the lowest part of the United Kingdom. Its origins pre-date Domesday Book. In AD 679 Hunna, personal chaplain to Etheldreda, retired to live at Honey Hill east of Chatteris, but there is architectural evidence of an earlier Stone Age settlement. Today it serves as a dormitory town for

Cambridge, Huntingdon and Peterborough but, in the early nineteenth century before the advent of the railway and with limited road access, it remained isolated and could at times be reached only by water. So at the time Daniel and his family lived here it was a remote area, at times cut off even from the county town of Cambridge. He did not stay very long.

When Daniel arrived in Cambridgeshire, the county's cricketing fortunes were at a crossroads. There are reports of Oliver Cromwell having played the game there two hundred years earlier when he was a student at the university, a time when cabbages were being grown on Parker's Piece – a short distance away from what is now Fenner's – which subsequently became a focal point for much town, county and university cricket.

Willie Sugg identifies three strands of Cambridgeshire cricket: in Cambridge town, in the university and, geographically separated and isolated by fenland, in the north of the county. At times they competed, at others they co-operated.

In the early nineteenth century there had been a Cambridge Club, but on its demise the emphasis had been on clubs based on public houses which were eventually to merge into the Cambridge Town Club. In the north of the county, out in the Fens and separated from Cambridge, Wisbech was a significant club. March and Chatteris, in the case of the latter mainly due to the patronage of Fryer, were becoming so too. The Town Club was *de facto* a county side, particularly when it played MCC at Lord's and recruited players from outside Cambridge, notably Dan Hayward of Chatteris. Thanks to Thomas Fryer's influence, the return match in 1832 was played not at the club's usual venue of Parker's Piece, but at Chatteris. Alongside all this ran the University Cricket Club, dating from 1817 and enjoying the equivalent of first-class status from that date.

The Town Club metamorphosed into Cambridge Town and County Club and having played very little for Chatteris, it was here that Daniel, quickly attracted by and adapting to the higher standard, played the bulk of his cricket. The Town and County Club folded in 1848 but by that time the career of 'Little Dan' (as he came to be known due to his small stature) was virtually over.

Chatteris was a club with confidence in its own ability, though clearly with a more parochial attitude, eschewing 'ringers' and 'given men' and expecting opponents to follow the same practice: 'The Chatteris Club are ready to play a match, home and away, with any club within 20 miles of them. As the Chatteris players are all resident inhabitants of the parish, they will expect those they play against to be inhabitants of and residing in the parish that accepts this proposal.'[7] Perhaps strategically, they omitted to mention that their own ringers (Fenner, Glasscock and Hayward) were resident in the town.

The development of cricket in Cambridgeshire cannot be separated from that in the university. Town-gown relationships are traditionally variable. The townsfolk, while welcoming the employment and commercial opportunities provided by the institution, resented the overbearing attitude and sense of entitlement of its students. Nevertheless, the annual early season fixture, Cambridge Town Cricket Club v Undergraduates of Cambridge – or Town v Gown, as it was popularly known – dated from 1817 and did much to bring the two communities together.[8]

In one of his earliest matches in his new county, at Swaffham in August 1830, playing for the Hoop Club (though *Scores and Biographies* says Cambridge Town), Dan scored 17 and 10, batting at number three, and took two wickets as a bowler. He turned out for Chatteris when able to do so, usually having a major influence on the result, as against Downham in 1835:

> On Wednesday and Thursday a match was played between the Downham and Chatteris Clubs at Downham. The following was the result of the game.
>
> Downham first innings 81 second ditto 59. Chatteris first innings 261.
>
> The batting of Messrs Hayward and West was very much admired, particularly Hayward, who got upwards of 100 runs without giving a chance.[9]

In the 1840s, having moved to St Ives for business purposes, Daniel turned out for the local team on occasions where the social nature of the event was at least as significant as the cricket.

> St Ives and March. The return match between the above clubs was played at St Ives on Wednesday week, and the weather being delightful, a goodly number of the 'right sort' assembled to witness the contest. Among other patrons of the noble game, we noticed J Linton, Esq of Hemingford, who, as on previous occasions, kindly lent his marquee for the accommodation of the fair sex.[10]

Hayward opened the batting and top-scored with 23 in an innings of 74.

He continued to appear for St Ives, still in the company of the 'right sort', including on at least one occasion the Earl of Sandwich who, in a large marquee 'profusely decorated with evergreens and flowers … presided over as goodly a number of the right loyal sort as ever assembled within the precincts of a cricket tent, between 70 and 80 sitting down to do justice to the tempting viandes.'[11]

Hayward had three wickets in each innings and, batting at number five, scored 13, the top score in the completed innings of 69. The result was probably secondary to the occasion, but for the record St Ives won, thanks in part, said the local press, to some superior wicketkeeping and long-stopping.

Dan's connection with his birthplace was not entirely severed, for he played for Mitcham against Gravesend in 1838 and the following year in the home and return matches against Town Malling.[12] His main cricket, however, was played at a higher level and his talent was such that he made a seamless transition from the kind of inter-town and inter-village cricket played by Chatteris, St Ives and Mitcham to the more significant matches in Cambridge Town's (at this stage fairly sparse) fixtures. These included a match against MCC at Lord's, his first appearance on that ground, in 1832, and later for the North (against the South) and Town and Gown of Cambridge as well as a number of single wicket matches.

Nonetheless, the dividing line between major and minor matches was not clearly defined, and by no means guilty of 'scorning the base degrees by which he did ascend', Daniel played for Cambridge Town throughout the 1840s in their less significant matches against Norfolk and Suffolk (usually beaten quite heavily, despite their propensity to adopt county titles) as well as town sides with which they had fairly regular fixtures such as Audley End, the Auberies at Bulmer, Bishop's Stortford and Bury St Edmunds. They also ventured further afield with travel facilitated by the railways, to the Lillywhites' club, Gravesend. The latter matches were usually fairly close and were often decided by narrow margins. There were useful performances on both sides, and alongside those some fairly hollow victories by an innings and plenty, for example in 1844 when Suffolk were bowled out for 28 and 63, or the following season, Norfolk for 22 and 24 and again for 64 and 44 in 1846. Bowling figures were rarely recorded at the time and catches and stumpings were not often credited to the bowlers, but when there were fewer bowling changes a number of five-fors at a cheap rate were taken by leading Cambridge bowlers, Francis Fenner, Thomas Snow and Charles Arnold. These matches kept the eye in and were excellent preparation for the more important encounters which enabled the Town and County Club to establish a name for itself and demonstrate that it was not punching above its weight when it took on the country's leading teams.

They won more than they lost, in both major and minor matches, but in August 1846, on Parker's Piece against the Auberies, they experienced 'the soundest "drubbing" we have yet to chronicle against the Cambridge Club'. However, 'Hayward stumped Honeywood very neatly' and 'Hayward added 24 by very excellent play'. He top-scored with 24 in an innings of 100.[13] It was a 'drubbing' only to the extent that the Town conceded when heading towards a probable innings defeat – 100 and 47 for four against 212. It did not begin to compare with the Nottingham results of 1834 (see next chapter) but was the worst in any of the 'minor' matches in which Dan played.

Towards the end of his playing days, he appeared for Huntingdonshire, as did a number of the Cambridge regulars, in a twelve-a-side match against the Cambridge Long Vacation Club. In 1848 on the new ground of Fenner's, his own team played against Fenner's team and later he played in the Cambridge Town v Cambridgeshire match. It was past meeting future and a not uninteresting encounter:

> On Wednesday last the dull monotony of a long vacation was somewhat relieved by a very excellent match, on Fenner's new ground, between eleven of the county of Cambridge, and eleven of the town. The weather was comparatively fine and the ground in good order, and it was extremely gratifying to find there was so much cricketing talent in the county as to produce a considerably better contest than the most sanguine could have anticipated. Hayward made his bow to Fenner and together they kept the game alive until 'Little Dan' was caught by Woodward.[14]

The Town and County folded that year, although a number of subsequent fixtures are attributed to a Town club.

A press report on the end-of-season Gravesend match on Parker's Piece demonstrates that there is nothing new in the conflict between the game and commercialism. A brief report on Dan's even briefer innings is followed by a few sardonic comments.

> [Hayward] is generally a careful old soul, and a great favourite as a batsman, but ill luck attended his first ball, he unfortunately depositing it for safety in the hands of Adams.
>
> The parties then went to refreshment, there being an interregnum of two hours, a most unnecessary long and tiresome period, and for which there could be no earthly reason, except the fear of giving offence to the booth proprietors, who like, for certain reasons, to see a game prolonged, especially when they are full of thirsty customers.[15]

4

MAJOR MATCHES

On his Lord's debut in 1832 – Marylebone with Lillywhite v Cambridge Town Club with Pilch and Caldecourt – and undeterred by such distinguished company, Dan kept wicket, had one stumping in the second innings and scored 24 and 22 in a match which the visitors to the metropolis from the country won by six wickets.

MCC and Cambridge Town, again supplemented by Pilch and Caldecourt, met in the return match at Chatteris in August, which the Town also won, this time by an innings and six runs. The choice of the venue was doubtless influenced by Thomas Fryer. It was the only 'first-class' match ever played on the ground.[16] By this time Daniel was well established on the national scene and over the next few seasons he played a number of matches at Lord's for various teams: Eleven Players against Sixteen Gentlemen, England against Kent and Sussex, the North against the South matches. In 1834 there was a new fixture, home and away against Nottingham, firstly on Parker's Piece and then on the new Forest Ground. It was in the middle of a phase where he failed to reach double figures in six consecutive 'first-class' matches, although in Nottingham he was joint top-scorer with 8 in a total of 29 all out in a match eventually lost by an innings and 114 runs. In the match in Cambridge the previous month, the team had been bowled out for even fewer, 23, and lost by 152 runs, but Dan had shown his versatility by bowling in the first innings and keeping wicket in the second. In 1838 he appeared again in the MCC v Cambridge Town match.

Of the significance and quality of the North v South fixtures, neither local nor national press had any doubt. Of the match in 1836 the *Brighton Gazette* reported, 'This match, which excited more than ordinary interest on account of the concentration of two-and-twenty of the most skilful players perhaps in the world, came off on Monday and Tuesday at Lord's and was decided in favour of the North.'[17] *Bell's Life* recorded: 'The great match between the North and the South players occupied Monday and Tuesday at Lord's. Clarke was caught out, after making a four hit, and Good and Hayward were still more unfortunate, for they were caught by Taylor and Milliard without having made a run.' In the second innings, Hayward had 'his stumps lowered by Mr Mynn with a score of three, which were got by one hit'.[18]

Earlier that year Dan had made what Cricket Archive has described as a debut for England at Lord's in a match against Kent and Sussex, but made only 1 and 3. His next 'first-class' match was not until two years later in July 1838 when the Town lost by an innings to MCC at Lord's, but his second innings knock of 17 ended a run of eleven consecutive single figure scores during which he had an aggregate of 29 runs. In the following year, 1839, also at Lord's, he was able to exact revenge of a kind, though this time playing for Surrey when he made 47 and was part of a team which dismissed the hosts in the second innings for 15 to win by an innings and 87 runs.[19]

Later, in 1841, Dan played for MCC as a 'given man' against the Undergraduates of Cambridge, which may have led Haygarth to mention that he was engaged on the Lord's groundstaff. It seems, however, to have been a one-off engagement and the MCC Archivist can trace no record of a regular contract.

Shortly afterwards Dan was selected to play for MCC v The North at Lord's. Roundarm bowling had been formally legalised half a dozen years before and now some bowlers tried to push their luck even further with an early attempt at overarm bowling.

Cricket Archive reports that, '*Bell's Life* describes The North as the Five Counties (as for the 1840 match). Several players were no-balled during the match, the umpires having received strict instructions to put the 10th law into full force when occasion should require it so that in no case was the bowler permitted to raise his hand above his shoulder in the delivery of the ball.'

Although his principal and first claim club was Cambridge Town, any contract was informal and not tightly drawn and the team played only one or two matches a season, so Daniel was free to ply his trade elsewhere and did so. The Cambridge Town Club was to all intents and purposes the Cambridgeshire county side, it was formalised as such in 1844 and apart from Gentlemen v Players and North v South was the highest standard of cricket available at the time. International cricket was still in the future and first-class cricket had yet to be defined, the nearest attempt at classification being 'great matches'. Bowling was still partly underarm, though roundarm had been finally legalised in 1835, and the art and science of pitch preparation was in its infancy.

After 1841 there is a three-year gap in Dan's playing career and in his fathering of children. The mystery of his whereabouts is solved by a description of his movements in a later insolvency case, from which it is learned that he was unemployed in Bedford, then living in Newmarket where he worked as a cricket instructor and journeyman gardener. In the spring of 1843 he had moved to 14 Covent Garden off Mill Road in Cambridge, a small terraced house, now replaced by Cambridge Econometrics. From 1844 he continued to play regularly, principally for Cambridge Town, their home matches on Parker's Piece, their away matches anywhere within reasonable travelling distance, now extended by the advent of the railways.

Dan also turned out in 1845 for a team designated 'England' against Fourteen of Nottinghamshire (though Cricket Archive has only thirteen) at Trent Bridge for £200 a side, and for MCC against the North. The England side comprised some of the leading names of the day. It was: N Felix Esq, Pilch, Dorrinton, Hillyer (Kent), Box, Dean, Picknell (Sussex), Cornwell (Cambs), Sewell, Martingell, Hayward (Surrey).

It is interesting to note that Hayward, despite being resident in Cambridgeshire for fifteen years, is categorised under Surrey, maybe because Cambridgeshire was more recently established and Surrey had a distinguished pedigree. He had already played for a Surrey club and against MCC for a team calling itself Surrey before the official establishment of the county club.

The 1846 Town v Gown match had a bizarre finish:

> Boudier, joint captain in 1843, played for the undergraduates, although he had taken his degree some time ago. At the end of the university second innings it was so dark that some of the players had left the ground, and so play continued the following afternoon with 7 runs required to win.

Although major matches were generally scheduled for three days, the lower scores which prevailed at the time meant that most were finished within two. Consequently 'fill up' or single wicket matches were on occasion played on what would have been the third day, but were usually neither recorded nor reported.

Later that year, in September, the Town and County Club (as it had now become) scraped home against the Gentlemen of England, with Alfred Mynn, Fuller Pilch and Dean, by one wicket. 75 and 90 for nine played 103 and 59, Israel Haggis (and more of him later) was left at the crease at number eleven with 1 not out.

The 1847 season was an eventful one. It began with a rare defeat in the Town v Gown encounter. Dan made his highest first-class score of 53, but Charles Arnold's running out of the backing-up University opening batsman, the evergreen George Boudier, can have done little to improve community relations.

Dan then made a debut for Surrey, now established as a county club, and participated in the first of only six ties in the club's history. The last three Kent wickets fell with the scores level. He also played in the return match at Aylesford, but those were his only two matches – his life, interests and legal and financial problems now lay in Cambridge.

Sometimes playing on Parker's Piece gave the Town side a clear advantage and certainly contributed to an outstanding result over MCC in 1847. The Cambridge Club had an impressive victory in

Detail from an 1851 painting by Felix showing Daniel on the left. It is the only known image of him.

which Hayward played his part, albeit in less than ideal conditions. The local press reported as follows:

Marylebone Club and Ground v Cambridge Club. The return match between these celebrated clubs commenced on Parker's Piece on Monday last, and from the general success of the Marylebone Club during the present season excited more than ordinary interest. The weather, which, for some weeks, had been all that man could desire very suddenly and with a wantonness peculiarly characteristic of our country, put on one of those threatening looks which tends so much to disturb the anticipations of pleasure seekers, whose hopes must ever hang upon sun and cloud. At a early hour on Monday morning the rain began to fall in a perfect deluge, and continued with a little less severity up to eleven o'clock at which time although there was a temporary lull, there appeared but little prospect of play. The ground was quite saturated at twelve o'clock – the time arranged for pitching wickets – but the absorbent nature of Parker's Piece being known to the Cambridge party it was proposed that, weather permitting, the game should commence at three o'clock and continue till seven o'clock, an arrangement which gave general satisfaction and enabled both sides to take a meal and coolly prepare for the toil of conflict.

Ringwood and Hayward were first placed at the wickets to the bowling of Hillyer and Dean; the bowling was good, but we thought we could observe an exchange of discouraging looks as the bowlers became aware of the sluggishness of the turf and the severe work which was evidently awaiting them. Ringwood played cautiously while Hayward imparted confidence by his neat and effective hitting: the pair scoring rather rapidly, although singles are more than usually predominant in the scores of both. At last, after a well-got innings of 23 runs Hayward was caught by Mr C Hoare off Dean.

The Marylebone were completely beaten by the general excellence of the play on the part of Cambridge, for never within our memory have we seen more cricketing talent displayed throughout every part of the game than combined in this match to distinguish it from its predecessors in all that constitutes cricket.

Cambridge 222. Marylebone 81 and 107.[20]

It was in this match that 'a great novelty presented itself to our notice; instead of the usual protection on the hand, a glove, Mr Ponsonby had adopted a basket.'[21]

By 1848, however, coincident with the opening of Fenner's new ground and ultimately occasioned by it, the Town and County Club ended its short life:

Town and County Club. A special general meeting took place at the Lion hotel on Thursday evening last for the purpose of considering the present peculiar position of the club.

One general feeling pervaded the meeting, namely regret that cricket in Cambridge this season had been so deplorably stagnant and that Parker's Piece, a spot ultimately associated with the earliest inhabitants, should have been so signally deserted.[22]

Daniel was now past his fortieth birthday and had problems off the pitch. In 1848 he played for the Cambridge Townsmen against the University and in 1849 for a combined University-Town side against the touring All-England Eleven in a match (unfortunately rain-affected) for Fenner's benefit. But the curtain was beginning to drop and in May 1851, Dan played the last of his couple of dozen 'first-class' matches, turning out one last time for a Cambridge Town side, captained by Ducky Diver, against the University at Fenner's. He failed to score, as did Francis Fenner and a couple more, but the team went on to win by six wickets, having totalled 119 and dismissed the students for 57 and 85. A little over twelve months later he would be in his grave.

Dan's final match brought to an end a career which had spanned two decades and brought him 420 runs with just one half century at 11.05, modest even at a time when batting averages were much lower. He also had nine catches, nine stumpings and five wickets at an unknown cost (it was unusual for bowling figures to feature at the time). Seventy years on, the numbers of his grandson were to be much greater.

5

SINGLE WICKET

In between his appearances for various teams, 'Little Dan' was prepared to back his own ability as a single wicket player. In 1832 He responded to a challenge in *Bell's Life*: 'Sir – A challenge having appeared in your paper, stating that Mr J Adams of Saffron Walden was prepared to make a match with any player in the county of Cambridge for £10 home and away, with a fieldsman, I beg leave to reply that I am ready to meet him on the terms mentioned. Yours etc. D Hayward, Chatteris, Cambridgeshire.'[23]

Consequently the two protagonists met, first at Chatteris in June, then at Saffron Walden the following month.

On Tuesday last the match between Mr J Adams of Saffron Walden and Mr D Hayward of Chatteris was played at the latter place, and terminated as follows: Hayward first innings 52. Adams 1st innings 0 2nd ditto 12 total 12.[24]

The return match of cricket between Hayward and Adams was played here (Saffron Walden) on Tuesday last. It had excited considerable interest by their both being clever batsmen. Adams had challenged the County of Cambridge for a single wicket man. The game came off as follows: Hayward 1st innings 16 second ditto 12. Adams 1st innings 20 second ditto 1.[25]

Another newspaper added that Adams was bowled by a ball which pitched wide but unexpectedly broke.[26] £10 was not to be sniffed at. It was about as much as the better ground bowlers could earn in a month, and more than sixty years later, the fee for playing in a Test match was no higher.

In 1848, Fenner's new ground (the present one) was opened. Dan played for the Town against the Undergraduates in May and in the following month in a two-a-side single wicket match to which his partner, Thomas Barker, made little contribution and they lost by a large margin to 'the two young ones', Claude Pell and John Walker. With a detail of scoring unusual at the time, the scores were recorded as follows.

	Balls	Hits	Runs	Balls	Hits	Runs
Barker	3	2	b Pell 0	3	2	b Walker 0
Hayward	10	9	b Walker 2	40	25	b Walker 10
			2			**10**
Pell	150	100	b ? 30			
Walker	60	45	b Hayward 15			
			45			

Pell and Walker won by an innings and 33 runs. There was no return match.[27]

In 1849, Dan played against the President of the Club, Frank Bavin: 'After the game a capital single wicket match was played between F Bavin Esq and Hayward the pet of the Cambridge Club. After a most interesting display of first-rate skills, victory crowned the efforts of the worthy President having obtained 27 runs and Hayward 23.'[28]

Although Daniel clearly had some success on the field he was unable to make a living out of being a professional cricketer and cricket instructor. At the time professional cricket was less well organised and certainly less secure than it was to become later in the century when the touring England elevens and, later, the county clubs were making their mark on the scene. The superstars of the time like Alfred Mynn, a fast bowler who played regularly but as an amateur, and Fuller Pilch, the outstanding batsman of the day who was always in demand and persuaded to move from Norfolk to Kent for

£100 a year, were probably able to make ends meet, but they were the exceptions.[29] Sir John Major, using as his source F Mandle's *The Professional Cricketer in England in the Nineteenth Century*, lists the backgrounds of professional cricketers. Almost all have secondary – or in most cases, primary – occupations to supplement their obviously insufficient incomes from the game. Of seventy-one studied, twenty-two were craftsmen in light industry, seventeen trade workers and shopkeepers, fourteen agricultural workers, fourteen clothing and textile workers, one clerk, one schoolmaster, one college servant and one coachman. Occupations may vary, but there can be no argument as to which of Disraeli's two nations they belonged.

Sir John goes on: 'None of these jobs offered high income or status. These men were in the terminology of the day, "working class", though many had artisan skills that lifted them socially above mere labourers. When their cricketing days were over, only a small minority returned to their trade. Uneasy economic conditions offered them few other jobs. The more successful became publicans, but others found employment at clubs or universities as coaches or groundsmen. Yet others coached boys at preparatory or public schools. But many ex-cricketers found life hard, and some died in poverty. Very few enjoyed ongoing reward for their cricketing skills: a ground-staff bowler at Lord's or The Oval earned only thirty to fifty shillings a week.'[30]

Denison paints a similar picture but with individual examples rather than statistical orientation. Of Daniel he says: 'Was born at Mitcham, in Surrey, on the 25th of August 1808 and is consequently in his 38th year [should be 21 August 1807 and 39th]. Hayward is a gardener, and in former years was a "young-un" in the celebrated "Mitcham Eleven" but having become a resident of Cambridge, joined the "team" of that distinguished club (the Town and County Club) – in the season of 1843, and quickly took his position as one of its "stars". He is an extremely showy hitter and an excellent "fast" field.'

Since leaving Mitcham, Dan had clearly developed skills beyond opening the batting and keeping wicket, though in financial terms life was a struggle.

6

OFF THE FIELD

Initially, Daniel had his day job as gardener to Mr Fryer which would have brought him a regular if not spectacular income, but by 1838 he had abandoned that to try his hand at a different occupation and become the licensee of the Three Tuns public house (still there but now called the Nelson's Head) on Merryland in St Ives in the adjacent county of Huntingdonshire. It is a pleasant building with two large rooms and a garden sloping down to the Great Ouse. Despite the location of the premises, being adjacent to the cattle market which brought local (and presumably thirsty) farmers into the town, the venture was not a success, possibly because there were fifty-four other competing hostelries in the town. It also brought him into contact with some of the rowdier members of society. After the relative tranquillity of gardening, it must have been quite a culture shock when two of his customers were convicted of criminal charges. Under 'Commitments to Huntingdon County Gaol', local newspapers reported: 'John Chambers and Thomas Osborne, convicted of having wilfully and maliciously broken four glasses and a pewter mug, the property of Daniel Hayward of St Ives, victualler, and also of having created a disturbance in the house of the said D Hayward.'[31] The miscreants – clearly not of the 'right sort' – were given the option of two months' hard labour or of paying £1 15s 1d.

A later case brought Dan into contact with his former employer, Thomas Fryer, though this time in the latter's capacity as a local magistrate. He was on the bench at St Ives Petty Sessions when Daniel appeared as a witness in a case of assault brought against Israel Haggis, a fellow professional cricketer and one of many trying to make ends meet. It turned out, however, that Haggis was the victim rather than the perpetrator of the assault:

> Ann Holmes charged Israel Haggis of Cambridge with having assaulted her at the Cherry Tree public house at Fletton. Daniel Hayward deposed that Mrs Haggis and Holmes went into the public room at the Cherry Tree, abused him and demanded money of him; he left and went to a private room where they followed him; they had abused Haggis at his booth, and both were very drunk. Two other witnesses corroborated this statement.[32]

Israel Haggis was a character as colourful as his name and the Fletton incident was just one of several. A playing colleague of Dan, he was a regular in the Town side, though his eagerness as a batsman meant few high scores and a vulnerability to run outs. Off the field he was one of Dan's drinking mates and a licensed victualler himself, landlord first of the Six Bells in Mill Road, then the New Inn on Parker's Piece. Like the bulk of his contemporaries, unable to make a living from cricket alone, he took earning opportunities as they arose. Haggis found employment in the University as 'manager of St John's College Cricket Club' and ran a dance band and booth at local fairs and events.

He had a harpy of a wife, Sarah, from whom he eventually separated. He met a sad and lonely end, bringing a salmon from London in contaminated water and contracting cholera as a result of eating it. Fearing contamination, no one ventured to go near him and he died after two days, alone in a tent. Sarah and his relatives engaged in an unseemly struggle over his possessions.[33]

The following year, Daniel was involved more personally in a legal case at the Cambridge County Court as he tried to deflect his creditors with a Petition for Protection in the case of his insolvency. It was one of five cases taken simultaneously and fell on a legal technicality. The barrister for the creditors argued successfully that the relevant Act required the annexed affidavit to the Petition to be sworn before a Master Extraordinary of the Court of Chancery and it had in fact been sworn before a Commissioner of Queen's Bench. Although the barrister for the Petitioners argued that it had been sworn before a Mr Prior who was a Master Extraordinary as well as a Commissioner and that the description of Commissioner was in error, the judge upheld the objection and the Petition failed.[34] On a resubmission in January, however, the legal technicalities were satisfied and Dan was able to benefit from the legal shelter of insolvency and protection from his creditors. His debts were almost £150, reduced to £20, but Hayward maintained that he was unable to meet the debt, even at £1 per month and the case was adjourned *sine die*.

Legal niceties aside, the court papers provide an enlightening insight into Daniel's erratic and itinerant lifestyle since leaving St Ives. In the summer of 1842 he was unemployed and living in Bedford, but presumably looking for work, then in the autumn of that year, living in Newmarket as a cricket instructor and journeyman gardener. For ten years he fathered no children. Presumably he was too busy looking for work or had left his wife and family in Cambridge. Significant in his later years was his association with the best known of his contemporaries, Francis Fenner, captain, secretary and leading all-rounder of the Town and County Club. They had met in Chatteris, the hometown of Fenner's wife, Mary, where both had featured in Thomas Fryer's supplemented team. By 1833, however, Fenner was back in Cambridge and instrumental in amalgamating pub sides into the Town team and later metamorphosing that team into the Town and County Club, equipped to challenge for county status. He was a tobacconist by trade (smoking during play was not at all uncommon) but his shop also sold cricket equipment as well as pipes, cigars and tobacco. It is likely, however, that Dan's gardening and groundsmanship skills were of use to Fenner in supplementing his entrepreneurship and administrative ability and establishing what was to become his lasting memorial, the University cricket ground:

A private ground situated at the back of the Town Gaol has been engaged by Mr Fenner, and during the whole winter men have been employed levelling and re-laying to the extent of 6½ acres. The ground is
now completed, and promises to be one of the best private grounds in
the country. The University club have arranged to play all their matches there, and the advantage of a well-conducted private ground most
people, we think, will be ready to appreciate.[35]

The Town and County Club declined an offer to use the ground
for £21 a year, preferring to stay on Parker's Piece, putting 'the wel-
fare and enjoyment of many hundreds who cannot afford to pay
ahead of the amusement and comfort of the few subscribers'.[36] It
was elitism v popularism in the raw. The University refused to play
the Town v Gown match on the now second-rate Parker's Piece and
went on to achieve first-class status while the Town and County
Club imploded. Cambridgeshire County Cricket Club was established in 1858, so to an extent the fortunes of Cambridgeshire cricket ran parallel to and were in part influenced by the Hayward family.

The family had moved to Covent Garden, off Mill Road, Cambridge in spring 1843 where Daniel senior continued as a cricket
instructor. The 1851 Census describes him as a gardener, though
when he died of what was then called consumption (now known as
tuberculosis) the following year the press refers to him as 'the well-
known cricketer'.[37] He was certainly that, but alas not well-known
for success in his business ventures. The next two generations would
turn things round, both for the family (or part of it) and Cambridgeshire cricket.

Part Two

DANIEL THE YOUNGER
AND THOMAS

(1832-1910 & 1835-1876)

7

THE FAMILY AFTER 1852

When Daniel passed on, leaving a widow and eight children, he handed the torch to the next generation but with very little to light it. Martha, now married, was back in Mitcham where she worked in the alehouse belonging to her mother's family. Jane was in service, living close to the family in St Andrew's Hill, Cambridge as a domestic servant in the household of an elderly lady, Sarah Attwood. In 1854 she married William Arnold, a mail cart contractor working for the Post Office. By 1861 they had three daughters. Eliza was also in service with an accountant, Henry Pearless, who kept a household for his three sisters and niece. In 1855 she married Alfred Brockett, a fly driver. By 1861, they had two sons, Alfred and (yet another) Daniel. Still living with their mother Eliza were her two sons, Daniel and Thomas, and three daughters: Mary Ann, entering her teenage years, and infants Emma and Caroline. It meant that financial responsibility was thrust on twenty-year-old Daniel and seventeen-year-old Thomas.

They responded in very different ways. Daniel concentrated on business, not getting married until he was thirty years old; Thomas concentrated on cricket and married his pregnant bride when still only nineteen. Both were successful but, inevitably, Daniel's business interests reduced his time for playing as much cricket as he might have wished and Thomas, despite making a not unreasonable amount, was careless with his money and was to repeat his father's financial and legal problems and end up in court. Both eventually had large families of their own, Thomas with seven daughters and Daniel with four sons and two daughters. So, at a relatively young age, Daniel found himself with the responsibility which comes to many people (but more often in middle age), that of supporting three generations: his own family, his younger sisters and, like his own father, his widowed mother, who was to survive more than thirty years until the latter part of the century. Dan and Tom's lives and cricket were to run roughly in parallel to the end of the 1860s, after which there is a divergence of paths; one to cricket, one to business.

The economic background was not the easiest. The Industrial Revolution meant that work, life and sport were becoming concentrated in towns and consequently areas like rural north Cambridgeshire were becoming isolated. With the Town and County Club now defunct, cricket in the county too needed a bit of an injection. It got one, leading to the formation of the Cambridgeshire County Cricket Club with first-class status in 1858, pioneered by some of the professionals employed by the University side, with three matches against Surrey in 1857 and 1858. It was to survive in that form for thirteen years when lack of finance, poor organisation and all the players getting old together led to it going the way of its predecessor.

For a decade or so Cambridgeshire was able to compete with the top county sides of Kent, Middlesex, Nottinghamshire and Yorkshire, as well as MCC and the University. Christopher Martin-Jenkins sums up as follows:

> For about ten seasons during the 1850s and 1860s Cambridgeshire ranked with the strongest counties and in 1864 actually won the three matches played against other first-class counties – Yorkshire (twice) and Nottinghamshire. Unfortunately the county found great difficulty in organizing and maintaining a properly constituted, and healthy, county club. The last Cambridgeshire club to attain first-class status was founded in 1866.
>
> For many reasons – not least the band of talented but undisciplined professionals on whom the side was based – it was always a struggle to maintain a strong foundation and the club was finally disbanded in

1869. The two county matches given first-class status in that season, and in 1871, were played by 'unofficial' sides representing the county. The current county club was formed in 1891 but although a regular competitor on the Minor Counties Championship it has never had first-class aspirations.[1]

During the brief period during which they enjoyed first-class status, Cambridgeshire played thirty-nine matches, winning a third of them, losing twenty-one and drawing the other five. In all of this, the Haywards played a major part; Thomas mostly on the field, Daniel mostly off it. With a sounder business brain than either his father or younger brother, Daniel set about repairing the ravages of earlier and contemporary mismanagement. He was an entrepreneur with fingers in a number of pies. Seeing the way the game was going, he set about providing support activities in the way of groundsmanship and providing players and spectators with the essentials of equipment, food and drink.

On the 1861 Census, Daniel and Thomas's mother, Eliza, described herself as 'gardener's widow', although at the time of her husband's death he was universally called a 'cricketer'. Eliza clearly understood that the gardening had brought in a steady, if not large, income while the cricket had not. Nevertheless, it was to cricket that both her sons turned initially.

8

MAKING THEIR OWN WAY

1852-57

The opportunities for Dan and Tom to make a living from playing cricket were immense compared to those afforded to their father. They were both included in a group of players paid by the University of Cambridge to coach students and bowl to them in the nets. From time to time these professionals had the opportunity to play in university and college sides as 'given men'. More and more clubs, many of them in the north of England, were also employing professionals as coaches and bowlers, but the greatest chances to shine and make money came from the All-England Eleven, a touring side of professional cricketers who travelled the country by the ever-growing railway network to play local sides of twenty-two players, occasionally fewer, occasionally more.

There are polarised views on the contribution of the All-England Eleven to mid-nineteenth century professional cricket. One is that it delayed the development of the county system, which may well be the case, but it was not known at the time that county cricket would be the future. As Kierkegaard observed, life can be understood only backwards, but it must be lived forwards. The other view is that the nationwide itineraries took cricket to and encouraged the game in all kinds of communities, raising its profile and demonstrating the standards which could be achieved. The two positions are not mutually exclusive and both have some validity.

Both brothers started their cricket careers with minor local club matches but these were also interspersed with games which were classified as 'major matches'.

These distinctions of 'minor' and 'major' follow the classification made by Cricket Archive between 'first-class' and 'miscellaneous'. It was a distinction not particularly significant at the time, particularly to Thomas Hayward who would have been more likely to grade them according to how much money they made him, so an All-England match well supported by the locals would have ranked higher in his estimation than a Town v Gown match on Fenner's or Parker's Piece. He was to represent the All-England Eleven on numerous occasions at numerous venues over a twenty-year period. Fixtures were well spread geographically from Cornwall to Glasgow and a number of well scattered venues in between.

Daniel junior, despite his business activities, over his playing career managed to play forty-three 'first-class' and eighty other matches recorded on Cricket Archive (and doubtless a number that were not), an average of around half a dozen a year.

The first recorded one of these was in June 1850 when, following in his father's footsteps, he played for St Ives, but twenty-two of them on this occasion including the Earl of Sandwich and two members of the Fryer family. The match (or mis-match) was against William Clarke's All-England Eleven, now in its fifth season, and played over three days. In the opposing team were such luminaries as Clarke himself, Alfred Mynn, John Wisden and George Parr. For the most part the locals were spared the pace of Mynn, but Clarke with sixteen wickets in the first innings and Wisden with sixteen in the second saw the star-studded visitors to victory by an innings and 154 runs, as forty-two wickets fell across both innings for 94 runs in all. There was only one double figure score. Daniel recorded a pair, bowled in the first innings, run out in the second, and Haygarth described this twenty-two as the worst team in England. There was clear scope for improvement.

Daniel did a little better two years later when playing for New-market against the offshoot of All-England, the United England Eleven, making 8 and 2 in a match which Newmarket lost by 95 runs, having been just one run behind on the first innings. Wisden, his allegiance now transferred, had twenty wickets in the match.

Additionally, Dan played for the newly established Cambridge Britannia Club against Newmarket on Parker's Piece in which 'Cambridge obtained 113 with the loss of six wickets; 46 were obtained in a very scientific manner by D Hayward, who proved himself a worthy successor of his father, the late "little Dan".'[2]

In consecutive seasons, 1852 and 1853, he played against the University Long Vacation Club, firstly for Cambridge Town on Parker's Piece, then for the Gentlemen of Cambridgeshire at Fenner's. The results, however, were the same. On both occasions, his team lost heavily by an innings. He had earlier played for the Britannia Club against the same opponents with slightly more favourable results, the University team winning on the first innings after he had made 27 not out.[3] Towards the end of 1853, he cashed in on his knowledge of groundsmanship by *inter alia* helping the Bishop Auckland Cricket Club in County Durham, where his younger brother was engaged as a professional, with the establishment of their new ground.

In 1854 Dan also made an appearance for the Britannia Club against the University (though probably not a full-strength side) and 'in a bold style (with now and then a chance)' scored almost a half of his side's runs – 33 out of 76.[4]

The Britannia was sufficiently strong to play well-balanced matches between its own members. One of these took place towards the end of the following season:

> An interesting and well contested cricket match took place on Parker's Piece between twenty-four members of the celebrated Britannia Club, selected in the most impartial manner to insure a good game, and the result proved the excellent judgment of those whose duty if was to make the sides as equal as possible. In consequence of the showery state of the weather only one innings each was played, but this afforded an opportunity of displaying the first-rate cricketing powers of some of

the members. D Hayward particularly distinguished himself by his fine hits – in one to the leg, for which he very leisurely obtained five, the ball ran across the road, and went with such force against Mr Talbot, the Surveyor's house that had he been at home he must have fancied he had an enemy battering at his doors. Dan, it will be seen, was ably seconded by his brother T Hayward.[5]

Daniel top-scored with 75 not out and Tom had 37 out of a total of 146. Only one other player and extras reached double figures. Tom also took three wickets.

Daniel had also started to play in major matches in 1852. He began at Fenner's in the Town v Gown match in what was even by the norms of the day a very low scoring fixture, Town running out winners by eight wickets in an encounter where no team topped fifty and no individual scored more than 18. 45 and 41 played 43 and 44 for two. His presence and performance were, however, noted by the local media: 'M Arnold was well caught by Stacey and retired without a run – 19 and seven wickets – making way for young Dan Hayward. Charles Arnold commenced hitting but presently lost the company of young Hayward, who, after making one fine leg hit for three and four square to the tent and a single, was well bowled by Pontifex.'[6]

If his father was there to see him play, it was the last possible occasion on which he was able to do so. He died less than two weeks later.

Dan junior distinguished himself by being the top scorer in both innings in the equivalent fixture the following season. Batting at number nine in the first innings and three in the second, he had put his team in a strong position in a fixture with higher totals than the previous year: University 103 and 80; Town 112 and, chasing 72 to win on a rain-affected third day, 40 for three. However, 'D Hayward joined Diver and the play on all sides became excellent. The bowling and fielding were unexceptional, and the batting of a very superior order. Hayward kept increasing the score by fine dashing hitting … shortly after Hayward played a fine ball from Pontifex well, but it rolled, touching the wicket and a bale [sic] dropped off. The young 'un had added to the score by fine play 22. Stumps were drawn at half-past five, in consequence of the boat procession on the river. Much altercation took place, the gown contending that the game was drawn, while the town insisted the game to be played out. We regret that this match, which has usually terminated so pleasantly should have ended unsatisfactorily.'[7]

In 1854, low scores were forgotten as the University followed on and hung on for a draw after a huge first innings score by the Town to which Dan contributed with what was to remain his highest 'first-class' score of 59 in a match in which his younger brother made his first-class debut, batting at number ten. The University replied to 318 with 110 and, following on, saved the match with 218 for five: 'The bowling on the side of the University was good for the first two or three hours; it then became very indifferent, which, in some measure, accounts for the Town making up the extraordinary score of 318.'[8]

Dan then went on to play his sole match for Surrey against Sussex at Brighton, a well-balanced one which ended up as a draw. The game itself drew plaudits from the press: 'Few matches for many years have shown finer cricket or more brilliant batting than have been exhibited in this grand contest.'[9]

Daniel's own performance, however, did not. He was part of a team of distinguished names: 'The Surrey Eleven – F Burbridge, F P Miller, Brockwell, Caesar, Caffyn, Hayward, Lockyer, Martingell, Matlock, Sherman, and Stephenson.'[10] Surrey had a first innings lead of 50 and, in an even match against a team including such legendary names as Lillywhite and Wisden, were 95 for five, pursuing a target of 150 in the fourth innings when time was called. Batting at number ten, Dan scored one, bowled by Lillywhite, and took a catch. That '1' remained his career aggregate and average for Surrey. He never played again and it has been suggested that his appearance on this one occasion was because the county were under the mistaken impression that he was born in Mitcham.[11]

The story seems unlikely. The club minutes have nothing to say about it and it would be almost two decades before rules on qualification by birth or residence were introduced. Sussex-born James Southerton made his Surrey debut that season and in 1867 was to play for three different counties (those of his employer, his birth and his residence) so the reasons for Dan's exclusion are more likely to be associated with his other commitments in his native county and in the context of a star-studded Surrey team at the time he was simply considered not to be good enough.

In 1855, the Town beat the University by seven wickets, Dan making a dozen out of 104 in the first innings and 'was caught by Wingfield after scoring with spirit one 4, two 3s and two singles'. In the second innings, requiring 46 to win, he was third out at 21, stumped for 11, but Ducky Diver and Fred Bell saw the team home with no further alarms. The following year the match was played on Parker's Piece rather than Fenner's and the University turned the tables, winning by two wickets with 55 for eight in the fourth innings, having been at one stage 29 for seven. Tom played as well and opened the innings, Dan batted middle order and failed to distinguish himself with one and four.

Tom had shown early promise, since not long after his eighteenth birthday he was appointed as professional to the Richmond Club in North Yorkshire, one of a series of early engagements which took him to Newport Pagnell, then back to the North Yorkshire/Durham area. The club and the local press were clearly pleased with their new acquisition and looked forward to a bright future.

North York Rifles v Richmond Club.

On Wednesday last the Richmond club played their first match this season on their new ground, which is picturesquely situated on the banks of the Swale, near to the beautiful ruins of Easby Abbey. Through the kind permission of his Grace the Duke of Leeds the splendid band of the North York Rifles enlivened the scene with their harmonious strains until after the close of the match, and during the afternoon a great number of ladies honoured the ground with their presence.

The game was very closely contested, and except congratulating the club on the very good choice they have made in selecting their professional bowler (Hayward of Cambridge) and giving the credit due to Mr George Morton for his excellent wicket-keeping, it would be invidious to mention the playing of others so steadily did everyone take his part in the game. Hayward is now engaged for the club and with the practice the members will get from his bowling they cannot fail to become the most formidable club in the North Riding.

Owing to the short time that could be spared for the match only one innings each was played and the riflemen were victorious with nine runs to spare.[12]

Tom had at least five wickets – five were bowled but other wickets are ascribed to catchers and the bowler does not get a mention.

Both brothers were retained by Cambridge University as bowlers and coaches for the students, which could sometimes bring about some extra practice. Daniel may have been surprised by the keenness of the students when a bizarre and unseasonal bit of cricket was witnessed (though not by many, in view of the heavy frost and snow) on Parker's Piece the following winter:

This celebrated and much frequented ground, owing to its being covered with snow, has had an unusually long rest, but the wind having drifted some of the snow left one part of it bare, sufficiently large to enable two gentlemen of Pembroke College to renew their cricketing on Monday and Tuesday last, and although the frost was very sharp all the time, they seemed much to enjoy the lessons they received from that celebrated bowler, Hayward, whom they unexpectedly dragged from his winter's retreat to commence the session. However great the novelty of such a scene it failed to attract the attention of many spectators.[13]

In what it is assumed were more congenial climatic conditions in 1856 – though in April at Fenner's perhaps not – along with his brother Thomas, Daniel played against the University for the 'Players engaged at Cambridge University', against the University. Thomas Hayward opened the batting and scored 19 and 26; Daniel Hayward, batting at seven, scored 12 and 0 out of total scores of 111 and 95. Neither bowled in a match played for benefit of Thomas Barker, the old Nottinghamshire player and current University umpire.[14] The *Cambridge Chronicle* dubbed it Gentlemen v Players, which it was, albeit a much diluted version of the encounters at Lord's and The Oval.

In the verbosely entitled 'Undergraduates of Cambridge v Eleven Professional Players Engaged for the Season at Cambridge' match at Fenner's, Thomas top-scored with 55 of 125. The pros trailed the students by 24 runs on the first innings and, in the second, the University scored 200, whereupon the 'players engaged' conceded the match, clearly not one of any great significance to them, as they had agreed to take on the fixture which should have been against the Household Brigade, who were unable to honour the commitment.

Thomas's first appearance in a first-class match was at the age of nineteen in the annual Town v Gown fixture of 1854 at Fenner's. He batted at number ten, made a single before being bowled by CWH Fryer, but did not have the opportunity of batting a second time, as the University followed on and comfortably secured a draw. It was not the most auspicious of debuts. Performances more impressive were to follow. Two years later he played in the equivalent match,

The old pavilion at Fenner's, the Cambridge cricket ground that gradually supplanted Parker's Piece during the later nineteenth century.

this time on Parker's Piece, opening the innings but making four and ten in a match which the University won by two wickets, despite needing only 55 in the fourth innings. Town turned the tables the following season, winning by an innings and 69. Thomas, batting number three, made 35, half the runs in a partnership with century-maker Henry Francis, which established the platform for Town's 294. It was more than enough for the University's reply of 130 and, following on, 96. Later that season, Thomas made his first appearance on the ground to be graced in later years by his as-yet-unborn nephew, the Kennington Oval. It was his Cambridgeshire debut but, again, not a particularly distinguished one, just a single in the first innings and half a dozen in the second, stumped Lockyer bowled Caffyn, as Surrey won in two days in a low-scoring match in which only one of the four innings struggled past three figures.

In family terms at least, Thomas was surrounded by women. He and his elder brother were sandwiched between half a dozen sisters, three older and three younger, and Thomas himself went on to have seven daughters; Emma, Lizzie, Fannie, Maude, Norah, Clara and Edith, born between 1856 and 1870. His only son, also Thomas, was born in 1860 and did not reach his first birthday, dying of a chest infection.

Thomas's bride was Lizzie Dell, whom he married in her home town of Newport Pagnell in January 1855 where eldest daughter Emma was born before the end of June, though not baptised until the following year.[15] So, like his father, Thomas married at nineteen and like his father too, his bride was pregnant on her wedding day. Thomas and Lizzie began their married life living with her parents in Newport Pagnell.

It was not unusual. It has been estimated that in nineteenth-century Britain, about one in three marriages was accelerated by a (usually unplanned or unwanted) pregnancy. In days when political correctness was an unheard of concept and when before the 1882 Married Women's Property Act, a wife's assets and earnings were the property of her husband, the conventional male wisdom was that you didn't buy a horse before trying it out. But, unlike the present day when births within and without wedlock are given the same social recognition, the stigma of illegitimacy was strong and marriage was the obvious way to avoid it, leading in most cases to an early entry on to the perpetual treadmill of pregnancy, birth and nursing, running from not long after puberty until menopause, the lot of most Victorian wives.

Not tardy to accept an earning opportunity, and with a growing family to support, in 1856 Thomas played as a professional for Jesus College in an early season inter-college fixture, providing a bit of balance to what may otherwise have been a one-sided match:

> Jesus College v King's College. This match was played on Jesus Piece on Friday May 2. The gentlemen of Jesus College were allowed by their opponents to play with Hayward, a professional bowler. At the same time it should be observed that three of their usual eleven were unable to play. The match was well contested, Jesus College winning by 2 runs only.[16]

Thomas's efforts were perhaps the difference – a third of the first innings total, 17 out of 52, run out for two in the second innings, a mode of dismissal that was to blight his whole career at all levels of the game. He also had eleven wickets in the match, seven in the first innings, four in the second.

Meanwhile, in July 1856, Thomas played for Stockton-on-Tees in an away match against the Grange Club in Edinburgh, Haygarth noting in *Scores and Biographies* that 'Thomas Hayward was engaged at Stockton about this time'. He made 9 and 2 and took a couple of wickets. Then in September, playing for Twenty-two of Stockton (with Hodgson and Joy) against a powerful All-England Eleven in a match lost by the locals by an innings, he fell to the superstars – caught Willsher bowled Jackson 3 and bowled Diver 1. He did have the consolation of a couple of wickets, but like many of these matches, even having twenty-two players did not help to bridge the gap. All-England had ten wickets to play with, Stockton 42, but the

All-England Eleven still managed more runs in their one innings than Stockton (even with their two 'given men') in two.

Daniel continued to play for local Cambridge teams. At the end of the 1856 season, he turned out for Cambridge Hope, another club formed in the 1850s, against Saffron Walden:

> The ground being dead prevented large scores being made but with patience and steady play for nearly three hours a score of 117 was obtained. The batting of Messrs G Masterton, R Addison and D Hayward was unusually good, they scoring between them more than 50 runs.[17]

Like the Britannia they had sufficient members to play a match among themselves, though there was probably some overlap:

> A match between the members of the above club took place on Parker's Piece on Tuesday last. Although the day was somewhat inclined to be wet, Sol at intervals enlivened the scene. There was some very good cricket shown on both sides. The most distinguished was the very excellent batting of Mr D Hayward and Mr G Masterton.[18]

In the second innings Dan was top scorer with 28 in a total of 100.

The following season, 1857, Dan played in the University trial match for the next twenty-two. As one of only three bowlers used, he made his contribution to an innings victory. Then the following week, loyalties and allegiances being fairly flexible, he appeared *for* the Undergraduates of Cambridge (of which he was not one) against the Gentlemen of Cambridgeshire who 'gave up the match'. To conclude that season, he played for Twenty-two of Stockton-on-Tees, where his brother was club professional, in a rare victory against the All-England Eleven, thanks mainly to a seemingly liberal interpretation of 'Stockton and District'. Daniel had little personal success, becoming one of John Jackson's nine victims. Thomas top-scored in the first innings and picked up four of the first five batsmen in the second.

Eleven of All-England v Twenty two of Stockton and District. The match came off on Monday, Tuesday and Wednesday (21-23) last on the Stockton ground. The weather was favourable and a large number of persons witnessed the game. The Stockton team proved too strong for its opponents.

The England eleven was not so good as we have seen it on former visits to the county; whilst the Stockton twenty-two was, without a doubt, the best which could be turned out in the north of England. With such players as Hayward, Joy, Morton, Hornby and Darnton, backed up by a legion of minor celebrities, the issue of the contest could not be doubtful and we were, therefore, not surprised to learn that the contest had ended in favour of Stockton by 17 wickets.[19]

Earlier in the month, both Dan and Thomas appeared for Bishop Auckland against Stockton. Daniel is also on record as helping Bishop Auckland Cricket Club to develop their new ground. This is the first indication of his later well-known skills as a groundsman.

Thomas was kept pretty well occupied as he split his time between Cambridge Town, the University, his northern commitments and a few games with the All-England Eleven. He played for both Stockton and Bishop Auckland against local opposition such as Crook, Middlesbrough, Redcar and West Hartlepool. Against Bradford, 'As soon as the bell rang the Stocktonians sent in Hayward and Darnton to the bowling of Lawson and Hodgson. Hayward commenced slashing the ball to all parts of the field. His innings amounted to 66, being one of the finest we ever witnessed on the Stockton Ground.'[20]

In 1857, Thomas was invited to join the All-England Eleven for two matches, a win at North Shields and a draw at Richmond, but did not travel to Scotland with them for an unseasonal three-day October fixture in Glasgow.

9

DRAWING APART 1858-59

Dan did not play 'major cricket' again until 1859 when he played in the Town v Gown fixture for three consecutive seasons, including a double header in 1861 when the teams met at both Fenner's and Parker's Piece. On no occasion did he do anything exceptional, now being eclipsed by younger brother Thomas. The second day of the two-day match was washed out completely. Thomas had a duck, but took seven of the thirteen wickets to fall and caught two of the others. The 1860 match was one of the closest, Dan doing nothing special, Thomas taking another five wickets and the Town just getting over the line with 96 for nine in the last innings. Honours were even the following season when the Town Club won the 'home' fixture by six wickets, Thomas again doing well with the ball, Dan scoring 20 not out in the second innings, as four wickets fell cheaply. Thomas did not play in the return match later in May, which might have had something to do with the result, University winning by an innings and 62.

In the University v Players Engaged at the University match of 1858 at Fenner's the totals were phenomenally high for the time, the University reaching 364 and the Players Engaged 208. As the match was scheduled for only two days there was time for no more. Thomas was now playing for the All-England Eleven against whom Dan played for Twenty-two of Grantham, though on this occasion Thomas was not in the team. Dan made 33 before being bowled by George Parr, who had taken over the management and captaincy from the now deceased William Clarke. It helped the Twenty-two to a first innings lead of 20 – 184 played 164 – but with a scoring rate of little more than one per over, there was no time for a fourth innings and the match remained drawn.

The following year, 1859, Dan again played in the usual fixtures, Town v Gown, University v Players Engaged at the University, Gentlemen of Cambridgeshire v the University. In the second of these, Dan outscored Thomas (just) by 41 to 40 in the first innings in a six wicket win. As given men for the Gentlemen of Cambridgeshire, in a total of 371, Dan (batting at number four) had 6. Thomas, one place higher, scored 220, almost unheard of as an individual score at the time. It marked a parting of the ways. A few months later, Thomas would be on tour in the United States and Canada and Dan pursuing his business interests. The split was symbolised in August when they played on opposite sides; Dan for Twenty-two of Cambridge Town; Thomas, along with Bob Carpenter, for the All-England Eleven. It was a match played at Fenner's rather than the usual venue for the Town's home matches, Parker's Piece.

For some time, the local press had excitedly anticipated the match, though it was initially assumed it would be played on Parker's Piece: 'For a long time – indeed many months back – a liberal subscription was entered into, not only by cricketers, but by the admirers of the game, to have a match on Parker's Piece, which, for importance in the annals of Cambridge cricket has never been surpassed, if, indeed, equalled. This arrangement was that the mighty Eleven of England's best cricketing sons should be invited to contest Twenty-two amateurs including two as bowlers viz. Fred Bell, a Cambridge professional and Grundy, great at "Lord's".'

At the end of the second (of three) days, at a dinner held at the Lion Hotel, George Parr (who because of injury was umpiring), said he 'thought that Cambridge was not strong enough in itself to take the All-England on even terms; but Cambridge and Nottinghamshire would stand a better chance.'[21]

Cambridge gave a reasonable account of themselves, scoring 91 and 69 against All-England's 86 and 78 for two, Jackson and Reynolds taking thirty-nine of the forty wickets to fall to bowlers (there were two run outs). Thomas Hayward got the other one and posted the highest individual innings of the match with 42 not out in the fourth innings.

In contrast to Dan, Thomas was going from strength to strength. That he was one of the leading batsmen of the day is not in doubt:

> The greatest cricketer in the Hayward family had been Daniel's brother, Thomas, who in the 1860s when Cambridgeshire were one of the strongest teams in the land, had been regarded the equal of any batsman playing. Never blessed with great strength or good health, his forte had been on-side play, especially the shot that forced the ball off the leg stump between mid-on and short leg. It was a way he had of conserving energy. He also excelled on fiery pitches.[22]

Whether he made the best use of that talent is another matter. It is almost a given that any professional sportsman wishes to compete at the highest level. He was capable of that and did it, but he attracted much criticism from his contemporaries and from the media for having a preference for single wicket contests and matches against the odds where the standards were lower but financial rewards the greater. It is much the same mindset which causes cricketers of the current day to opt for the more lucrative IPL, CPL and Big Bash rather than the more prestigious Test matches and one-day internationals. Such an attitude may not appeal to the cricket-following public who wish to see first-class, especially international, sides represented by the best players available, but it is defendable on the grounds that professional sport is a short career and those good enough to follow it have a right to maximise their earnings to support their wives and families. Not that Thomas did.

His strength was working the ball on the leg side, a skill always likely to gain him an advantage at a time when the emphasis was on off side bowling and stroke play. A number of his contemporaries and near-contemporaries praised the technique. He was also a more than competent medium-pace right-arm bowler and no slouch in the field, the ideal combination for success at single wicket. His health was never good and he was lacking in strength and physical fitness, but despite these apparent handicaps, in skills and technique he stood head and shoulders above most of his contemporaries.

Surrey's William Caffyn played with and against Thomas Hayward throughout his career and shared tours to North America and Australasia. He is therefore in a better position than most to make a judgment on his temperament and technique:

> Volumes almost have been written about this player, and little can be said of him which has not been said already. He was a beautiful player to watch, and was a remarkably effective bat, as well as possessing a graceful style. He had a decided flourish in his style of defence, which might have been considered bad form in a less skilful batsman, but the flourish in Thomas's case was natural, and was never the cause of his getting out. He was one of the very best 'on-side' players I ever saw, his finest stroke perhaps being made between short-leg and mid-on. He also drove freely, but somewhat loftily. His wrist play was perfect. He was remarkable for the way he could put down a rising ball, and was also very safe at stopping a shooter. He was seen to great advantage on a fast wicket. His style of defence may be considered as forward and 'half-forward'. The latter stroke he used more frequently than any player I ever saw, and used it to a ball which most batsmen would play back to. Though in my opinion he was not as reliable as Carpenter, he was of course a more attractive one to look at. For a first-class bat, he was, I think, the worst judge of a run I ever saw, and should say he was responsible for more 'runs out' to his side than almost any other player. As a bowler he was also very good, being medium pace, with a break back. He was also an excellent field at cover-point. He was a thin man of medium height, had a very dark complexion and rather a 'sour' expression of face. Soon after he appeared in first-class cricket he joined the All-England Eleven and made many large scores for them for years.[23]

George Freeman too was able to put Hayward' s talents into a historical context in later years:

> 25 April 1895. Cricket Notches: an evening with George Freeman by Rev Holmes.
>   To my mind, barring WG and putting in the most unstinted appreciation of others, Thomas Hayward I have always considered the

greatest batsman of my days. I used to like to see him run up big innings against us, just for the pleasure of watching his every movement of the bat. Daft had a more perfect style perhaps, Jupp wanted shifting and Bob Carpenter on our modern wickets would never have been got out by medium and fast medium bowlers. But Hayward I place above them all.[24]

HS Altham puts Hayward's skills into the context of contemporary Cambridgeshire cricket and draws a genetic link with the next generation, with which he would have had personal experience:

The modern cricketer may well find it surprising to hear that for some years in the sixties Cambridgeshire were among the strongest counties in England; but such was indeed the fact. In AJ (or, as he was generally called, 'Ducky') Diver, they had an excellent all-rounder player who formed one of Stephenson's American Eleven. In John Smith, the fastest outfield in England; in Tarrant, a bowler who, for speed and destructiveness ranked second only to John Jackson; and in Thomas Hayward and Robert Carpenter such a pair of batsmen as no other county could claim.

It is interesting that these last three names should, forty years later, again become almost household words in cricket. The Cambridge bowler was, so far as I know, not related to the famous Australian and Middlesex player, but Thomas Hayward junior was the senior's nephew, while Herbert Carpenter was Robert's son. These two would, with Richard Daft, have been for some years first choice as batsmen for an England side, but in physique and style they were curiously dissimilar. No one, in Daft's opinion, with the exception of Arthur Shrewsbury, rose to such heights of batsman-ship from such slender physical resources as did Hayward. He was rather below medium height and very spare of frame, weighing little more than nine stone when he first began to play in big matches; added to this he was never blessed with good health, or with the happy temperament that so often goes along with it. He looked, indeed, but a frail figure as he stood at the wicket, holding the bat very lightly in his hands and at the end of its handle, and yet in all England there was no more graceful or masterly batsman, with the possible exception of Dick Daft himself. Hayward was essentially a forward player, with something of the pendulum correctness of swing that Pilch possessed. He was a beautiful off-driver, but his real forte was his on-side play, and especially his ability to force the ball off the leg stump and his legs, between mid-on and short-leg, a stroke which his nephew played to perfection, and surely must have inherited. In spite of his natural disadvantages, Hayward was at his very best on fiery wickets, when his ability to keep down the rising ball was most marked. Like the younger Thomas, he was a more than useful medium-paced bowler, and an excellent field at cover. His long scores are innumerable. In 1859 he scored 220, playing as a given man for the Gentlemen of Cambridgeshire against the University, and twice he obtained a century for the Players against the Gentlemen at Lord's, an example which his nephew was to follow at an interval of thirty years.[25]

After the University v Players Engaged match in 1858, Thomas joined the All-England Eleven for four matches in June, playing against Eastwell where, in the intervals of play allowed between the rain breaks, the match was fairly well-balanced. Off the field, however, the gales were of such force that, according to Cricket Archive, they overturned the tents specially erected for the occasion – and this was mid-June. Whitehaven were turned over by an innings and 111 runs, Thomas top scoring with 70 at number nine, though the *Nottinghamshire Guardian* recognised the difficulty for batsmen and fielding captain of coping with a fielding side of twenty-two: 'The Whitehaven cricketers fielded tolerably well, though, in our opinion, there is always a degree of awkwardness in placing a field of twenty-two in such positions with advantage.'[26] Broughton and Derbyshire then beat them by nineteen and twelve wickets respectively.

Thomas's out-of-Cambridge cricket continued to be with Bishop Auckland, though he still managed the occasional match for Stockton, as in the trans-Tees derby against Twenty-two of Middlesbrough.[27] He remained popular with his home teams and with opponents, both for his performances as a player and for his groundsmanship and assistance in preparing pitches:

Durham City v Bishop Auckland at Durham City ground Friday last. Hayward, finding his round bowling was not so telling as he could have desired, commenced bowling 'slow' which, however, was not much more effective. Hayward, whose professional assistance must have been of much value to the Bishop Auckland club, proved himself 'a good man all round' and as well by his style of playing as by the pains he took in preparing the wickets, obtained much credit and warm praise from the members of the City club and their friends.[28]

At the end of the season Bishop Auckland showed their appreciation:

The members of the Bishop Auckland cricket club played their last match of this season on Tuesday last, after the conclusion of which they adjourned to Mr Moore's Shepherd's Inn, where a most sumptuous dinner was provided for them. A subscription having been entered into by the members a fortnight ago for the purpose of presenting their professional teacher 'Mr T Hayward of Cambridge' with a suitable testimonial. As soon as the cloth was withdrawn and the usual toast proposed and drank with much enthusiasm, Mr John Lee, the Chairman, rose, and in a neat and flowery speech decanted on the many excellent qualities of Mr Hayward, who merited the warmest praise, not only as a complete master of the manly game of cricket, but for his untiring and unremitting exertions to bring the club to its present state of efficiency. Mr Lee then, in the name of the members presented Mr Hayward with an elegant and valuable gold watch, the case of which was most elaborately chased and engraved. Mr Hayward rose, and in feeling terms thanked the members of the club for this unexpected mark of their approbation and respect.[29]

In 1859, after a couple of matches at Fenner's, one for the 'Players Engaged', the other for the Gentlemen of Cambridgeshire in which he contributed to an innings victory with three wickets followed by that individual score of 220, he supplemented his first-class cricket with a further nineteen matches for the All-England Eleven.

There was some scepticism about the quality of the bowling against which he scored his double century: 'T Hayward's enormous score was not, it must be observed, made against the best bowling of the day; still, the Undergraduates were young and by no means to be despised.'[30] The value of any innings has to be seen not only in statistical terms, but in the context of the match as a whole and the strength of the opposition. That said, however, a double century is a double century and far rarer in the nineteenth century in any form of cricket than in the twenty-first.

Thomas was now beginning to supplement his batting with some impressive bowling performances. In the match against Suffolk on the Ipswich School ground he had five for 14 as a foil to Jackson's fourteen for 18 in 33.2 overs, then twelve for 27 in the second innings as only one Suffolk player managed double figures in either innings.

In other matches, the All-England Eleven generally came out on top, in large part because of the pace of John Jackson which, in most cases, was just too much for the local batsmen. In the match against Twenty-two of Cornwall at Redruth, he had the surreal figures of ten for 1 as the Cornish were bowled out for 22. All-England then replied with 226 before, still in the first day of a two-day match, Cornwall did slightly better in the second innings, getting to 30 for seventeen before conceding the match. They were spared John Jackson this time round, but Hayward's ten for 13 and Reynolds' six for 9 were effective enough. Against East Cornwall a few days later, Thomas followed up with six for 19. His highest with the bat was 85 against Buckinghamshire, so overall it was a satisfactory season. It came to a wet end at Bradford as the local side replied to All-England's 98 with 23 for eight when rain washed out almost two days of a three-day match.

On balance, given the different strengths of the teams, eleven v twenty-two worked out fairly well. The All-England Eleven were generally at a disadvantage batting as all twenty-two opponents would usually take the field, though scorecards suggest that not everyone was present for the whole match and among those who did take to the field smoking was not uncommon, so speed in getting to the ball was not always an issue for the batsmen to consider when thinking of sensible running between the wickets.

By 1859, Thomas's family had increased. Two more daughters were born, Lizzie (after her mother) and Fannie. He was now living in Cambridge at 74 Burleigh Street. The house is no longer there, having been replaced by a Cambridge Co-operative department store and then a large branch of Primark. They were later to move round the corner to 16 Clarendon Street.

Thomas now took a break from fathering children to go to America as his performances with the All-England Eleven had sufficiently impressed that team to invite him to join the 'Champion Band', the first English overseas touring team.

10

NORTH AMERICA 1859

Thomas was a member of George Parr's trailblazing squad that embarked from Liverpool on the *Nova Scotian* on 7 September 1859 upon England's first overseas tour. It was made up of players from the two touring sides, the All-England Eleven and the United England Eleven. The first international cricket match was not Australia v England as popularly supposed, but Canada v USA in 1849. Cricket is now very much a minority sport in North America, played mostly by Caribbean and Asian immigrants, but in the mid-nineteenth century it was vying with baseball for supremacy.

Whatever the origins of cricket (unsurprisingly historians differ in their opinions) and whatever its antecedents might have been, there is no doubt that it emerged as a game and for most of its participants over the years it has remained that way. However, when small bets began to be placed on the outcome of matches or players' performances, it started to emerge as a business within a game. When the aristocracy took over the sport for gambling purposes and a class of professional players infiltrated the hitherto-amateur ranks, it began to be a game within a business. That was certainly how William Clarke, founder of the All-England Eleven, and other pioneering entrepreneurs perceived it and, whatever noble sentiments might be expressed about spreading the game within Britain and overseas, at its roots the professional game was about money. While overseas tours were privately organised (as they were before the establishment of the Board of Control in 1898), 'how much?'

and 'when?' were the determining factors for overseas tours. A trip across the North Atlantic might conceivably have taken place earlier, the idea having been first mooted in 1856, but it was deferred until the end of the 1859 season when the financial terms were right. As far as playing in more favourable climatic conditions was concerned, summer 1860 would have been preferable, but the organisers were anxious to rake in the takings before the various parties involved changed their minds.

Contemporary press reports, William Caffyn's reminiscences and Scott Reeves's *The Champion Band* all give a flavour for an unprecedented tour:

> On the 7th September 1859 the first team of English cricketers set sail to America from Liverpool in the *Nova Scotia* [Caffyn consistently referred to the ship as the *Nova Scotia*; it was actually called the *Nova Scotian*]. We all arrived at Liverpool overnight and put up at the George Hotel, while we were photographed on a vessel in the docks before proceeding on board the *Nova Scotia*.
>
> We were just over a fortnight making the voyage and experienced some rather rough weather. Some of us were very bad sailors, the worst being John Lillywhite, HH Stephenson and old Jackson. Parr, Wisden, Hayward and Carpenter were just the same as if they had been on land. Towards the end of our voyage we passed some enormous icebergs, which were very beautiful.
>
> We landed at Quebec on the 22nd of September, and proceeded to Montreal by special train, where we were to play our first match.[31]

The outward crossing was extremely rough, some of the players vowing they would never leave England again. Thomas Hayward was not among them and remained one of the few unaffected by sea-sickness. The tribulations of the outward voyage behind them, they settled into their first match and won comfortably by eight wickets.

> Our first match was delayed for a day owing to rain. There was great excitement on the day of the match and several thousands of spectators were assembled long before the time for commencing play. We were to encounter Twenty-two of Lower Canada and as we lost the toss we had to take the field.[32]

The pattern of fixtures was that the tourists would play against a home team of twenty-two, beat them easily, then follow with an eleven-a-side match between themselves on the time-honoured patterns with which the players were familiar in Britain: All-England v United or North v South, with the locals making up the numbers.

There had been huge excitement in Montreal and elsewhere about the forthcoming tour, concern about the delay on the journey and the weather, coupled with anxiety as to whether the tourists would actually feel like playing after the traumas of the crossing. But, despite a delay for rain, the match had gone ahead, accompanied by lavish civic hospitality:

> The unexpected delay in the arrival of the *Nova Scotian* has thrown into confusion all the arrangements of the Montreal Cricket Club. They had advertised it extensively that the match would commence on the 21st inst. and the greatest excitement prevails in the city in consequence of the non-arrival of any intelligence respecting the missing steamer. It is,

The pioneering overseas tourists of 1859.
Back: Robert Carpenter, William Caffyn, Tom Lockyer. Middle: John Wisden, HH Stephenson, George Parr, James Grundy, Julius Caesar, Thomas Hayward, John Jackson. Front: Alfred Diver, John Lillywhite.

however, sanguinely anticipated that the English players will arrive here tomorrow so as to enable the match to commence on Thursday. In this we think that due allowance is not made for the fatigue and prostration of strength incidental to a transatlantic voyage, and the eleven representatives of English cricket may very reasonably protest against such an immediate commencement of the great match, before they have fairly recovered the effects of their sea voyage.

It is arranged that a grand public dinner shall be given to the English cricketing visitors on Friday 23rd inst. at the St Lawrence Hotel, the principal place in Montreal, and that the public shall be allowed to participate in the affair by the payment of five dollars each. As might have been expected the forthcoming match is the sole subject of conversation among all classes among the numerous devotees of cricket here.

The managers of this match, prominent among whom is WP Pickering Esq., the originator and one of the most accomplished cricketers in Canada, have used every exertion in getting their ground into as fine a condition as possible. Situate about half a mile from the city, off St Catharine Street, the natural beauties of the locality cannot be surpassed. On the one side is the well known Mount Royal, covered with varied coloured foliage to its very summit; on the other is the distant prospect of the 'silver city' of Montreal. A more beautiful cricket ground, we really believe, does not exist and every effort has been used to render it worthy of the great match about to be played.[33]

As sportsmen, and in the interests of diplomacy, the cricketers probably refrained from expressing opinions on American politics, delicately poised as the country was on the brink of Civil War. But a visit to the stage version of Harriet Beecher Stowe's anti-slavery novel, *Uncle Tom's Cabin*, albeit in Canada, must have raised awareness of differing attitudes.[34]

All-England v United England was resumed in late September, part of the English season, although on the other side of the Atlantic. Indeed, it was All-England v United England plus, as the six Englishmen on each side were supplemented by five Canadian players:

As the game was over early on the Tuesday, another match had been arranged to commence as soon as the first was concluded. The six All-England men were put on one side and the six United on the other; five gentlemen of Lower Canada assisting each to make up eleven a-side.

The United batted first and scored 188. All-England were got out for 90, and having to follow on, were got rid of for 44, thus losing the match by an innings and 54 runs.[35]

The party then moved across the border into the United States at a time well before 9/11 had its impact and before President Trump and the Department of Homeland Security imposed their political and bureaucratic border controls.

> On the following morning we left Montreal very early to proceed to New York. After a long and tedious journey and a lot of changing we arrived at Albany. I recollect that Fred Lillywhite's printing-tent was a great nuisance to us on the journey. It was a most complicated arrangement, and took a lot of carting about, and he was always complaining that the railway porters did not stow it away properly, until at last George Parr lost all patience and in pretty plain language consigned both Fred and his tent to an unmentionable region.
>
> We arrived at New York on the Sunday morning and put up at the Astor House Hotel. There was great excitement evinced on our arrival, about 2,000 persons![36]

The *New York Herald*, in welcoming the players to the city, sympathised with their plight of being required to perform after so brief a period of acclimatisation and on so 'dead' a ground:

> In the first match which the English Eleven played at Montreal against Twenty-two of Lower Canada, they were not in a proper condition to display to perfection the beauties of their scientific game. They had just arrived, after having passed the ordeal of a severe voyage across the Atlantic and were consequently not in proper trim for playing a game which requires such steadiness of nerve, quickness of eye and activity as cricket. Notwithstanding this, they were able to beat their opponents easily by eight wickets, although, from the heavy rains which had fallen, the ground was not in sufficiently elastic condition to do justice to the admirable bowling of Jackson, Caffyn and Wisden.[37]

From the hotel and luxury unexceeded in the United States at the time, it was a trip across the Hudson River to the delightfully named Elysian Fields, home of the St George's Club in Hoboken:

The ground was that of the St George's Club, and here on the Monday morning was a great crowd of nearly 10,000 people. We were absolutely mobbed when we arrived on the field, so eager were they all to get a look at us.

We won the toss and put our opponents (Twenty-two of the States) in to bat. The bowling was entrusted to George Parr and Jackson. The twenty-two did not appear to at all understand the break on George's lobs and as there was a stiff wind blowing they attributed the break to that. They were all disposed of for the small score of 38. Hayward and Carpenter opened the innings of the Englishmen to the strain of 'Rule Britannia', and the two quickly knocked off the runs. Our innings closed for 156, Hayward being the largest scorer and his fellow towns-man next with 26. The twenty-two only made 54 in the second innings.

We had a dinner given to us at our hotel in New York, and very enjoyable it was, there being some excellent music and singing.

On the Saturday night we left New York for Philadelphia, arriving there about eleven o'clock. An immense crowd awaited us at the sta-tion. A grand supper also awaited us at our hotel, to which many of the Philadelphian gentlemen sat down, and it was very late before we adjourned to bed.[38]

Not mentioned here are Caffyn's own absurd second innings bowling figures of 34-25-24-16 when the United States' Twenty-two did marginally better, totalling 54 in sixty-eight overs. Their first innings had used up only 57, the highest individual score across both innings was seven. The opening partnership of Hayward and Carpenter with 33 and 26 respectively dwarfed their opponents' two meagre innings and the disparity between the teams was as large as anything seen on their domestic tours. And yet the novelty of the occasion attracted a near five-figure attendance.

The match was followed not by an All-England Eleven v United or North v South this time, but by T Lockyer's XI v HH Stephen-son's XI. From the names it could have been a Surrey warm-up match supplemented by a few Americans and players from other counties. Hayward and Carpenter both played for Stephenson's team in what appears to have been a none-too-competitive encoun-ter. Julius Caesar top-scored with 52 for Lockyer's side, Carpenter matched it for the opposition with the same score not out. Carpenter batted through from number three as none of his partners after Jackson, who had opened the batting, made more than half a dozen. Hayward bowled in both innings with 41-16-64-4 and 17-9-21-0, but batted at number ten with Diver at number eleven. They were the two highest scorers in the second innings, but their last wicket partnership fell 75 short of what was required to win the match.

The tour and tourists had proved extremely popular so much so that the *New York Herald* regularly carried an advertisement for a photograph of the players and ground.

> English cricketers – An Imperial photograph of the 'All-England Eleven' now in exhibition at Bray's Gallery, 643 Broadway, also a fine stereoscopic view of the cricket ground with cricketers playing. Copies of the stereoscopic view for sale.[39]

The next stop was Philadelphia where there was a delayed start because of rain. It was not the massacre of New York, but still a fairly straightforward seven-wicket win against the country's premier club. Thomas, restored to his usual opening spot with Carpenter, was the match's top scorer with 34:

> The match was against twenty-two of Philadelphia, nine of whom were got out on the first day for 40 runs. On the next day we had no cricket, owing to an election taking place. On Wednesday, however, we had a full day. An immense number of people were on the ground. about a thousand ladies, whose brilliant costumes lit up the whole scene, occupying one stand. We defeated the twenty-two by seven wickets.[40]

The squad then divided into North and South camps for what was essentially another internal exhibition match supplemented by the locals. It was rain-affected and there was play only on one day during which the South were all out for 59 and the North replied with 120 for five. Hayward had three wickets and followed up with an aggressive sixty, the highest innings of the tour so far.[41] Despite the weather and the low-key nature of the match, around 2,000 spectators were curious to witness the tourists in action. Because of

illness, George Parr did not play in the match, though he was well
enough to travel to Buffalo and on to Hamilton for the next fixture
on the itinerary:[42]

> On the Saturday afternoon we proceeded to Buffalo, on our way to
> Hamilton, where we were engaged to play our next match v Twenty-
> two of Upper Canada. The journey to Buffalo was a very tedious one,
> and we went a great length of time before we were able to get anything
> to eat. We arrived at Buffalo on Sunday morning, from whence we had
> arranged to go on to Niagara; but when we arrived at Buffalo we found
> the train for the Falls had already started, so we were obliged to take a
> conveyance, and we were nearly five hours doing a distance of twenty-
> two miles or so. It was evening before we reached our destination and
> took up our abode at the International Hotel on the American side. Ar-
> riving so late prevented us from seeing as much of the world-renowned
> Falls as we could have wished.
>
> On our arrival at Hamilton we were met by so dense a crowd of
> people that we had great difficulty in getting out of the station. Fred Lil-
> lywhite's printing-tent had been lost on the journey, and consequently
> there were 'no cards' on the first day at Hamilton. The weather was
> terribly cold, it now being the 17th of October. The twenty-two batted
> first and scored 66. The English team scored 79 and the twenty-two
> made 53 in the second innings, leaving us about 40 to win, which we
> obtained without the loss of a wicket.[43]

It was not as clear-cut a win as in the previous matches, but it was
a win and ensured the tourists kept up their unbeaten record. The
North v South match which followed was a one-day single innings
affair, abandoned with the South hanging on at 33 for nine in reply
to the North's 52 all out

The final match of the tour, against a combined Canada-United
States Twenty-two at Rochester, was an elongated affair: a three-day
match spread over five and interrupted by snow, a game of baseball
and a trip to Niagara Falls to compensate for the earlier truncated
visit caused by railroad delays. The match itself resulted in a comfortable innings victory and had a Hayward half century, the only
one of the tour in the matches against American opposition. There
were thirteen ducks in the North Americans' first innings, eight

in the second and two men were absent. In their two innings the Canada-United States Twenty-two fell 70 runs short of Parr's team's single innings score:

> We left Hamilton that night and travelled to Rochester. It had been intended that our match at Hamilton should be the last of the tour; but while we were at New York the match was arranged to be played against twenty-two of Canada and the States combined. It was morning before we arrived at Rochester and the cold was now intense. We got the twenty-two out for 39 on the first day. On the second there was no play owing to a fall of snow, so we had a turn at base-ball. Sunday intervening, we all took the opportunity of going to Niagara Falls – a long journey – and we were thus able to view them from the Canadian side. The visit well repaid the trouble of getting there, the sight of the Falls being most impressive, in fact never to be forgotten. Returning to Rochester, we resumed our match on the Monday and scored 171 runs. When we took the field for the last time most of us had overcoats and gloves on![44]

Thomas did not feature in the baseball match, though with his batting strength in hits to leg, he might have done well. As in the secondary cricket matches the teams were mixed, Oriel's team overcoming Lockyer's team by 17 (or maybe 18 – the scorecard does not balance) to 7. After two innings, Lockyer's team were ahead 3-1, but the third went 6-1 to Oriel's team who, after that, never looked back. It was an interesting diversion, perhaps indicating the relative significance of the two sports at the time. By the end of the century and beyond it would be very different.

Caffyn indicates there had been a 'practice' baseball match on the 'snowed off' day prior to the one which substituted for what would otherwise have been a 'fill up' match after the cricket:

> The English cricketers have just agreed with the delegates of the Base Ball convention of New York and Brooklyn to play a match at Base Ball on Wednesday and Thursday next. If this time is not agreed to, the match cannot be played as they leave Quebec for Liverpool on Saturday. A snow storm is falling here and the cricket match is postponed until Monday.

There was no cricket played today but the Rochester baseball players invited the English cricketers to practice this afternoon. The baseball players were amalgamated with the cricketers and nine innings a side were played, the scores being eleven and thirteen. The cricketers did not make much headway from want of knowledge of the technicalities of the game.[45]

There had been strong moves from baseball's administrators to try to set up a more representative match along USA v England lines, no doubt in the belief that the cricketers' 'want of knowledge of the technicalities of the game' would enable the Americans to gain some kind of revenge for their heavy defeats at cricket. Lockyer's wicketkeeping abilities embraced what would in later years be deemed 'transferable skills' and enabled him to put up a reasonable performance as catcher, but pitching, batting and fielding skills were not identical with those of cricket. Moreover, the baseball people were willing to provide some financial incentives and with the professionals, money usually talked:

> Base ball Convention. A meeting of the presidents of the base ball clubs of New York, Brooklyn, Williamsburg and others, was held last evening at Astor House, for the purpose of entering into arrangements for playing a friendly game of base ball with nine players of the All-England cricketers. The Chairman stated that it was the general wish of the American players that direct communication should be held with the All English Eleven for the purpose of ascertaining whether, in the event of certain guaranteed conditions being secured to them, they could remain long enough here to play a game of base ball.
>
> In the course of discussion it was stated that, at a meeting held in Brooklyn, though the proceedings there were informal, a sum of $5,000 had been subscribed for the purpose of remunerating the English Eleven for the delay and expense they would incur in the event of their accepting the friendly challenge. This sum of $5,000 will be forthcoming at any time, and an immediate guarantee will be given to the Eleven for its transfer to them whenever the preliminaries are satisfactorily settled upon.[46]

Some days earlier, the Englishmen had indicated to the press that, notwithstanding the financial carrot, they were unwilling to participate in a game with which they were not familiar, especially if it meant prolonging the trip. They were contracted to play four cricket matches (later extended to five by the addition of the Rochester match) and wished to stick at that.

> We have the authority of the English cricketers for contradicting the statements lately made in reference to a contemplated base ball match. Our reporter saw them at the railroad station yesterday afternoon, just as they were on the point of leaving Philadelphia, and they assured him that the statements made of their having offered to play a match for a certain amount of money, of having received a specimen base ball and book of instructions etc are false in every respect. They never play for money; they have never received a challenge to play a match at base ball or offered one; they came here on an invitation from the representatives of cricket clubs in Montreal and New York with whom they were acquainted, to play a series of four matches at cricket, and they never purposed entering into a match at a game with which they were unacquainted.[47]

'They never play for money' may be taken with a large pinch of salt, but that apart, the sentiments are absolutely understandable. It had been an arduous tour, following a busy season in Britain and the players were anxious to get home, in appropriate cases, see their neglected families and put their feet up for the winter.

For similar reasons an invitation to extend the tour to Baltimore was declined:

> Cricketers' Convention. Pursuant to a call this Convention met last evening at Metropolitan Hall. The Convention was called to order by Mr Gould. On motion of Mr Bowen, of the Franklin Club, WW Glenn, Esq of the Maryland, was called in the chair, G Holloway, of the Pickwick, Vice-President, Mr Iglehart Secretary. The following clubs were represented: Maryland, Pickwick, Franklin, Chesapeake, Atlantic, Patsco, Monumental and Baltimore. On motion a Committee from each club was appointed to take into consideration the expense attendant upon inviting the English cricketers to Baltimore. The report of

the committee was that the expense would be $450, exclusive of the cost of an entertainment at the close; also that the match should be played on the Cattle Show grounds on Charles Street. On motion of Mr Schofield of the Patapsco, a committee of three was appointed to go to Philadelphia and invite the English players to come to Baltimore. Carried.[48]

The end of October was quite late enough to be playing in this part of the northern hemisphere. There would be other opportunities in the future.

We left Rochester that evening and very early in the morning found ourselves at a place called Rome. There were no beds vacant at the hotel there so we had to get a few hours' rest as best we could in the smoke-room. We next took a train to Cape St Vincent, from whence we proceeded in a river-boat up a narrow canal to Kingston. On our arrival there we found the railway station was several miles away, and that we should never get there in time, with our great quantity of baggage, to catch the train to Montreal. One or two gentlemen, however, drove over to the railway in a trap and induced the authorities to delay the starting of the train for an hour. This saved us waiting at Kingston till the following day, but as it was, we reached Montreal that night. Having spent a day there, where we went to a steeplechase meeting, we proceeded to Quebec, whence we were to return to England in the *North Briton*. About two hundred miles up the river we passed the *Nova Scotia* which had brought us out. The captain of the *North Briton* ordered a large board to be brought on deck and chalked on it in large characters 'won all our matches' This was no sooner seen by those on board the *Nova Scotia* than they began to cheer lustily, waving their hats and clapping their hands like anything. After a few days' fairly smooth sailing a fearful gale sprang up. Our jib-boom was broken, and one poor old sailor had both his legs broken while he and some of the crew were endeavouring to set matters right. We arranged a concert in the saloon a few days later for his benefit. The poor fellow died of the injuries he had received a few days afterwards. We had had, on the whole, a most eventful trip, and had experienced the greatest kindness from everyone both in Canada and in the States.[49]

Thomas Hayward, youngest player on the tour, topped the averages ('internal' matches excluded) with 22.57 and, as well as his 50 in the final match, also had the next two highest scores: 34 against Philadelphia and 33 against the United States. Next came Lockyer with 31 not out against Philadelphia. A number of his fellow tourists were coming to the end of their careers. At twenty-four, Thomas's best years lay ahead.

The tourists shared £1070 between them, enough to indicate that overseas tours to places where the enthusiasm for the game was growing provided not only evangelical and missionary opportunities to develop and spread the game, but more significantly for entrepreneurs and players, the chance to make some money.

Hayward and Carpenter were duly honoured with a dinner on their return to Cambridge. Recognised for some time as being the country's leading players and now established as 'internationals', they saw the occasion as a catalyst to launch a decade of Cambridgeshire as a 'first-class' county:

Reception of Hayward and Carpenter at Cambridge. The admirers and supporters of cricket at Cambridge met the 'heroes of the American matches' at the Castle Inn on Wednesday evening at dinner. The party was large and included many of the old cricketers of the town.

After dinner the loyal toasts were proposed and responded to in an enthusiastic manner. Then came the toast of the evening, the health of Messrs R Carpenter and T Hayward was drunk in a manner which showed the respect the admirers of the game in Cambridge bear towards two of the best cricketers in England.

Mr Carpenter responded and alluded to their reception in America, but he stated that he was more pleased and gratified by the good feeling expressed towards them by his fellow-townsmen that evening. He went on to say that Cambridge should form a Town and County Club and that himself and T Hayward would assist as much as laid in their power.[50]

11

By schisms rent asunder

1860-63

It was in the period between his two overseas tours that Thomas played the bulk of his first-class cricket without letting up on the more lucrative All-England matches. Of 118 matches in his first-class career, fifty-four were played in these four seasons. While his batting performances remained reasonably constant throughout his career, it was during these years in his mid to late twenties that his medium-pace roundarm bowling (at the time it had to be roundarm or underarm) was at its most effective. In 1860 he had fifty wickets at 9.4, a season which also saw his career-best nine for 30 against Sixteen of Kent at Lord's. Overall, between 1860 and 1863 he bowled almost sixty per cent of his first-class overs (1432 of 2413.3 four-ball) and had a similar percentage of his wickets. It was also in 1860 that he had his highest first-class innings of 132 for the Players against the Gentlemen at Lord's, ironic as it was a ground on which he rarely performed particularly well with the bat. Over the four years, he had just under 2,400 runs (about half his career total) and his lowest annual average was 24.35, more than acceptable for the time.

There was by now a pretty well established pattern to the first-class season. For Thomas it was the Town v Gown match, followed by in varying order; Gentlemen v Players, North v South, North v Surrey, England v Surrey, England v Kent, All-England Eleven v

United England Eleven and two or three Cambridgeshire matches thrown in on the way.

Unlike the previous year when rain had affected a low-key Town v Gown match with some of the leading players for personal and organisational reasons not making themselves available, in 1860 'The Town won a fine match by a solitary wicket, after some moderate scoring, Hayward carrying his bat through the innings for 86 runs.'[51]

In the match against the United at Lord's, George Tarrant made his first-class debut and celebrated it with six for 28. Thomas mopped up the tail in the second innings with four for 10 and the All-England Eleven won by 21 runs. The American tourists then reunited as the 'England Eleven to North America' to play against the imaginatively titled 'Another England Eleven' at Old Trafford. Another England Eleven won by three wickets, recording the highest total of the match in the fourth innings. Thomas's contribution was negligible, 0 and 7, two catches and the wicket of Richard Daft in the second innings.

For England against Kent at Lord's in June he had his best bowling figures, nine for 30, after six for 19 in the first innings. Kent won a low-scoring match by 32 runs, but then again they did have sixteen players. Notwithstanding that, the match was subsequently deemed to be first-class.

Surprisingly Thomas did not make an appearance in the Gentlemen v Players fixture until 1860. Maybe he was never invited or, more likely, he preferred the more lucrative All-England and single wicket matches, but when he did so he made an immediate impact in the back-to-back fixtures at The Oval and Lord's in June 1860. He had four for 33 at The Oval (Carpenter was the main contributor with the bat with 119) and followed up with a maiden first-class century at Lord's with 132 which was to remain his career best. The Players won both matches quite easily, one by eight wickets, then by an innings and 181 runs. It was typical of the period. Richard Daft puts the fixture in its historical context:

The results of these Gentlemen and Players matches were at this time generally in favour of the latter, and for eleven years after this date [1854] they had it all their own way. There are many reasons to account for this. It is perhaps not saying too much to remark that man for man the Players were superior to their opponents as batsmen, and when one comes to consider their great strength in bowling it is easy to be seen that the great annual contest was at this period a one-sided one. Then, too, the Players played together throughout the season in the All-England and United matches, and consequently knew each other's play to a nicety, while some of the Gentlemen scarcely ever met save on the occasion of the great encounter at Lord's.

The tables were turned in after years, when the Graces, the Walkers, the Lubbocks and many other great batsmen appeared on the scene. The Gentlemen became stronger while the Players became weaker. Dissensions between the North and South, the All-England and United, to say nothing of other mushroom 'England XI's' which sprang up, were too often the cause of the Players' XI not being representative. And even had they always put their full strength in the field against their opponents they would not have been so formidable as they had been in the years past. Lockyer, the greatest of wicketkeepers had gone; George Parr was by no means what he had been; Carpenter, getting on in years when he began first-class cricket, could not last so long as he would otherwise have done. His great rival Hayward's day was done before his own, although he was five years his junior. The dreaded Jackson and Tarrant were men of the past and Caffyn was out of the country.[52]

A decade after Thomas's death, a correspondent of *Cricket* produced a set of statistics for the Gentlemen v Players matches for the preceding forty years which showed him top of the Players' list with 36.12 and in the two sets combined behind only WG Grace and WW Read.[53]

In the 1860 Surrey v England match, the county took a first-innings lead and were well on the way to respectability and maybe even avenging their defeat of the previous year when rain washed out the final day. With six for 26 (five of them bowled) Hayward had the best bowling figures of the match, running through the lower order after a sound Surrey start. They were eventually all out for 174. England were 26 runs short of that and by the close of the second day Surrey had extended their lead to 120 with seven wickets remaining. Then it rained:

> To the disappointment of numbers, owing to rain, this great match was not resumed on Wednesday at the Surrey ground, Kennington-oval. As far as it went it was one of the best matches of the season.[54]

Additionally that season Thomas had 28 (run out – not unusual) and 67 against the United England Eleven, 43 for the England first Eleven against the Next Fourteen and a similar score for the North against Surrey, four for 35 in the North v South match at Rochdale and an economical 9-7-2-2 in the equivalent fixture at Sleaford.

The 1861 Census discovered Thomas Hayward in Rugby staying as a visitor at the address of one of his colleagues from the All-England Eleven – he had been appointed to assist Ducky Diver with the coaching at Rugby School – so he does not appear on the census in Cambridge and Lizzie describes herself as head of the household.[55] However, she would probably have welcomed the extra income that the coaching appointment brought. Intriguingly, the roles are reversed ten years later when Thomas is at home with the seven girls and Lizzie nowhere to be found on the census.

In the 1861 match against Surrey at Fenner's, a century on each side, one by Caffyn and one by Hayward, supported by a half century from Carpenter, ensured no result other than a draw was possible for a fixture scheduled for only two days:

> County of Surrey v Cambridgeshire. The splendid batting of Hayward drew forth much applause and, despite the changes of bowling he succeeded in scoring 112. The batting of Hayward, Caffyn and Carpenter was so much appreciated that Mr J Perkins collected £10 for them in the pavilion, £4 each being presented to Hayward and Caffyn and £2 to Carpenter.[56]

Caffyn himself was later to recall:

> Surrey and Cambridgeshire met this year at Cambridge. This was a great run-getting match, we totalling 252 and Cambridgeshire 325.

Two centuries were made, I scoring 103 and Thomas Hayward just beating my score by 9 runs. This match was left unfinished. In the return we were defeated by two wickets. In this match no fewer than three centuries were made – Caesar 111 for Surrey, Hayward 108 and Carpenter exactly 100 for Cambridge. Three centuries had not been scored in one match since 1817.[57]

Three days were allowed for the return match the following month at The Oval and once again Hayward and Carpenter were to the fore with a century each. Their stand of 212 for the third wicket was, says Rowland Bowen, the first certain partnership of over 200.[58] Julius Caesar had a century for Surrey and Cambridgeshire won a close fought encounter by two wickets, Hayward capturing three wickets in each innings:

> Surrey v Cambridgeshire. The Surrey and Cambridgeshire match was marked by a most wonderful exhibition of batting on the part of Carpenter and Hayward. The former went in when the score was at 7 and left it at 222 and the latter when it was at 10 and left it at 227. They both made runs amazingly fast, only giving one chance between them, and never being more than seven runs apart, and the subscriptions flowed in to the tune of £18 when the 'Cambridge Clippers', one with 100 and the other with 108 for his score, came up to the pavilion to receive the public acknowledgment of their masterly defence and hitting.[59]

Alongside Thomas during the mainstay of Cambridgeshire cricket at its zenith in the 1860s were Bob Carpenter and George Tarrant; according to contemporary reputation, respectively the best batsman and best bowler in England. The batting styles of Hayward and Carpenter complemented each other. Tarrant's fast roundarm bowling, said to be second in speed only to John Jackson of Nottinghamshire, was effective against first-class opposition and devastating against the twenty-twos which were generally mismatched with the powerful All-England Eleven, for which Tarrant appeared regularly in the 1860s. Carpenter accompanied Thomas on both his overseas tours, Tarrant on the second one to Australia in 1863/64. The three also formed a deadly combination in lucrative single wicket matches.

Back at The Oval in early August, Thomas opened both batting and bowling for the All-England against the United, had five for 90 in fifty overs and followed up with a top score of 36. There was little support, however, the All-England Eleven's 106 failing to match the United's 171. Despite Tarrant's five wickets they built on that to establish a lead of over 300. Thomas had a second innings duck and, although Stephenson and Caesar had 72 and 40 respectively, his team lost by115 runs.

In between the two Surrey matches, Cambridgeshire entertained Kent on Parker's Piece in conditions which were 'intensely cold for the time of year'.[60] Thomas had a half century and five wickets in the match in a win by 72 runs.

Other noteworthy performances that season were three for 23 for the All-England Eleven against the United, contributing to a win by five runs, participating in two huge wins for the Players against the Gentlemen in the same week, an innings and 60 at Lord's and then an innings and 68 at The Oval. The disparity between the amateurs and professionals was marked at this time, though was later to narrow – at least on the field. At Old Trafford he finished off the United lower order after Willsher and Jackson had done the bulk of the bowling. Then for the North against Surrey he had 66 and five for 85 in 50.1 overs. It was insufficient to win the match, however, Caffyn and Lockyer having got Surrey out of gaol in the second innings.

By this time Hayward and Carpenter were national celebrities and in June 1862 John Lillywhite was advertising for sale 'the beautifully executed photographs of Hayward and Carpenter just published'.[61] One appeared in the *Illustrated Sporting News* with a 'compare and contrast' profile which praised Hayward's defensive play as second to none with Richard Daft as the only comparator, and Carpenter's more aggressive and still developing style.[62] The fielding of both came in for favourable comment, Hayward's at long-stop, Carpenter's at point, as did Hayward's prowess as a bowler, referring to his 'clever medium pace and true bowling'. It concluded with an earlier accolade by the same journalist, resurrecting what he had said a year earlier on the occasion of Hayward's century and Carpenter's half century against Surrey at Fenner's the previous year:

> A pair of better batsmen of one county could hardly, if at all, stand to their wickets. Both masters of all the craft of the game, while still young enough for sustained vigour, activity, and endurance in carrying out all their skill contrives, both alert and acquainted with each other's style. They made the most runs every hit would possibly afford, and not seldom stole runs well, because they stole with cleverness, discretion and decision.

Thomas played an attractive innings of 77 in the Gentlemen v Players match at The Oval. Following his five wickets in the first innings of the match, 'Hayward's batting was perfection, his dashing style eliciting frequent encomiums, and upon reaching the Pavilion where he was presented with a new bat on behalf of the Surrey Club, the applause was great. Among his hits were a five, three fours, three threes and ten twos.'[63]

The presentation of the bat by Surrey had a touch of irony about it. Later in the decade Hayward was to be part of a group of players who, as part of the great North-South schism, declined to play at The Oval.

Thomas came down to earth with a duck in the equivalent fixture at Lord's, but his second-innings half century helped set up a two-day win for the Players. He top-scored with 54 in a ten wicket win for the North against the South at Broughton, then took part in but made little contribution to the All-England Eleven's four-wicket win over the United England Eleven. He was in the collapse to 6 for five, then 14 for six, before Clarke and Anderson pulled it round to achieve what initially had seemed a not too challenging target of 53.

Thomas had 117 in the Surrey v England match at The Oval in August before being bowled by Lockyer, taking a break from keeping wicket, but it was not for that that this match is memorable, nor for the 503 that England made in the first innings. Edgar Willsher was no-balled on six occasions by umpire John Lillywhite for raising his arm above shoulder level, illegal at the time. England walked off the field, the umpire was changed and Surrey eventually escaped with a draw, having followed on. There were longer-term consequences, however. On the positive side, the Law was changed to allow over-arm bowling and on the negative, it exacerbated North-South hostilities (Willsher was a man of Kent, VE Walker of Southgate the captain, but the team had a northern and *ipso facto* bloody-minded bias against the South and Surrey) and caused a deepening of the already existing schism.

William Caffyn, who played for Surrey in the match, recalls the acrimony caused by the incident:

> The great match Surrey v England was played this year at the Oval, when the notorious 'no-ball' incident of Willsher's career occurred. This was a remarkable match altogether. The England side was a very strong one indeed. They won the toss, and on an excellent wicket compiled the enormous score of 503. Thomas Hayward scored 117, Jemmy Grundy 95, Bob Carpenter 94 and Willsher 54. When Surrey took the bat Willsher was promptly no-balled by John Lillywhite half a dozen times. I have alluded to this unpleasant incident before and have stated how the England side left the field (with the exception of the Hon. CG Lyttelton and Mr VE Walker). There was no more play that day and the next morning the England team refused to go into the field unless another umpire was provided. So at this pass Street was substituted for Lillywhite. We were easily defeated. The 'no-balling' caused a lot of unpleasantness for a long time afterwards, some of the Northern players becoming bitterly prejudiced against Surrey and the Oval.[64]

When Samuel John Stone wrote in the 1860s of an institution 'by schisms rent asunder' he was thinking of the Christian Church, but the form of words could equally apply to the state of professional cricket at the time. The no-balling of Willsher by John Lillywhite, largely assumed to have been instigated by Surrey, was just one aspect of the dissension in the game which had its origins in the composition of the team which toured Australia in 1861/62 under the captaincy of HH Stephenson of Surrey. The team had a heavy southern bias, though whether that was due to selection or the intransigence of the northern players in declining to accept a lower fee than that to which they believed they were entitled remains a matter of speculation. The animosity was further exacerbated by what was perceived to be biased umpiring. For a few years, Nottinghamshire declined to play against Surrey, as did five of the Yorkshire professionals, and the Cambridgeshire trio of Carpenter, Hayward and Tarrant refused to play at The Oval. Fixtures and loyalties were thrown into confusion as North v South fixtures clashed with Gentlemen v Players matches and the long-established Canterbury Festival was disregarded in the arranging of fixtures at The Oval. The dispute led ultimately to the formation of the United South of England Eleven, partly in protest against the All-England Eleven with its roots in Nottinghamshire, and ultimately to the spawning of a number of other professional touring sides, a number of them very short-lived.[65]

The North-South divide is part of economic and political history but in the 1860s it spilled over into a decade of cricket history. Hayward was not directly involved in the politics, except in so far as his association with 'northern' Cambridgeshire affected the matches in which he was willing to play. The ferocity and acrimonious nature of the dispute are apparent from a Surrey general meeting and a letter of a few years later from Fred Lillywhite about *inter alia* the arrangements for the 1861/62 Spiers and Pond tour to Australia. There was no love lost between Lillywhite and Parr after 'a bit of previous' in the hassles involving the logistics of transporting the tent and printing press around the United States and Canada.

A letter from George Parr to *Bell's Life* points to a further cause of the deepening rift owing to a misunderstanding with the Surrey Honorary Secretary, William Burrup, over availability for a Surrey v England fixture which clashed with Canterbury week. Burrup had also been involved in the gate-crashing of negotiations for the 1861/62 tour. Established as a county club in 1845, Surrey was now beginning to flex its muscles and challenge other longer established institutions and traditions. The Northern professionals were having none of it:

In the opening of last year Mr Burrup asked me to play in England v Surrey. I promised to do so provided it did not interfere with the Marylebone Cricket Club matches. Afterwards I found out that Mr Burrup's match clashed with England v Kent at Canterbury. As it was impossible for England to play in two places at the same time and, as I subsequently discovered that the Canterbury week had for very many years been held at or about the same time for which Mr Burrup had fixed his match at the Oval (which he, as Secretary of the Surrey Cricket Club must, or at all events should have known), I refused to play inasmuch as England matches are played under the immediate direction of the MCC which is the senior club of the two, and I thought that my interference in their one at Canterbury was unwarrantable. My example being followed by many of my brother professionals, the old-established Canterbury week remained the same and the days of the Oval match were changed. For this reason, coupled with the fact that I could not agree with the sentiments Mr Burrup expressed in his letters to me last February with regard to the dilatoriness of the MCC in not fixing their matches until the end of January, I have incurred the displeasure of the Secretary of the Surrey Club. I have now for many years been a professional player, and no one is more grateful than I am for the kind support which I have met with at the hands of the public. I have played for the MCC for nearly twenty years and have always, with the rest of England, considered that club the fountain head of cricket. To them I owe my allegiance and owing to giving it to them I have incurred the displeasure of the Secretary of the Surrey Club, but I cannot serve two masters.[66]

The 'Lion of the North' was biting back.

As the weather warmed up for the 1863 season, the All-England lost to the United and the Players had their customary win over the Gentlemen at Lord's, Thomas 112 not out, before Tarrant and Jackson cleaned up twice to win the match with a day to spare. The pair did a similar demolition job for England against Kent (with thirteen players) at Lord's, Tarrant with a career-best ten for 40.

Because of the deepening schism and the Parr-Burrup dispute, the trio did not play for the North at The Oval though in logic there was no reason why they should not have done except for sheer bloody-mindedness and to demonstrate solidarity with their northern professional colleague. They had missed out on the 1861/62 Australian tour because of the Burrup-Lillywhite intervention, but that could not have been a major consideration as Carpenter and Hayward had played and starred in the subsequently controversial Surrey v England match of 1862. However, opportunities for more lucrative engagements elsewhere may well have been the determining factor. The *Sporting Life,* more in sorrow than in anger, opined: 'We are sorry to say that this, which ought to have been one of the great hits of the season, is really no match between the North and Surrey through the weakness of the Northern team owing to the refusal of Parr, Tarrant, Carpenter, Hayward and several other well-known men to play against Surrey on account of some rupture between Parr and the secretary of the Surrey Club and we must say it is a pity that any such private misunderstandings should be allowed to interfere with this, one of the most important matches of the season.'[67]

The season over, the London *Evening Standard* took a distinctly non-London view in siding with the 'secessionists':

As to the so-called 'cricket schism' which has made such havoc this year with the best 'Oval' matches, I heartily agree with the 'Church and State' review that the Surrey management is responsible for it. I do not see any necessity for the cricket world to submit to a Surrey dictatorship, and can, from what I have seen, both understand and sympathise with the determination of our best players not to take part in a match of which the Surrey secretary has the management. And I know that this feeling has been intensified by the endeavours made through the medium of the papers to shift the onus of blame from the right shoulders to the Notts and Cambridge professionals, and to lecture a most respectable set of hard-working men as if they were a body of spoilt schoolboys. The North, let me add in conclusion, can generally nowadays beat the South but if tables should be again turned, I believe and trust that the North will revenge itself on the cricket-field and not by attacks on men of inferior social position to whom their cricketing character is their daily bread.[68]

Thomas did nothing distinguished in the South v North match at Lord's, nor in the Kent v England match at Canterbury, but was top scorer with 34 for the North against the South at Liverpool.

Shortly before that, along with brother Dan, he had played for Cambridgeshire against MCC at Lord's and with George Tarrant shared nineteen wickets in the match as the hosts, 106 in arrears, were obliged to follow on. However, the 'senior club' converted that to a lead of 101 before bowling out the county cheaply in the fourth innings. He had 44 in the first innings, but was part of a final innings collapse which cost the match.

It epitomised a less successful season than usual and in November, the *Sporting Life* summing up the year as was its custom, pointed out that Hayward no longer stood at the head of the list of 'leading batters', but his season had been good enough to earn him a comparison in the newspaper's columns with EM Grace. It is unlikely that either would have read the correspondence. By this time both were well into a journey to Australia:

> We have annually since 1860 been in the habit of laying before our readers the season's performances of the leading batters of the day. Thomas Hayward, until this year, has stood at the head of our list, but circumstances have occurred during the present season which have prevented this great batter taking part in some matches in which he has usually been engaged. Nevertheless we find him running a good second. He is at the present moment on his voyage to Australia, where he is sure to give a good account of himself.
>
> Mortlock's performances entitled him to the first notice.
>
> Hayward commenced the season early at Cambridge and against the University made a good score; nor did his average suffer in his contest against the United at Lord's, where he made a fine innings of 30; but his great performance of the season, and one of which he may justly be proud, was his not-out innings against the Gentlemen at Lord's. He also worthily defended the honour of his county in the contest against the MCC and Ground in which his first innings produced 44, to which he subsequently added 5. He played a fine innings in a match against odds at Redditch where he made 71 (not out) and 4 in the second attempt; but his greatest score in any of these matches was against twenty-two of Longsight where he made 86 in one innings. At

Ashton-under-Lyne, his two innings fell only two short of that number (84). The numerous spectators of Harrogate and Scarborough were also gratified by a fine exhibition by this master-hand on the occasion of the All-England Eleven visiting these fashionable places of resort for autumnal visitors.

Thomas Hayward played in ten eleven-a-side matches and made 392 runs in sixteen innings; was not out once, bowled five times, caught nine, stumped once and run out once. The average per innings being 21 and 8 over. Also in twenty-four odds matches he made 759 runs in thirty-eight innings giving an average of 21 and 17 over. In these matches he was not out four times, was bowled nine, caught twenty, stumped twice, leg before twice, hit wicket once and run out four times. His aggregate number of runs in thirty-four matches amounted to 1151 for which he played fifty-four innings averaging 21 and 17 over.[69]

12

THOMAS'S MINOR MATCHES

1860-63

Thomas returned from North America in top form and began the season with a 74 in the University v Players Engaged match before another outstanding performance in the Town v Gown match the following week.

In early June he played for a team called Old Cambridge Men against the University. It was not his most memorable performance. His team lost by an innings and 60 runs, having collapsed to 21 all out in their second innings. He made four in the first innings and failed to score in the second, but demonstrated his versatility as well as his genetic inheritance by keeping wicket and effecting a stumping.

Then against Lansdown in Bath, he was run out (not unusual) without getting off the mark (not unprecedented), but followed up by sharing the ball with Jackson and dismissing the twenty-two for 28, Jackson seven for 10 and Thomas thirteen for 16 in thirty overs each. A rare defeat followed as Lincolnshire's 60 and 34 beat All-England's 37 and 46 in a match presumably not in batsman friendly conditions where the scoring rate was well below one per over. It was followed by defeat by eleven wickets at Broughton. No longer were the touring All-England Eleven carrying all before them. For sheer imbalance, the Broughton first innings scorecard takes some

Thomas Hayward (left) photographed with his Cambridgeshire teammate Robert Carpenter. Both are wearing the distinctive spotted shirts of the All-England Eleven.

beating. There was one century, two in double figures and of the remaining nineteen, none got past nine.

Walsall were not too dissimilar in the next match, dispatched for 49 with just one batsman making it to ten, as once again Jackson and Hayward shared the wickets between them. Sometimes Thomas bowled through the innings, sometimes not at all. Likewise, though Thomas usually opened the batting, he also batted sometimes in the middle order. It was all very flexible. Against Gainsborough, Willsher and Hayward were the only bowlers used, splitting the second innings wickets equally between them after Willsher had shared the attack with Jackson, Reynolds and Tinley in the first. It was not unusual for one or more of the opposition batsmen to be marked 'absent'. Sometimes they may have been injured, sometimes had work to do or maybe just not shown up. Professionals were expected to play for three days. Then as now amateurs had more of a choice.

There were some commendable performances by Thomas's colleagues. Against Eighteen of Hallam at Hyde Park, Sheffield, a match which All-England won by an innings and 156 runs, Bob Tinley with his slow lobs had ten for 54 in the first innings, then a rare, maybe even unique, 'all seventeen' for 58 in the second.

The versatility of the All-England side continued. As well as matches against town and city sides, against somewhere-and-district and against teams purporting to represent counties, they also played a bit of country house cricket. In the match against Shugborough on the Earl of Lichfield's ground on the edge of Cannock Chase, Thomas's bowling was bracketed for commendation with that of the leading performers of the day:

> All-England Eleven v Twenty-two of Shugborough. This was a three days contest, commencing on Thursday the 2nd in Shugborough Park, the seat of the Earl of Lichfield and terminating on Saturday, the Eleven winning by nine wickets, the bowling of Jackson, Tinley, Willsher and Hayward being very effective.[70]

Despite the improving railway services, the travelling must have been absolutely exhausting, even for those who had experienced North America. In August and September they played at Barnsley and Leeds, not too far apart, except the itinerary took them via Plymouth, Dublin and Belfast, then a brief trip south to Leicester, before heading north again to end the season in Glasgow, where against the Caledonian Club, they collapsed to 20 all out in eighteen overs to lose by 28 runs. It had been a long season. It was presumably worthwhile financially or they would not have considered going such distances.

In 1861, Thomas was helping Ducky Diver with the coaching at Rugby School, staying with him at his home and playing in a trial match, First Twelve v Next Ten, beginning on 1 April (early for the time) and spread over four afternoons.[71] Then, back in Cambridge, he top-scored with 37 and had five for 69 for the 'Players Engaged' against the University.

Later Thomas turned in a couple of reasonable performances for the All-England Eleven against Twenty-two of Bradford and District: 'Hayward was early substituted for Jackson as a bowler and the change proved most effective, he obtaining nine wickets and only 21 runs being got from his 44 overs.'[72] Then, in the second innings, 'The bowling of Hayward was again most destructive, no fewer than 12 wickets falling before him.'[73] Twenty wickets for 74 runs was a useful enough contribution, but it was insufficient. Bradford won by 17 runs.

Now in his mid-twenties, Thomas's bowling was perhaps at his peak. He helped demolish Hallam and Staveley at Sheffield with eight for 16 and six for 48. Willsher's ten for 18 in the second innings ensured a win for the tourists by 54 runs.

Then, against Twenty-two Gentlemen of Walsall with two professionals, he scored 60 and took twelve wickets for 13 in the first innings.[74] Richard Daft batted through the innings for 114. Walsall were bowled out for 50 and 78 as All-England won by an innings and 177.

At the end of the 1861 season, Thomas and Dan resurrected their connection with the North East, taking a Cambridge team to play against Twenty of Bishop Auckland and District with two professionals.[75] On the way Thomas had played for the All-England Eleven at Middlesbrough, taking five wickets in each innings.

In addition to his first-class matches, Thomas had played twenty 'miscellaneous' matches in 1861. It was nearer a couple of dozen in each of the following two years. Most were for the All-England Eleven, some against regular opponents, others against new ones or one-offs, such as Captain Handley's team at Hungerford, Rossall School and Old Boys in Fleetwood. As well as the Cambridge matches, he had occasional excursions elsewhere, such as for the Players at Lord's against a combined Oxford-Cambridge University Sixteen and, according to Cricket Archive, for Phoenix against I Zingari in Dublin September 1862 when he batted at number ten and did not bowl. It can only be assumed that was a different T Hayward as Thomas is also recorded on the same days as batting at number four and taking six for 27 to help All-England beat Harrogate at the Swan Hotel Ground.

It has been said that proficiency at billiards is the mark of a gentleman, but to play too well is a sign of misspent youth. Thomas Hayward was certainly no gentlemen, in either a social or cricketing sense, but was good enough to win the local tournament in the winter of 1863:

> The second great billiard handicap of the season took place at Mr Saunders's Billiard rooms on Wednesday January 21 and following days. The play of some of the competitors was exceedingly good, especially that of the renowned Thomas Hayward of cricket notoriety who won the handicap in fine style.[76]

However, he began his summer activities early, as a given man for the Next Fourteen against the St John's Club First Eleven, then for the Players Engaged against the University:

> This match was played in rather unfavourable weather. The University won the toss and put the Players in and disposed of them for 106, no large number considering that the three single wicket champions were included in the team.[77]

Maybe the three 'cracks' were affected by the cold, though as all were natives of the county, it could not have come as a great surprise to them in late April and early May. However, thanks in part to Thomas's 40 in the second innings with support from brother Dan's 22 not out ('The brothers Hayward were in great force' according to *Bell's Life*) the Players won by 5 runs.

13

DAN'S PLAYING CAREER

AFTER 1859

The record of Dan Hayward junior in first-class matches was not among the most distinguished. He played forty-three matches, mostly for Cambridge Town and the newly established county club of Cambridgeshire, never bowled, took eighteen catches, scored a couple of fifties and his average of 10 (690 in sixty-nine completed innings) was slightly below that of his father. Nevertheless, Cambridgeshire's first-class fixtures during their brief sojourn at the top level were against the leading counties of Kent, Nottinghamshire, Surrey and Yorkshire. Dan's return, at a time when batting averages were lower anyway, compared well with many of his contemporaries and were certainly better than those who, then and now, failed to make the starting line. Furthermore, unlike his brother who made professional cricket his career, for Dan it was supplementary to his business interests.

In 1860, both brothers appeared in the Players Engaged match, but only Dan in the double header Town v Long Vacation Club matches at Fenner's and on Parker's Piece. Likewise in 1861, both played in the Players Engaged match, Thomas again outscoring Dan over the two innings and taking five for 69 in the first innings. The Town, with Dan but without Thomas, were hammered by the Long Vacation Club to the extent of an innings and 96 runs, the Town having no answer to the Vacation Club's massive total of 450. Dan opened the bowling, came back later and had a couple of lower order wickets. Cricket Archive comments that the Cambridge Town Club should have been called the second eleven as all the 'cracks' were away. In September the Players played against the Long Vacation Club, Dan scoring 17 in the first innings and the top score of 16 in the second.

The Players Engaged match in 1862 provided an extraordinary finish. The Players Engaged required just 17 to win the game in the fourth innings, but a heavy shower between innings made the pitch almost unplayable as Henry Plowden followed up his first innings five for 74 with six for 6. Thomas Hayward and Bob Carpenter, convinced of victory, had already left the ground. When the seventh wicket fell, George Tarrant – who was still on the ground but had changed – was obliged to change back again quickly and see his team home; officially by three wickets, effectively by one:

> A remarkable match was played in 1862 between the University and Cambridge players. The latter had in their innings only 18 runs to get to win, but before they went in a heavy shower fell and made the ground very queer. Plowden's slows 'skirt up' or shot very quickly, and the wickets fell so fast that seven men were out for 16 runs! The two cracks, Hayward and Carpenter, had left the ground, thinking the match as good as over. Tarrant had changed but like the good sports-man he had stopped to see the end. He came in and made a hit for which two runs were got, and a third, unnecessarily, attempted, in try-ing for which he was run out. This of course did not count, the runs required having been made.[78]

Later that year Dan played for the United England Eleven against the Gentlemen of Hampshire and, in June of the following year, against MCC at Lord's. From July 1863 to 1865, however, his allegiance was to the All-England Eleven. In 1866 he flitted to and fro between both touring sides and in 1867, apart from the usual Cambridge matches, his loyalty was to the United. Between 1868 and 1873 he played little cricket, but towards the end of the 1872 season attracted the attention of the local press in a Youngsters v Veterans match when youth succumbed to experience:

> There was a match on Parker's Piece on Monday last between eleven 'youngsters' and a similar team of Veterans of Cambridge. The odds were in favour of youth before the battle but the sequel proved that the preference was miscalculated.
>
> The Veterans put together 73 before luncheon, leaving Dan Hayward and Cornwell in possession of the wicket. Dan proved himself to be in his 'old form' and was repeatedly encouraged by the plaudits of the spectators.'[79]

The 'Youngsters' had 69; Dan 17.

From that point until his last match in 1869, apart from one match for the All-England Eleven against Yorkshire at Barnsley (the only first-class match ever played on the Shaw Lane ground) and one for a combined Cambridgeshire-Yorkshire XI against Nottinghamshire at Newmarket, his first-class cricket was entirely for Cambridgeshire. Of the thirty-nine matches played by the county in the brief period of their first-class existence, Dan featured in thirty-one, just behind his brother (thirty-five) and Bob Carpenter (thirty-two) and level with George Tarrant. His overall batting average for the county was 8.78 and he never bowled. That compares with batting and bowling averages of 33.34 and 17.51 for Thomas, 31.64 and 14.18 for Carpenter and 17.82 and 12.25 for Tarrant, principally a fast bowler. The other three are prominent in the averages and statistics for the thirty-nine matches, Dan appears just once, as a participant in the highest eighth-wicket partnership of 36 against Yorkshire at Ashton-under-Lyne in 1865. By no means were all matches on a home and away basis. Ashton-under-Lyne is in neither Yorkshire nor Cambridgeshire, and the same season one of the Cambridgeshire v Nottinghamshire matches was played at Old Trafford. The previous year the same counties had met at Lord's when Cambridgeshire won by 18 runs, the Midlanders never recovering fully from Tarrant's first-innings seven for 30. Dan opened in both innings, first with Tarrant, then with Ducky Diver:

The Cambridgeshire men began the batting with Tarrant and Daniel Hayward to the bowling of Jackson and Wootton. Some good, free hitting and not very good fielding enabled Cambridgeshire men to score 34 runs before a wicket was lost. At 82 for three Daniel Hayward left for a well-played 37, a good leg-hitting innings.[80]

In 1867, batting at number nine, he had his second first-class half century, 58 not out, against the University at Fenner's. The county had followed on 121 behind and, at 84 for seven, an innings defeat was on the cards. But Dan managed to avoid that and took the final total to 187. The University knocked off the runs for only two wickets, but the extent of the humiliation had been reduced. It was one of the many matches in which he distinguished himself as long-stop.[81]

Daniel often opened the innings, usually with little success, although there were exceptions. At Dewsbury in 1867, looking to avenge an earlier one-wicket defeat by Yorkshire at Wisbech when the tenth wicket had added 15 to win the match, Dan (having made 3 not out at number six while wickets fell like ninepins at the other end) opened in the second innings and made 24 before being bowled by Emmett. Thomas followed up at number four with 44 not out and Cambridgeshire were able to add 105 to their first innings lead of five. It was insufficient. Yorkshire still won by four wickets but overall, in the eight matches played, Cambridgeshire came out on top, winning four and drawing one of the eight encounters. Thus, they remain – and are likely to remain for the foreseeable future – the only county side to have more wins than defeats against the White Rose county, although all the others have played a few more matches.

Daniel's final match for the county side, however, was one of complete humiliation. At Hunslet, Yorkshire totalled 352, the tenth wicket partnership of 72 coming close to Cambridgeshire's 40 and 46. Thomas Emmett, bowling through the match with George Freeman, had seven for 15, then nine for 23. Dan had 4 and 0, bowled by Emmett on both occasions. Time to call it a day. His contribution to Cambridgeshire cricket, to the game as a whole and to his own bank balance, lay in other areas.

Appearances for the All-England Eleven at Maldon and appropriately against the Cambridge Town Club on Parker's Piece brought down the curtain on his playing career in 1873.

Towards the end and slightly beyond it, he umpired in five first-class and fourteen miscellaneous matches. It may have been more. Records are incomplete, but his last appearance on a cricket field seems to have been as umpire in the Surrey v Nottinghamshire match at the Kennington Oval in August 1875.[82]

14

AUSTRALIA AND NEW ZEALAND
1863/64

The first tour of an England team to Australia was in 1861/62 under the captaincy of Surrey's HH Stephenson and the early sponsorship of Spiers and Pond, proprietors of the Café de Paris in Melbourne. A fee of £150 was insufficient to attract some of the more financially aware members of the team, including putative captain George Parr and Thomas Hayward, which two years earlier had crossed the Atlantic, though the eventual proceeds were sufficient to pay them considerably more than that. Instead they filled the coffers of Spiers and Pond. An upward movement to £250 for 1863/64 made a difference and once more a strong side of a dozen English cricketers – eight of whom were regulars in the All-England Eleven – packed their bags for a journey to the other side of the world. In October, they set sail from Liverpool in the SS *Great Britain*, among their fellow passengers were a variety of livestock including sheep, pigs, goats, chickens, geese, ducks and turkeys.

> The Cricketers for Australia. The twelve cricketers who are in a few months to uphold the sporting fame of the mother country at the antipodes, are all now in London, making the necessary preparations for their long voyage half round the earth. They were to receive the sum of money £50 per man which had been munificently sent over as the price of their engagement, and they are now occupied in making purchases

for their outfit. They were to have embarked early this month in the Great Britain but the start has been delayed to the 15th in order that this splendid steamship may be fitted with larger boilers. It is calculated that this alteration will have the effect of shortening the trip by six days. Some little alteration has been made in the original list. We believe that the following is a correct list of those who will sail from Liverpool on Thursday.

G Parr, Jackson, RC Tinley and A Clarke (Nottinghamshire); Caffyn, Lockyer and Caesar (Surrey); Anderson (Yorkshire); Hayward, Carpenter and Tarrant (Cambridgeshire); and Mr EM Grace.[83]

As in North America four years earlier, Caffyn's memories and press reports are invaluable in reconstructing the tour and recapturing something of the pioneering spirit of those involved:

It was owing to the Melbourne Club that the visit of the second team to Australia was brought about. George Parr was entrusted to get up the team, and amongst others was told to try and get Dr EM Grace, HH Stephenson, Mortlock, Griffith and myself. Cambridgeshire sent the famous trio, Hayward, Carpenter and Tarrant.

We were entertained to a farewell luncheon at the Adelphi Hotel by Mr Whitaker, a great supporter of cricket, before we proceeded on board the *Great Briton* [sic] in the afternoon. We had not been many hours in the open sea before the vessel began to roll a bit, causing several of our team to retire to bed.

We had a very pleasant voyage altogether, and used to beguile the time by day with a little cricket practice, 'bull-board' etc. We had some great fun when we started 'cock-fighting'. This game was played between two opponents, who had a stick passed at the back of their knee-joints and held it there with their arms. While in this position each had to try to knock the other over. In the evenings we sometimes had a concert in the saloon, at which several of our men assisted. On another occasion we had a most enjoyable magic-lantern entertainment. Then there was often dancing on deck on fine evenings. At one part of our journey we encountered large flocks of 'Mother Carey's chickens'. I recollect seeing a hawk capture one of these, which he came and devoured on one of the masts of our ship. When we sighted the Canaries there was great excitement, caused by the appearance of a large whale. When we crossed the line a lighted tar-barrel was thrown overboard. This we could see after we had left it miles behind, and it produced a grand effect in the darkness of the night. On Sundays when it was fine we always had divine service on deck, and when the weather was unfavourable it was held in the saloon. To see the sailors attending these services, all attired in beautiful clean white jackets and trousers was very pleasing. We had rather rough weather towards the end of our voyage which lasted sixty-one days.[84]

The tour opened on New Year's Day, against Victoria at the MCG. Unlike the United States and Canada, cricket was well established in Australia and a repeat of the one-sided contests which had characterised the 1859 tour was not anticipated and did not materialise. The arrival of the cricketers was eagerly awaited:

> The arrival of the twelve English cricketers, who were passengers by the *Great Britain*, has been one of the events of the past month; and now that they are among us, people are looking forward eagerly to their first appearance in the field against double their number. The team are in fine health and spirits, and now that they have regained their 'shore legs' they have been pretty hard at work in practice on one or two of

Parr's tourists gather at Lord's before journeying to the other side of the world.
Back: Julius Caesar, Alfred Clarke, George Tarrant, George Parr, EM Grace,
Robert Carpenter, George Anderson, William Caffyn.
Front: Robert 'Cris' Tinley, Thomas Lockyer, Thomas Hayward, John Jackson.

our suburban grounds. What with the international matches, and an inter colonial match, or rather a trial of strength between an eleven of the Albert Club of Sydney and an eleven of the Melbourne Club, which begins on Boxing Day, we shall have quite a 'carnival of cricket' presently.'[85]

The enthusiasm was such that a good number of Melbourne residents eschewed the pleasure of last-minute Christmas shopping to watch the tourists at practice:

> Those who were so fortunate as to be present on the Melbourne ground yesterday afternoon enjoyed quite a treat in the way of cricket as several of the All-England Eleven were practising. A more perfect and finished state of play than that of Hayward and Carpenter would be impossible to imagine. Every ball appeared to be played exactly at the proper moment and in the right way.[86]

Caffyn was certainly pleased with the beginning of the tour:

> We had a fortnight to prepare for our first match, which was to take place on New Year's Day. On Christmas Day we were invited to Sandridge to visit the ships Dover Castle and Agincourt. A few days later we had a picnic at Sunbury which was very enjoyable. Between the time of our landing and New Year's Day we had some excellent quail-shooting. We killed over forty brace one day.[87]

The local reporter was spot on in recognising Hayward and Carpenter as the key batsmen. In the first innings against Victoria, they had a half century each, the only players in double figures, and added 125 for the fourth wicket:

> 22 of Victoria v Eleven of England. Three men out for only ten runs was regarded as a most favourable state of affairs by the Twenty-two but when Carpenter joined the other Cambridge player (Hayward) and the two were known as the safest bats in England, the backers of the English team were still hopeful of a large score being obtained; and right well did they sustain their reputation, increasing the score from 10 to 138 before they were parted ... Hayward whose splendid batting was a great feature of the day's play. No fairer display of batting was ever seen

than was displayed by Hayward in obtaining his score of 61 runs – the highest score of the first innings and he was enthusiastically cheered on his return to his tent. From a sharply thrown in ball Hayward was struck severely on the forehead, but continued to bat with undiminished vigour.[88]

Bell's Life was in no doubt about the significance of the match. Nor were the thousands of spectators who paid at the turnstiles:

> The greatest cricket match ever played in Australia – the four days tourney in which the flower of the cricketing chivalry of England was engaged, is now at an end; and although the Victorian Champions claim the merit of a drawn battle, there is no doubt that the English knights of the willow would have gained an easy victory over their twenty-two opponents had the battle been continued but a short time longer. As it was, on the termination of the play on the fourth day, the Old England Eleven reached within 8 runs of the number required to win and had yet six wickets to fall. As showing the interest taken in the play of the Eleven from England, we may state that over 40,000 persons paid at the gates, and that the pavilion and the tents on the MCC's reserve were crowded.

In more measured tones, Caffyn summarised:

> The match lasted four days – a Sunday intervening. The twenty-two of Victoria scored 146, the English Eleven beating this total by 30 on the first innings. Hayward and Carpenter made a long stand, the former scoring 61 and his fellow townsman 59. The Australians put on 143 in their second innings, leaving us 114 to win. We were within 9 runs of winning, having 6 wickets in hand, when time was called, the match being drawn.[89]

The match in the gold-mining town of Bendigo was affected by the weather, but there was still time for Parr's XI to win by 144 runs:

> The favourable weather which has hitherto attended the All-England Eleven on their public appearances in this Colony was broken on Saturday at Sandhurst. Early in the morning the wind changed to the northwards, and for some hours, as it blows very hard, the town was

enveloped in a cloud of dust. Shortly before twelve, the time at which the play commenced there was a light fall of rain and this was but the prelude to other and more violent visitations of the elements, which from time to time caused the players to take shelter in the pavilion. About five it commenced to rain steadily: an adjournment took place and after waiting some half an hour, the Eleven, who were fielding, resolved to continue the game in the wet – and with a ground never in particularly good condition, what the rest of the innings was may be easily imagined. The weather prevented any great number being present, and at no time during the day could there have been more than four hundred on the ground.[90]

Ballarat was as much a social occasion as a cricket match. The players were welcomed and entertained with great enthusiasm and afterwards, there were a few sports during which EM Grace and Thomas Hayward ran a race of 100 yards in which Thomas was just defeated.[91]

A change of plan meant that the party travelled to Ballarat a day later than originally intended, on Monday morning, much to the disappointment of those assembled at the station to greet them on Sunday evening. An enthusiastic welcome when they did eventually arrive at 11.30, followed by a drive to the hotel in a carriage and four and a late 'breakfast' meant that the planned starting time of noon was rescheduled for 1.15. Lunch was taken at 2.30 and lasted an hour, so by 3.30 there had been just over an hour's actual play.

In the evening the team visited the Theatre Royal. It was, however, a three-day match, so there was ample time to win by an innings and 12 runs and play a single wicket match afterwards. *Bell's Life* reported on an injury to Hayward's hand, which caused him to be dismissed cheaply, and an extraordinary journey to Ballarat:

During the day an old man, verging on sixty years, and who had travelled nearly 310 miles – a third of it on foot – to witness the match, was introduced to several of the Eleven, by whom he was warmly welcomed. The old man stated his intention of accompanying the Eleven to Araret [sic], to see them play once more and that then he should return to his garden and his work contented and happy. This old man stated that forty years ago he had played in several matches of note at St John's Wood and that he could not rest contented until he had once again witnessed the play of the Old England Eleven.[92]

There then followed an up-country tour, first to Ararat, then on to Evaraly and Maryborough where they accepted a lunch invitation and then were met 'by the Mayor of Maryborough and a considerable number of the inhabitants of the town who, on horseback and in vehicles of all descriptions had gone forth to bid the Englishmen welcome. A procession was formed to Maryborough and on arrival there the Eleven were received with great cheering and conducted to their quarters at the McIvor and Commercial Hotels.'[93]

Tom made a useful contribution to the innings win at Maryborough, taking nine wickets in the first innings while Tinley cleaned up at the other end, then chipping in with a useful 30 as ten of the local side had a turn with the ball, and finally conceding a miserly 14 runs from his forty-one overs, as Tinley matched his first innings take with another eleven and Jackson's pace accounted for six for 5.

Hospitality was lavish throughout. Special trains were laid on, timetables rearranged, the party met by civic dignitaries, conveyed around Melbourne by horse-drawn carriages in a procession comprising 'numerous horsemen', welcomed by flags and cheering crowds and treated to high level entertainment.[94]

It was then on to New Zealand for matches in Dunedin and Christchurch where the assembled crowds were equally if not more welcoming on piers, railway stations and at the grounds.

En route to Dunedin to play XXII of Otago:

We started for Dunedin in a coach-and-six, driven by a famous coachman called 'Cabbage-Tree Ned' accompanied by a large number of carriages and horsemen by way of escort. The road was across the mountains, and had been newly made. The scenery was grand. We had a tremendous reception when we arrived. The people seemed to have fairly gone mad with excitement. The wicket was a very rough one. The twenty-two scored 71 and 83. We made 99 and 58 for one wicket, thus obtaining a victory by 9 wickets. Thomas Hayward secured 15 wickets in the first innings of the twenty-two and 9 in the second.[95]

Tom in fact bowled through both innings, 47-29-34-15 and 41.1-25-36-9.

On the second day of the cricket-match the ceremony of laying the foundation-stone of the Exhibition buildings took place. A large procession was formed on the cricket-ground, and marched from there to the site of the building. Before leaving Dunedin we each planted a memorial tree on the cricket-ground, as in the case of the first English team at Melbourne two years before.[96]

For the burghers of Dunedin the town was *en fête*. Employers in the city declared a half holiday on each day for their staff and a public holiday on the third.

The spectators were compensated for their disappointment at the defeat with a fill-up match against Canterbury and Otago in which Thomas, having already done his bit in the main match, bowled but a handful of overs and batted at number eleven – at least it is categorised as a fill-up match by Cricket Archive and Parr's side probably saw it that way, but for the New Zealanders it was something more. The Canterbury players had remained in Dunedin following an interprovincial fixture in anticipation of such a match and amalgamated with their previous opponents to become, rather grandiosely, Twenty-two of the Southern Hemisphere.[97]

In addition to that there were also some sports, probably enjoyed far more by the participants than the elaborate receptions and presentations:

Some sports were got up at the conclusion of the cricket in which we all took part:
 Jackson v Tinley. 100 yards. Jackson won by a yard.
 Caffyn v Caesar. 100 yards. Caesar won easily.
 Grace v Holmes. 1/4 mile. Holmes won as he liked.
 Hayward v Wills. 100yards. Hayward won by a yard.
 Grace v Tarrant. 600 yards. Tarrant won by a yard.

Anderson v Jones. 100 yards. Two dead heats.
English Eleven handicap. 120 yards. Caffyn won (9 yards start).
Caffyn v Jackson. 100 yards. Caffyn won.
Hurdle race. 600 yards. Tarrant won.[98]

EM Grace was the only amateur on tour, but in the more egalitarian environment of Australia and New Zealand where being one of 'the right sort' was of less significance, he seems to have integrated well with the rest of the party and shared their leisure and social activities.

There was no financial risk to the tourists in New Zealand. A willing sponsor was unearthed, prepared to risk losing money in the interests of seeing the cricketers were not out of pocket and that his fellow countrymen had the opportunity to witness some high quality sport:

> How it has happened that we can boast of having the English cricketers in our midst is so well known that little need be said on the subject. Long before they left England the Dunedin club and some friends held a meeting and talked over the possibility of making arrangements to bring the team down here. The terms offered by Mr Marshall, who had engaged the Eleven seemed to forbid all hopes of successful negotiation. But all that was wanted was that the matter should be taken up by some enterprising man and not left to a committee, by whom the necessarily prompt action could scarcely be taken apart from the very important question of how to raise the necessary money. Such a man was found in Mr SFR Jones of the Provincial Hotel. With nothing guaranteed, but content with the promise that as much as possible should be collected he took the risk of making an engagement with the Eleven; he bore the cost of erecting a stand which is one third larger than that in Melbourne, and which will accommodate nearly 3,000 people and he has also had the ground temporarily fenced and otherwise prepared.[99]

The *Hawke's Bay Herald* reflected the excitement of the occasion but clearly felt the preparations were excessive:

> Otago: from our own correspondent. How we shall contain ourselves when the All-England Eleven come among us, I do not know I am sure.

Where are we to get a sufficiency of grey horses from, which are to draw the carriages in teams of fours, sixes and eights is puzzling everybody. The number of places and occasions at and in which the immortal cricketers are to stop and partake of champagne certainly pre-supposes that All-England Elevens and champagne are closely allied in a dissoluble bond, although it may be difficult to explain upon what grounds.

The All-Englanders being delivered in the Port Chalmers jetty in good order and sound condition, they will be received by the various provincial clubs. On leaving the jetty the whole are to be champagned at the leading hotel at the public expense, raised by general subscription. Then the grey horses attached to carriages will take all on to Dunedin where they are to champagne at Shadrach Jones's 'Provincial'. Then once more into conveyances and onto the cricket ground where there is to be more champagne. The All-Englanders will then have some practice with bat and ball and wicket among themselves. Afterwards follows a spread attended with more champagne.[100]

Their arrival, however, had to be stage managed. Because of weather conditions they had arrived in the middle of the night, so had to be sidetracked, in order that their quayside reception could be timed for a more convenient hour:

Arrival of the All-England Eleven. The *Alhambra* was anxiously watched for and it was known that Captain McLean would do his best to come to anchor at the time named as most suitable for a triumphal procession from the port to Dunedin. But mail steamers on the Suez route will, as the dwellers in these colonies know to their sorrow, get behind time; and so it happened that, when going overdue, the steamer with the November mail was telegraphed just when the *Alhambra* should have left and she was detained to bring on the bags.

The port had never before looked so gay as it did on Saturday. The wretched little jetty was so disguised with flags and wreaths of fern, with festoons and flowers, that it looked quite picturesque.

There was scarcely a building in George Street that did not show at least a flag or some evergreens. But the *Alhambra* did not arrive until after midnight on Saturday, and during Sunday, as there could be no public demonstration if the Eleven had landed, they were taken by Mr Jones to the Maori Kaik near the Heads where they fraternised extensively with the dusky and tattooed residents. Yesterday the landing did take place and the Eleven had to endure, during the ride to town, an infliction in the shape of wind and dust which they may rest assured was exceptionally severe.

An over-elaborate reception then followed, arrangements severely hampered by freak weather conditions. Spearheaded by the iconic Cabbage Tree Ned and accompanied by the provincial brass band, a procession of half-a-dozen carriages, trimmed with ferns and club colours, made its way to Port Chalmers. Amid strong winds they arrived at the hosting hotel to find a collapsed tent and roofless stables. Then, after lunch and speeches of welcome from the cricket clubs:

> The procession was soon reformed. The pull up to the Junction Hotel was rather a long one but it was effected without the slightest accident. We know that the Eleven expressed themselves delighted with the romantic scenery through which they passed. We also know they did not like the dust. Cheer and cheer was given as the men alighted and entered the hotel. A much needed wash was obtained and then came another luncheon. By four o'clock the coach and six was once more in motion; and the team was driven rapidly to the ground.
>
> Painful evidence of the strength of the gale was afforded by the Grandstand which was almost wholly stripped of its galvanised iron roofing. The men speedily got their bats in their hands and went in for about an hour's rollicking practice. There was some great hitting, but the men seemed rather to desire to stretch themselves than to make play.[101]

It was all well-intentioned and the attention to detail and response to the adverse weather conditions were commendable. But did the players really want this kind of attention? These were working-class men who knew their place in the class-structured deferential society at home. To be met with arrangements which would not have been out of place for a state visit would have been unexpected and embarrassing. Certainly Thomas would have felt more at home in a pub with a billiard table and a few betting slips. At the post-match presentations, not on the scale of the welcome reception but nevertheless at the Princess Theatre rather than at the ground, he chose to absent himself, to the obvious surprise of his captain who with a bit of quick thinking dredged up the unconvincing explanation of Thomas's injured finger as a reason for his not being there:

> Mr Hamilton: It is said that the best of guns is of no use without a ball and I have a ball here which I have the pleasure of presenting to one of the greatest guns ever known. I am sorry that a slight accident on the ground prevents Mr Hayward being present. But I must say that Mr Hayward has made the best 'analysis'. I present this ball to Mr Parr for Mr Hayward.
>
> Mr Parr: I am called upon unexpectedly in this matter. Mr Hayward received an injury to one of his fingers which I presume has caused him to be absent, but I am sure he will be glad when I tell him how enthusiastically his name was received. I thank Mr Hamilton on behalf of Mr Hayward.'[102]

The correspondent of the *Lyttelton Times* could not have been alone in his opinion that the tour's organisational arrangements had been totally over the top, not unlike contemporary Olympic Games where at times competition between host venues for the most elaborate opening and closing ceremonies seems to exceed in importance competition between the athletes:

> To the Editor. Sir,
>
> Is it too late to beg that we may not be made ridiculous on the arrival of the English cricketers by the interference of people who know nothing about the game?
>
> The English Eleven is composed of very worthy fellows who would appreciate what they are accustomed to at home – the hospitality and welcome which it is the duty of the cricket clubs to offer. But a Superintendent and a Town Council Chairman with their coaches and six, and their speeches are more, I should think, than they bargained for.
>
> I shall be told that Victoria and Dunedin have set us the example, but examples have been set before often enough in New York.
> Yours, An Old Cricketer.[103]

Certainly the cricketers on both sides might have wished that less attention had been paid to the peripheral glitz and more to the quality of the conditions in which the actual cricket was to be played.

The *Otago Witness* described the ground as 'in very poor condition and bumpy and rough to a degree'.[104] *Bell's Life* would comment a week later that it was in 'wretched condition'.

The hospitality and entertainment contrasted markedly with the quality of and local interest in the cricket, though for the visitors the Maori war dance was something different:

> The arrangements made by Mr Jones were of the most complete and liberal character. The players were taken to and from the ground each day in a coach and six, a good band under the leadership of Mons Fleury on the ground each day, and an excellent lunch provided, at which the usual speeches were repeated.
>
> The accommodation at the Provincial was of a first-class character and Shadrach's cook is a man to be worshipped. The Dunedin people did not appear to hold cricket in very great estimation, as the attendance on each day, both on the ground and stand, was considerably less than was expected.
>
> On the last day the Maoris who had come up from Port Chalmers to see the match, perpetrated a war dance, of the propriety of which the less said the better. It was certainly an eye-opener to the English visitors.[105]

Arrangements had been put in place for those who wished to travel to Christchurch for the Canterbury match:

> The SS *Queen* will leave for Lyttelton on 5th February and arrive there in good time for those who wish to see the greatest treat ever offered to New Zealand lovers of cricket, namely the match of the All-England Eleven with the Canterbury cricketers. For this occasion return tickets will be issued at reduced prices.[106]

Canterbury were dismissed for 30 and lost by an innings. Another fill-up match was played, Parr's Eleven v Anderson's Eleven. The mixing of the teams produced a much closer result. Parr's Eleven, for which Thomas played, winning a close match by seven runs, Thomas starring with six wickets in each innings.

The attention lavished on the tourists and the attention to detail would rival that afforded today to pop stars and royalty, one newspaper even taking an interest in the colour of their eyes:

'There is one fact,' says the Ararat Advertiser, 'which we have not seen recorded in any of our Victorian journals in reference to the English cricketers and that is that all of them possess blue eyes. Even Mr Caesar, whose complexion is darker than that of most men, has eyes of a dark blue; and as it is well known that all the crack English rifle shots have also blue eyes it would almost seem that this colour is indispensable in any occupation where quickness or strength of sight is requisite.'[107]

They returned to Dunedin for the second fixture with Otago which again resulted in a heavy defeat for the twenty-two. The tourists wore different coloured caps as an aid to identification, an idea perhaps borrowed from contemporary football and a forerunner of squad numbers on shirts:

As the general public must naturally desire to be able to distinguish the different celebrated players from each other, it has been settled for the Englishmen to wear caps of varied colours, and these colours will be named on the 'authorised card' published early tomorrow morning. The same card will also inform purchasers of the places taken in the field by the champion players, both plans being entirely novel and a most useful boon to the public.[108]

So, alongside a futuristic idea, there is also a reflection of a contemporary feature: that of rigid field placing. Indicating the fielding positions of each player suggested that a fielder would remain there for the duration of the match. It was only later in the century that field placing became less rigid and flexibility introduced to allow for the state of the match or strengths and weaknesses of each batsman.

This match was brought to a conclusion yesterday and resulted, as was expected, in an easy victory for the English team. The great feature of the day was the appearance of his Honor the Superintendent in the company of cricketers; and it was imagined that the champion cricketers would do their spiriting gently in order to allow so distinguished an opponent the chance of scoring. This was soon proved to be a popular fallacy inasmuch as Jackson's second ball sent the wickets of the Superintendent flying.[109]

The glamorous peripherals and celebrity treatment concluded with an elaborate farewell dinner:

Last evening Mr S Jones gave a farewell dinner to the All-England Eleven and to most of those who have been in any way connected with the cricket campaigns.

After dinner Mr Jones returned thanks for the Eleven for the hearty manner in which they had supported him and said that though the speculation had not been satisfactory in a pecuniary sense, as all the world knew, still he did not regret it. The mistake was that the speculation was before the times. He then handed each one of the All-England Eleven a handsome shield pin, made of New Zealand gold.

In testimony of the esteem they felt for that gentleman they presented a handsome silver cup bearing the names of the Eleven and the date of their visit.

It is uncertain when the cricketers leave for Melbourne but it is probable that they will sail today in the *Omeo*.[110]

The *Omeo* certainly took the team back to Australia, where in the first match, Hayward had 21 against Castlemaine and took fifteen wickets:

We reached Melbourne on the last day of February, having had a very pleasant passage, although one or two of our men had not been able to escape from sea-sickness. The next day we proceeded to Castlemaine, where we easily defeated another twenty-two by an innings and 37 runs. A scarf pin was presented to each member of our team as a memento of our visit.[111]

Bell's Life reported in some detail on Hayward's style and approach to batting:

Hayward was next and for a time he kept to the scientific system and the result was a scarcity of runs. Hayward then contrived to work up a few, first by singles, obtained principally at short leg, and then he increased his score by one or two doubles, but they were not obtained rapidly, as both batsmen were playing with caution.

When the play was resumed, Carpenter joined Hayward. Then both batsmen commenced to let out, but the ground being rather dead, it was impossible to get the balls far away from the wickets.

Hayward, by cautiously playing the straight balls and punishing the loose ones succeeded in adding considerably to his score. Hayward was at length bowled by Makinson after he had been at the wicket upwards of two hours and scored 21.[112]

Caffyn recalled that:

Our next match was at Melbourne – George Parr's eleven against George Anderson's. Caesar, Tinley, Tarrant, Carpenter and I played for Parr, while Dr Grace, Hayward, Lockyer, Clarke and Jackson were with Anderson. The two elevens were made up with Australian players, as at Christchurch. Anderson's side was victorious, defeating us by 4 wickets.[113]

This was the only first-class match played on the tour when the team split in two, Anderson's XI v Parr's XI, each side supplemented by the locals. What Caffyn does not say is that the match was delayed by over an hour because the supplementary players could not – and eventually did not – agree terms. They were more financially savvy than their American counterparts had been. If they were to play alongside the English professionals they were entitled to similar financial rewards. The authorities were having none of it and simply replaced them with amateurs. Nonetheless the match retained its first-class status and although 'timeless' took only three days to complete. In an all-Cambridgeshire scoreline in the second innings, Hayward was caught Carpenter bowled Tarrant 1:

Once more the English Cricketers are at work on the Melbourne ground. The twelve Englishmen have for this once divided themselves fairly into two parties, the ranks of each being completed by Victorian players.

It became apparent that a misunderstanding of some kind had arisen and considerable interest prevailed as to its nature and extent. It soon became known that the difficulty was with the Victorian professional players who declined giving their services except on terms higher than Marshall and the English cricketers had understood them to have been willing to accept. So far as inquiries have been carried out, it is difficult to ascertain the real merits of the dispute since the statements on both sides are conflicting. There is one point in the dispute, however, which cannot and ought not to be passed over in silence. It will be admitted, we think, that such a dispute, no matter what the right or the wrong might be, should never have been allowed to come before the public at all. Surely the difficulty could have been arranged in private and prior to the commencement of the match, in an English and cricketing spirit.

The difficulty occasioned by the defection of the professionals was at length got over by the substitution of gentlemen players.

An hour and a quarter was consumed before this arrangement was effected.

Jackson and Wills were the first to take up the bowling with Lockyer of course behind the wickets; the long stopping being entrusted to Hayward and Grace in turns.[114]

Caffyn's recollection was:

During our stay in Melbourne this time we attended the theatre, where Mr and Mrs Kean were performing. A photograph was taken of the English team here, from which a large picture was produced by an artist. Whether this afterwards came to England or remained in Australia I cannot now recollect. The same artist also painted a portrait of each one of us separately. They were all good likenesses except that of Thomas Hayward's, the artist never being able to obtain a satisfactory portrait of him, although he made many attempts to do so.

On the 11th of March we set out for Sydney in the Alexandra and arrived there on the 14th. The next day was Sunday, and we passed it in driving about the country. On the next day we had an address presented to us at our hotel. The day before our first match at Sydney was excessively hot and made some of us feel quite ill. Rain fell at night, however, and cooled the air a good deal. Our match was against twenty-two of New South Wales. There was a huge crowd to witness it, fully 20,000 people being present. The twenty-two made a good show against us in their first innings. The twenty-two totalled 137 in their first venture. In our first innings we compiled 128, thus being 9 runs behind. The spectators were very delighted at the success of the twenty-two, and there was a feeling that they might be successful in lowering the colours for the first time of Parr's renowned eleven. A heavy rain coming on, however, altered the condition of things, and they only managed to knock up 50 against us in their second innings. This left us 60 to win, but we lost six wickets in obtaining them. The match was concluded on the day before Good Friday. The return match was begun on the Saturday before Easter, the ground being in a very wet state. The game ended in an even draw.[115]

There were in fact three matches played in Sydney against a New South Wales Twenty-two, all at The Domain. The first was timeless and spread over nine days – although there was rain on five of them – and won by four wickets, the second drawn and the third won by one wicket, as Tinley, coming in at number eleven with the scores level obtained the required single.

Then another Anderson's v Parr's match, though without first-class status this time, and the tour concluded with drawn matches against Ballarat when Carpenter had 121 and Victoria, where because of the state of the ground, a different pitch was used for each innings. Then it was time for home:

On the evening of the 7th of April we went on board the steamer *Wonga Wonga*, bound for Melbourne, after partaking of a farewell luncheon in Sydney. When we had got a few miles outside The 'Heads' we came into collision with a small sailing vessel called the *Viceroy*. The *Viceroy* was sunk almost immediately. A boat was lowered and we succeeded in saving the crew. Our vessel was a good deal injured in the forward part, so much so that there was nothing for it but to put back to Sydney for repairs, where our arrival caused the greatest astonishment. We were not able to start again until two days later. The mosquitos were so troublesome on our voyage to Melbourne that we were obliged to sleep on deck and a few of us caught bad colds in consequence. Eventually we arrived at Melbourne about two in the morning of April 11.

Of the sixteen matches played (all against twenty-twos) ten had been won by us and six drawn. Carpenter came out at the head of the batting averages with 22, his large innings in the last match but one having pulled him up a good deal. He also totalled the highest number of runs (396) and had the honour of scoring the only century. I came next to him, having made 348 runs for an average of 18. Thomas Hayward also averaged 18, but scored 22 runs less than I did. We each cleared £250 from the trip, after paying all expenses.[116]

In terms of results and finance, the tour was a success, for the players at least. There was also an undoubted public relations element. Australians had flocked to the cricket and New Zealanders had enjoyed the social side. The Auckland-based *Daily Southern Cross* took a more jaundiced view – albeit a more realistic and measured one. It repeatedly expressed the view that Auckland should not have been omitted from the arrangements and that a combined New Zealand team might have fared better than the two provincial teams. The financial arrangements had benefitted neither host nation and the mercenary attitude of the players attracted some criticism:

> In some respects, indeed in not a few, the All-England Eleven's visit to New Zealand was a failure. Gloss it over as we may, we cannot altogether get rid of this unpleasant conviction. The contractor who brought over the team was obliged to confess that he had suffered a loss by the affair. The public did not seem to take an interest in the play sufficient to give up their ordinary occupations to see it. They might go once to see the great English cricketers but they could not take the trouble to go again in the hope of seeing play between sides so utterly unequal.
>
> The people and cricketers of Otago wanted the All-England Eleven to come and play there; and the wish was reasonable, and one to which no objection could well be raised. Dunedin was indeed the natural place for a cricket match to have been played between the All-England players and a twenty-two representing the colony. This the Otago people appear at first to have fancied they could get amongst themselves; to do them justice they soon shook themselves clear of such an idea it would seem, but they still clung to the notion of a twenty-two of Otago as the correct thing. Had the object been to get a game of really good cricket, the best obtainable in this part of the world, the course of inviting all the provinces to join in sending their very best would have been the natural one. Auckland has no jealousy of Dunedin and we chance to know that Auckland could and would have sent at least two or three players equal to any who did play, if not superior, to have assisted our Southern cricketers to uphold the credit of New Zealand's cricket.[117]

Well, the matches are over, the cricketers gone and now there's nothing left but a muddy ground and three beatings to remind us of the great Eleven; – yes, there's one thing more – an unpleasant deficit in the funds of the speculators, a deficit that it was in the power of no one to prevent – that cruel rain that deadened everything and heaped disappointment as it fell day after day, and prolonged each game to such an extent that the most enthusiastic at last began to weary. On only two entire days during the visit of the English were we without rain, and it was only on the first and last days that the ground was nearly fit for cricket; on the other occasions it could only be called a bog. Under such a misfortune it may perhaps be considered fortunate that so much as £5,000 was taken but we can't help thinking what a great success fine weather would have brought.

The English cricketers are getting into rather bad repute. They have exhibited a grasping spirit, and a determination to make themselves disagreeable. They have evidently been here too long and have too much money. It is said that each will walk off with his cool thousand. Not so bad for cricketing, that.[118]

From a cricket point of view, the second edition of *Wisden* had no doubts about the success of the tour or the quality of the team.

There cannot be any doubt in all unprejudiced minds that the Eleven now leaving these shores is greatly superior to anything the colonists have previously seen in point of cricketing excellence. The previous Eleven showed nothing equal to the wicket-keeping of Lockyer, the batting of Hayward and Carpenter, or the bowling of Jackson, Tarrant and Tinley.[119]

Already in April preparations were in progress in Cambridge to welcome them back to the town:

Testimonial to Hayward, Carpenter and Tarrant, the Cambridge cricketers. Lion Hotel Tuesday evening.

On their return home anticipated in June next from their brilliant career in Australia, their cricketing friends desire to testify their approbation of their prowess in the field and the manner in which they have represented their town and county by presenting them with a testimonial, the preliminary of which was the purpose of the meeting.[120]

When the players did eventually arrive home with the 1864 season already half over, there was speculation on the financial success of the tour:

> By the Australian mail the English cricketers have arrived from Australia. As a pecuniary speculation their visit has proved a very great success and each man will, after payment of all expenses net something like a thousand pounds.[121]

£1,000 was something of an exaggeration; the actual amount was nearer £250 (well over twice the amount the average manual worker could earn in twice the time) plus expenses, plus various gifts bestowed upon them, particularly on the New Zealand leg.

15

DAN THE BUSINESSMAN

Dan went into business on three fronts. Eventually he acquired the Prince Regent public house close to Parker's Piece. In addition to being a well-established watering hole it was, under his management, to become a meeting point for local cricket teams and their functions and also for the embryonic Cambridgeshire Football Association. Linked to the pub business was a lucrative sports outfitting operation, but his business started more modestly with hiring out tents for the use of the clubs who played on the Piece.

The financial arrangements, however, were messy. In 1857, Dan followed the pattern set by his father and continued by his brother in having a brush with the law in a case regarding non-payment of rents for the tents. The case ended with the hope that a tidier system would be in place for the following season:

> Cricketing Tents. Numerous summonses having been issued against the tent-keepers on Parker's Piece for arrears of rent, several of the defaulting appeared this morning (Thursday). It appeared that there were 11 informations against Haggar and Snow, who are partners, 12 against Hayward and 13 against Ringwood. Last year the late Treasurer used to send the collector Mr Thomas Brown to gather the money of the tent-keepers, but this formed no part of his duty. According to the terms of the Corporation bye-laws the tent-keepers have a right to pay before the tents are erected, but when Mr Brown called upon them they referred to certain clubs, who, they contended, had previously paid and would pay again, stating 'if you don't get the money we'll see you paid in October'. This being an unsatisfactory way of 'doing business' the Commons

Committee ordered the Town Clerk to proceed against the tent-keepers and summonses were issued against them 'by wholesale'. Snow, Haggar and Hayward were present this morning and after the case was heard Mr Cooper said he could not offer terms, but would willingly listen to any offer they had to make; and it was eventually agreed that the cases should be adjourned to the 4th of September, it being understood that in the meantime the defendants should pay all claims and costs, each of the summonses being 2s 6d. This saved the cost of conviction, which would be 1s 6d more. The Bench have the power of inflicting the penalty of 10s upon each information which, upon Haggar and Snow, would, if carried out, amount to 22/- and it was thoroughly explained that for the future the money for the tents must be paid before erection, and no other persons will be looked to but the tent-holders.[122]

In 1864, Dan was again in court, though not about financial matters this time (at least, not directly) and admittedly only as a witness, but it was clear that he had exceeded the authority given to him for cutting the turf on Parker's Piece. The prosecution wished to have the witness convicted, but the Magistrate's Clerk quite correctly disallowed this. Nonetheless it is difficult to avoid the impression that Dan was becoming to regard the Piece as his personal

The Prince Regent in Cambridge, a Hayward family home from the 1860s.

patch and private cricket area rather than the public amenity it was intended to be:

Sessions and Police Intelligence. The Question of Right to dig on Parker's Piece.

George and Stephen Arber were summoned for digging Parker's Piece. The defendants were cricketers and the Town Clerk, who appeared for the corporation, said they were charged with disturbing the turf upon Parker's Piece under the Malicious Trespass Act.

James Seale stated that on Monday he saw the defendants cutting up the soil upon Parker's Piece. He spoke to Hayward and he said he should cut up what he liked; that he had permission from the Commons Committee and that the Mayor was not upon that committee. Hayward told witness that he had no right to interfere.

Mr Cooper said practices of this sort could not be put a stop to by the infliction of a small fine, because the fine was paid by certain parties while the offender escaped punishment. He should, therefore, ask in this case for the defendants to be punished in some other way, under the Act of Parliament.

Mr Hayward, cricketer, now entered the court and the defendants wished to call him as a witness.

Mr Cooper: Then I prefer a charge against him also. I ask him to be taken into custody also.

The Magistrate's Clerk: Not upon this charge. You cannot do that.

Hayward being admitted as a witness stated that he asked permission of the Mayor two months ago to repair the Piece.

The Mayor: Yes and I told you that you might cut the turf against the gaol and that you were to leave the ground in its usual condition.

Seale was recalled and stated that Hayward said he should do it, notwithstanding the Mayor, as he had nothing to do with the Commons Committee. The Mayor addressing Hayward reminded him of his application to repair the cricket ground, when he (the Mayor) told him that he might cut where the hills were, against the gaol, and that the holes were to be filled up. Shortly afterwards he received complaints of holes being left nearly opposite to Park Terrace, although he had shown him, Hayward, what spot to take the grass from, and pointed out one particular place. The Mayor proceeded to say that Parker's Piece was for the benefit of the inhabitants of the town, and it was not to be cut up by certain individuals as they choose, and large holes left large enough to put coffins in. The Piece was to be properly repaired and kept in good order, and not cut up by persons as if they had the sole power and exclusive right over it. Parker's Piece was one of the finest pieces of pasture in the whole kingdom, left for the benefit of the town and must be preserved.

Mr Ald. Hurrell: What you want, Mr Cooper, is to prevent it for the future.

Mr Cooper: We can't do so by a fine.

The Mayor said with a hope that these things would be prevented for the future, the Bench would be as lenient as they could, but if another case came before them they were by no means prepared to say they should allow a fine. The Defendants, this time, would be fined 2s 6d and costs.[123]

Nevertheless, despite his hard-headed business sense, Dan was to the fore when it came to helping a seriously ill friend and colleague:

Frederick Bell of Cambridge. We very much regret to hear this professional, so well known at Eton, Cambridge and as one of the old United Eleven is now lying dangerously ill at Cambridge. It is stated a subscription list is started to minister to Bell's comfort in his sickness, and we are further informed that a University gentleman – a prominent and popular member of this year's Eleven – recommends Bell's case to public sympathy. Carpenter or Daniel Hayward of Cambridge will kindly receive any aid kindly proffered to poor Bell.[124]

By 1863 Daniel was in a position to marry and start a family, although on his marriage certificate he is still described as 'cricketer' despite his other interests by that time. His bride, Emma Martin, was the daughter of an innkeeper. Two sons, Arthur and Daniel Martin, and two daughters, Emma Martin and Alice, were added to the family in six years. It was then, in the late summer of 1869, that he embarked on his most lucrative business adventure, linking his tent-hiring business to his acquisition of the Prince Regent Inn:

Dan Hayward Begs to inform his Friends and the Public that He has taken the Prince Regent Inn, 55, Regent Street, Cambridge And hopes to meet a share of their patronage N.B. Good beds, stables and Coach-houses. MARQUEES FOR SALE OR HIRE.[125]

It was a deliberate and conscious change of direction. In 1861 and again in 1863, he had described himself as a cricketer.[126] Henceforward he is an innkeeper, and thereafter a licensed victualler with other sidelines not mentioned on the Censuses.[127] The Prince Regent Pub would become the centre of family life and Daniel and Emma's last two children, Thomas Walter and Frank, were born there in 1871 and 1881 respectively. By 1891 however, his son Daniel Martin, then aged twenty-five, is listed as an athletic outfitter, so that part of the business had clearly been developed and delegated. Tom is a wood turner; Frank, aged ten, still at school. Emma and Alice, twenty-four and twenty-two respectively, have no profession or occupation recorded against their names, but the likelihood is that they were occupied helping out in the Prince Regent.

Echoing the experience of his father in the licensed trade in St Ives, Daniel was never far away from the criminal fraternity. At the County Petty Sessions on 22 February 1871, in a case of pocket-picking in Bury Corn Exchange, James Watson and John Harrison were charged with stealing money from a gentleman's pocket. Emma Hayward gave evidence:

> Emma, the wife of Daniel Hayward, landlord of the Prince Regent public-house, Cambridge said 'The prisoners slept at our house on Tuesday night, in a double-bedded room. They had tea on the Tuesday evening and breakfast the next morning. One ordered for the two but I don't know which; Harrison paid for both. They left the house at about half past nine. It is about ten minutes walk to the railway station from our house. They went towards the station.'[128]

Daniel was clearly an astute businessman and while he may have pushed the envelope of legality to the limit, he does not seem to have been engaged in any fraudulent activity, though with an astute eye on cash flow, he was not keen on parting with his money if he did not need to:

Cambridge Borough Petty Sessions. Tuesday.

Dan Hayward, publican, of Regent Street was charged with assaulting John Williams in Regent Street on Saturday last.

Complainant said: 'On Saturday evening last about seven o'clock, I went to defendant's house in Regent Street. He was putting the shutters up. I said "Please Mr Hayward are you going to pay me my money?"

He replied "I'll money you, you nasty young scamp. If I catch you on my premises any more I will summons you."

Because I did not go away defendant took me by the collar, shook me and said "I will learn you."'

Ernest Pigg corroborated the above evidence.

Defendant, in answer to the charge, said complainant did not come to work on Friday but came on Saturday morning and said he was not coming any more. He came in the evening for his money and I said I would pay him when he had done his week's work.

The case was dismissed upon defendant paying the expenses.[129]

The cricket and other sports teams using Parker's Piece and, in consequence, Daniel Hayward's tents, obviously needed equipment, so a new advertisement was brought to their attention:

D Hayward Cricket, Lawn Tennis & Football Outfitter 55 Regent Street, Cambridge Has now in stock about seventy Dozen of well-seasoned cane-handled BATS, from the principal makers; also Twenty Dozen of practice Bats, suitable for clubs from 6s each. All goods first-class quality and low prices. Marquees of Every Description for sale or Hire.[130]

Diversification beyond the licensed trade and cricket was an obvious move and soon he was hiring his tents and renting out the premises to other organisations. A newspaper report mentioned that he would provide the tents for the Cambridge and Isle of Ely Agricultural Society's show and he was not slow off the mark to develop a business relationship with the newly established Cambridgeshire Football Association. Cambridge was one of the pioneers of the game. The earliest rules were drawn up there in 1846, providing some guidance to the Football Association, established in 1863 when they made an attempt at conformity. In the wake of that County Associations were established and they needed meeting rooms.

> Cambridge Football Association. A meeting of this recently formed association was held on Saturday evening last at D Hayward's the Prince Regent, to draw up rules and arrange matches for the season. It was ultimately decided to play matches with Middlesex, Norfolk, Lincolnshire and Huntingdonshire.[131]

Later, he had a 'football room', where the association met to discuss major and minor policy issues. The room was clearly intended for exclusive use, but would not have been made available free of charge:

> Cambridgeshire Football Association. A meeting of the committee of this body was held on Wednesday evening in Mr Hayward's football-room. Attention was called to the practice of Clubs not adhering to their registered colours with reference to teams playing in League matches.[132]

16

THE SCHISM CONTINUES

1864-72

Within days of their return from the Antipodes, in the summer of 1864, most of the tourists were in action at Lord's in the Gentlemen v Players match – not that much action was required from most of them. Thomas had a modest half dozen but the Players' total of 187 was more than enough as Willsher and Tarrant bowled through both of the Gentlemen's innings taking all twenty wickets between them and bowling them out for 60 and 59.

Then it was back to more competitive cricket with Cambridgeshire, England and the North and, bizarrely, because of the schism rending asunder the tidy North-South arrangement, for Cambridgeshire and Yorkshire against Kent and Nottinghamshire at Newmarket. During Cambridgeshire's first match against Yorkshire, played a week after the Gentlemen v Players outing at Lord's, the opportunity was taken to combine the cricket with the recognition of the local trio's success on the winter tour:

> The first match between Cambridgeshire and Yorkshire will be played on Monday, Tuesday and Wednesday next on Parker's Piece. A dinner will take place on Tuesday at the Lion Hotel when the testimonial to Messrs Carpenter, Tarrant and Hayward will be presented.[133]

Against Nottinghamshire at Lord's, 'Two conspicuous scores were made T Hayward 40, comprising fours, threes and twos, and Carpenter 29.'[134]

Before the multi-county affair at Newmarket, played late in the season in October, a normal North v South match had taken place at Old Trafford, suggesting that the schism was players v administrators and not players v players. Thomas's 66 helped the northerners to a nine wicket win.

However, the *Sporting Life,* in its Christmas Eve issue, was highly critical of the Cambridgeshire set up and its continued refusal to play Surrey, notwithstanding that there had been the possibility of reconciliation, at least between the players on the previous winter's Australasian tour:

> There must be something rotten in the state of affairs cricketical in a county possessing so many first-class professionals as does Cambridgeshire – the non-existence of a regular county club and the reduction of its matches to three in a whole season, and only one of those played on its own soil – needs not the wisdom of a philosopher to discover; but to arrive satisfactorily at the causes of this deplorable state of things, if not a very difficult, is certainly not a very pleasant task; but it becomes our duty as the staunch advocates of county cricket, to endeavour to probe it. That the county possesses talent of the highest order there can be no doubt whatever, and that that talent properly organised and exercised can successfully hold its own against the strongest elevens in England is equally certain; but that the gentlemen who find the sinews of war, and who give their time and energies to the promotion of the noble game, will continue their support, or take further trouble in advancing the interests of men who, however talented, are indifferent, or something worse, is rather too much to be expected. That such has been the case for the last two or three years and is likely to continue for some time to come, we fear is more than problematical. We have no desire to recur to the past, beyond expressing our regret that the Cambridge eleven have of late afforded the cricket loving public so few opportunities of witnessing their prowess, and as regards the future, we are in a position to state that the Surrey committee, being desirous this year of renewing their annual contest with Cambridgeshire (the only first-class county omitted from their programme in 1864), recently for-

warded a challenge for a home-and-home match to Mr H Perkins, the respected honorary secretary of the late Cambridge county eleven, offering, if lack of funds should be an obstacle to the arrangement, to bear the whole of the expenses of the match at the Oval. The reply received in due course from that gentleman was that R Carpenter, T Hayward and G Tarrant had positively declined to play at the Oval at present, and therefore the match could not come off. We state these facts in order that our readers may be well posted as to the cause of the omission of this great county eleven from next year's Surrey programme, and to afford them an opportunity of judging what probability there exists of the three eminent professionals before-named appearing upon the Oval for some time to come, if ever again.

The county of Cambridgeshire during the season 1864 played, as before stated, three matches only, and can say what no other county is enabled to, viz – that they won them all.[135]

Disorganisation continued to dominate in 1865, as witness the Yorkshire v Cambridgeshire match at Ashton-under-Lyne when Yorkshire won the toss and took advantage of the fact that four of the Cambridgeshire players had not arrived by inviting them to bat. Thomas was to score 84 and take six wickets in the second innings.[136]

In a departure from their matches against twenty-twos, the All-England Eleven demonstrated their ability to play in eleven-a-side matches with an overwhelming innings victory at Bramall Lane. Carpenter and Hayward had a century each, Carpenter a career-best 134, the partnership between the two taking the score past 300 before the fourth wicket fell. Captain George Parr then chipped in with 78 as the All-England Eleven ran up a mammoth 524 in 320 overs the innings concluding just before the close on the second day. There was time for one wicket before the close, Hayward catching debutant William Smith for a duck. Yorkshire were then dismissed twice on the third day, George Wootton taking all ten in the second innings including that of Smith for a second duck, an inauspicious start to his first-class career.

Cricket being the great leveller that it is, in the next first-class match in which Thomas played, South v North at Canterbury, Wootton had no wickets at all, which allowed space for Thomas to take the last five in the South's second innings. The North, however, failed to reach their target and lost by 27 runs.

Alongside the disorganisation, the malice, backbiting and repercussions continued. *The Sportsman* ran a long article about a letter from 'Stumps' in an earlier edition following the continued refusal to appear at The Oval of Carpenter, Hayward and Tarrant, suggesting that the public had been 'bamboozled' in paying admission for Surrey v England, only to witness an England bereft of three of its stars.[137]

The actions of Parr and Hayward were defended on the grounds of being a justifiable response to the criticisms made of them: 'Can it be wondered at, after the treatment Parr has received that he should decline to play at the Oval again? And further can it be wondered at that Hayward and others follow in his wake.'

Then there is reference to *The Guide*, that is, Fred Lillywhite's *Guide to Cricketers*, so not exactly unbiased, which has critical comments on Parr and Hayward, suggesting that money is their primary motivation:

> Parr, George ... His time is now devoted to other purposes far from promoting the game of cricket. He appears to be manager of the United as well as the All-England Eleven. Was the able manager (when out of his bedroom) in America and took an Eleven to Australia fortunately after he had received a benefit at Lord's Ground – receipts not known.
>
> Hayward, Thomas, a remarkably 'big' bat, showy but effective. He likes a good wicket but does not choose to play upon all those he can get; may be seen slogging the poor 'slaves' employed on a twenty-two side against the renowned elevens. His driving when last seen in *good* matches among talent was much admired; he is also a good change bowler and a first rate long stop and field anywhere. One of the North 'patients' and a free and grateful acceptor of the 'talent' money at the Oval Ground, and a member of any eleven, coupled with coinage.[138]

The trenchancy of such comments led to MCC withdrawing its support for what was popularly known as Fred's Guide. It was subsequently absorbed into the other Lillywhite publications, the *Companion* and the *Annual*. They continued in various forms until the end of the century when *Wisden*, which had run alongside them from 1864, took over and had the field to itself as the definitive record book for the twentieth century and beyond.

Away from Cambridgeshire, the schism was being deepened by a refusal of Nottinghamshire to play against Surrey following what was apparently a very poor umpiring decision which cost Nottinghamshire the match. The report is based on the *Nottingham Guardian*'s version of events, though in the interests of balanced reporting several opinions were sought and none seem to deny the accuracy, nor be in much doubt that Surrey-Notts relations are further soured and the schism anything but shallower:

> In respect to the decision of Lee the umpire near the finish of this recently played match on the Oval, the Nottingham Guardian of July 22 states 'Sewell made 8 runs when he played a ball from Jackson (going out of his ground) which Biddulph fielded and ran Sewell out. He pocketed the ball, naturally considering the game over and he and other of the Notts players were on their way to the dressing room, when they were called back by the Surrey umpire who stated that he had said "not out". Sewell then obtained the required runs.'[139]

The acrimony seems to have been directed at administrations (and umpires appointed by them) and not spilled over into relations between the players themselves which remained harmonious:

> North v South at Canterbury. If there are any believers in the statement that enmity exists between the professionals of England the friendly feeling and good fellowship exhibited on all hands in this match would completely negate such an hypothesis.[140]

Surrey members felt they had a right to know what was going on and at a general meeting in early 1866 received an explanation from the Honorary Secretary of the events of 1861, when the first cracks had appeared:

The principal object of the meeting was to elicit from the then Secretary or some other official, the cause of the present unfortunate disturbance in the cricketing world.

Mr Wm Burrup, before responding to an attack made upon him and the Surrounding Clubs as to their arrangement of matches and conduct towards professional cricketers of the north, begged that he might resign his position as Secretary.

He proceeded to endeavour to explain the non- attendance of some of the northern 'cracks'. He said it was in 1861 that a representative from Australia arrived in this country from Messrs Spiers and Pond, the now large purveyors in this country, and it was said that, owing to his influence and advice, the Northern players were left out and nearly all Surrey and south players were engaged. This he denied being the case, but admitted he had rendered Mr Mallam that assistance he asked for in a friendly manner. A large dinner was given at Manchester, and Parr, having in an abusive manner refused to have anything to do with the said match, the whole of the players were asked to it excepting that individual, and, in consequence Mr Mallam, it appears, had been informed of his management in America. Parr, however, Mr Burrup proceeded to say, attended uninvited, and, after the repast, a discussion ensued, which resulted in Parr, Hayward and Carpenter declining to go, as they themselves thought they were better cricketers and worth nearly double the money, that is, if the offer of £130 was made to such as Caffyn, or other players as good, if not of more importance, they, Carpenter and Hayward, were worth £230. The representative, therefore, was determined to have nothing to do with them, and these respective three great 'North doers' for a time were to rule cricket on behalf of England. This could not be allowed, and it was thought by them that the Surrey Club had accomplished their task through the Secretary, hence their 'proud' position now in the north of England.

The blame, consequently, was thrown upon George Parr and Mr Burrup, having thus exonerated himself at a public meeting called almost for the purpose, it only remains for Nottingham to act. The meeting re-elected Mr Burrup almost unanimously.

After some further conversation on the subject which did not elicit the real facts of the case, the company dispersed, knowing but little more than they did upon their arrival.

Burrup's half-hearted and unconvincing explanations were supported by a letter from Fred Lillywhite. There was very clearly no love lost between Lillywhite and George Parr and the Sussex man followed up with a trenchant and critical letter which made no contribution to healing the rift.

Fred Lillywhite and the Northern Cricketers. To the editor of the Brighton Gazette.

Sir, I perceive, by the enquiries made at the meeting of the Surrey Club members on Friday last, that they wished to know how the first twelve were got together and the cause of the present disturbance between the north and Surrey.

The facts are these and will doubtless throw some light upon the subject then and now under discussion. Mr Mallam was sent to me from Messrs Spiers and Pond and who can, no doubt, substantiate the fact. On his arrival he applied at my house, in the Oval, but I had just left for the Canterbury week, so he immediately followed and his first interview was with me at Canterbury. From that time until the twelve actually signed their names to proceed Mr Mallam acted under my professional advice. I told him at once to have no transactions with George Parr, as manager, as I had experienced his management while in America, where favouritism and jealousy existed, detrimental to England. I advised Mr Mallam to act with gentlemen of the Marylebone or Surrey Clubs, and treat with them as the Honor of the country was at stake, and that it was not with them a matter of money alone, but the furtherance of cricket. The Marylebone season had then closed. The next match that took place at the Oval, after Canterbury week, the whole matter was gone into and the representative from Australia was fairly on his feet and could feel his way, having been posted sufficiently with information as to the manners and customs of professional cricketers in England to act more upon his own judgment.

George Parr, with his recent confederates and his whole band of followers, such as Hayward, Carpenter, Tarrant etc. are, therefore, the principal cause of the present disturbance, and I am the individual as far as the south is concerned. I can entirely exonerate Mr Burrup and the Surrey Club from all blame. I did what I thought, and do think, was right. George Parr has been a great opponent of cricket and the Press generally, since the introduction of printing of Cards, throughout the country in 1848, and consequently the day has now arrived that the 'Press gang' can confirm him and the public of the fact. I am very anxious to avoid personality, but to get to more facts I must do so, and state that Parr did his utmost to prevent my press and tent going to

America because (after I had first made the arrangements) he was selected as Captain. He was unfit for the duty the whole of the time he was
away, whether on board of ship or in the cricket ground, and, on one
occasion, was so ill at Philadelphia for a week that he was compelled
to send for my assistance to carry out his arrangements. Thus from the
treatment I have received from him and other professionals, I not only
properly advised Mr Mallam how to act on a second continental trip,
but endeavoured to make the public aware of their proceedings in the
publication of the *Guide to Cricketers* of last May, which, being under
the patronage of two distinguished clubs, was withdrawn from sale after
about 10,000 copies had been issued. George Parr was written to by me
months ago on two or three occasions, to arrange matters, but he never
replied. These are the facts of the 'Cricket feud' and the only persons to
be blamed are George Parr and school …
Your obedient servant, Fred Lillywhite.[141]

Parr may well have had a case for libel, but even had he chosen
to pursue it, it would have been frustrated. Fred Lillywhite died later
that year.

Burrup, with Lillywhite's backing, had made a half-hearted attempt to justify his actions. Arguments raged back and forth in the
sporting press. Few had the full picture and the reaction was split
largely among class lines. It was the perennial gentleman-player, amateur-professional, south-north confrontation, though in a number
of cases, the attitude was a plague on both your houses. For the sake
of the game, let's get this sorted.

So the 1866 season began with no thaw in the icy relations between North and South. That, however, did not affect the Yorkshire v Cambridgeshire match at Bradford which drew a sizeable
attendance most of whom would be disappointed with the result
– an overwhelming victory for Cambridgeshire by an innings and
67 runs after an encounter which, apart from the first few overs, was
dominated entirely by the usual Cambridgeshire suspects. Hayward
had 78, Carpenter 97 not out, then Tarrant cleaned up with six for
30 and seven for 47:

The first match between these celebrated counties took place on Monday, Tuesday and Wednesday last, and upwards of 3,000 spectators assembled to witness the contest.

Two wickets, 9 runs – Hayward came to the rescue, but soon lost his partner Mr Warren. Carpenter joined Thomas and soon the leather-hunting became hot. For three hours did these batsmen worry the field by their brilliant hits and magnanimous defence; at length, when they had made 78 each, Thomas let one of Isaac's get past his bat. His runs were a treat to witness, his hitting superb, and he reminded us of his batting of three years since, when he carried everything before him.

Carpenter's hitting had put together 85 and had to go on but, strange to tell, not one could stay long enough to allow him to get his hundred, Dan Hayward contributing 7, although he suffered from a very sore hand.

In consequence of the splendid batting of Carpenter and Hayward they both received from the Bradford Managers the talent money amounting to £3 each.[142]

The schism was not total and did not affect the MCC v Cambridgeshire match at Lord's which MCC won by two wickets. Apart from five overs, Tarrant and Hayward bowled through both innings, dividing the eighteen wickets equally between them. Later in the season, in the two-day innings victory over Middlesex at the Cattle Market ground in Islington, the same pair did bowl through both innings, but this time the split was 12 to 8 in Tarrant's favour. Batting at number seven, Tarrant with 64 was also the highest individual innings in the match. Wicketless in the next game at Trent Bridge, Thomas compensated by 73 and 30 with the bat in a drawn match.

The propensity to run outs continued and in the return match:

The return match between Cambridgeshire and Middlesex was resumed yesterday morning at Cambridge. Thomas Hayward joined Mr Collier and the latter, after exhibiting some spirited cricket, was run out.

T Hayward who had by this time got fairly settled down to his work was unfortunate enough to misjudge a run and so was run out.[143]

Lord's CC Ground.

M.C.C. AND GROUND v. COUNTY OF CAMBRIDGE.
Monday and Tuesday, May 14 and 15, 1866.

CAMBRIDGE.	First Innings.		Second Innings.	
C. Warren, Esq.	hit w, b Wootton	0	c and b Wootton	15
J. Smith	run out	41	b Walker	30
C. Marshall, Esq.	l b w, b Wootton	0	c Biddulph, b Grundy	11
T. Hayward	b Grundy	3	b Wootton	5
R. Carpenter	b Walker	38	c and b Wootton	5
G. Tarrant	b Walker	9	c Buller b Walker	3
H. B. Saunders, Esq.	c Balfour, b Walker	18	b Walker	0
D. Hayward	c Wootton, b Walker	3	not out	12
G. Munsey	c Fitz-Gerald, b Wootton	4	b Grundy	0
H. J. Browne, Esq.	not out	0	b Wootton	1
H. Perkins, Esq.	c Bisset, b Walker	2	b Grundy	0
	l-b 5, b 4, w , n b	9	l b 1, b 5, w , n b	6
	Total	127	Total	88

M.C.C.	First Innings.		Second Innings.	
J. Grundy	b Tarrant	6	c and b Tarrant	17
Hon. T. De. Grey	b Tarrant	9	c Tarrant, b T. Hayward	19
A. Lubbock, Esq.	b T. Hayward	2	c Tarrant, b T. Hayward	1
R. Balfour, Esq.	b T. Hayward	6	b Tarrant	3
C. F. Buller, Esq.	b T. Hayward	55	b T. Hayward	10
R. D. Walker, Esq.	b Tarrant	4	b T. Hayward	0
T. Hearne	c D Hayward b T Hayward	39	c Carpenter, b Tarrant	1
R. A. Fitz-Gerald, Esq	b Tarrant	5	c Marshall, b T. Hayward	4
H. Bisset, Esq.	b Tarrant	1		
G. Wootton	b Tarrant	7	not out	9
S. Biddulph	not out	0	not out	0
	l-b 7, b 2, w , n b	9	l-b 1, b 2, w 1, n b	4
	Total	143	Total	73

Umpires......Royston and Nixon
Price Twopence.]   [List of Matches, see over.

The 1866 MCC v Cambridgeshire match survived the schism but was not a great success for Thomas as a batsman, but he did well with the ball (4 for 54 and five for 37), sharing eighteen wickets and 175 of 180 overs with George Tarrant.

Although the University won the match against the county side in 1867, Thomas had 55 not out and 20 and his brother also made a contribution.

> Tom Hayward bringing out his bat for a truly scientific fifty-five, made up of two fours, six threes, five twos etc. A purse of £4 was gathered in the ground and Mr Perkins, in very complimentary language, presented it to Hayward in the pavilion.[144]

Against Nottinghamshire at Fenner's, Thomas and Dan shared a third-wicket partnership in what ultimately turned out to be a lost cause:

> The Cambridge team having to get 218 in their second innings to win, sent in Dan Hayward and Smith to the bowling of JC Shaw and Wootton. In the second over, after Smith had scored two, he was bowled by Wootton. Tarrant then appeared and after playing a few good overs, and making a fine cut for four off Shaw he was caught. Now Thomas Hay-

ward joined his brother and for some time the play was very good, the brothers treating the spectators with some excellent cuts and drives.[145]

The tables were turned the following month, however, as Thomas's 52 helped towards a nine-wicket victory. It was Cambridgeshire's highest innings, just ahead of Carpenter's 46, but eclipsed by Richard Daft's 62 not out.

The 1868 Town v Gown match was played for Carpenter's and Hayward's benefit.[146] The county side saved the match, having been obliged to follow on, but at least it was to the advantage of the beneficiaries that the match lasted three days, rather than being completed in two.

The schism finally came to an end in 1869 in a way the professionals understood – by having money thrown at it. It was an appropriate method. The Cricketers' Fund Friendly Society had been established in 1857 and had been of assistance to players' widows as well as to the professionals whose opportunities had been restricted by accident or illness. MCC had made a contribution initially, but having declined at first to intervene in North-South hostilities, established a new fund, the Marylebone Professional Cricketers' Fund, but restricted it to those players who 'have conducted themselves to the entire satisfaction of the Committee'. Realising that they would be excluded from that category, the 'secessionists' complied with the effective cease-fire imposed by the game's rulers and came back into the fold.[147]

For the All-England Eleven against the United at Dewsbury that year, Hayward had the top score of 46, but the West Yorkshire weather had the last word and little play was possible after that.

The Fens, where cricket had been played on the ice the preceding winter, thawed out eventually in 1870, as did the frosty relations between north and south. For the first time since 1866, Thomas appeared at Lord's, in the Left-Handed v Right-Handed match and subsequently in the North v South and Gentlemen v Players matches: 'We are glad to see the old cricket sore has been healed and no doubt the appearance of Hayward and Carpenter at Lord's will be hailed with satisfaction by the Metropolitan fanciers.'[148]

The media welcomed the end of the schism and looked forward to a concentration on cricket rather than finance:

> We hope that Carpenter, Hayward and the other well-known cricketers we shall so gladly welcome back again to Lord's and the Oval will find out the advantage of playing *cricket* instead of cramping their style and destroying their reputation in catch-penny speculations for the benefit of publicans.[149]

The Gentlemen v Players match was a tight affair, the amateurs scraping home by three runs. The presence of WG Grace was beginning to make a difference in what had previously been usually one-sided matches. He started off with 109 before Hayward, who made a negligible contribution with the bat – just a single in each innngs – caused him to play on, the first wicket of a hat-trick:

> The chief feature of the game at present has been the bowling of Hayward. He bowled the two Graces and Mr Francis in three consecutive balls. He took care to collect the money from his fellow players for his richly-deserved new hat. At the same time Mr WG Grace's stumps were lowered rather by virtue of good luck than of a good ball. He had made 109 when Hayward appealed to the umpire as to his being leg before wicket, and while he was waiting for the verdict the ball trickled, as it were, off the great scorer's pads into his wickets.[150]

Later in the season there were also North v South matches at the Canterbury Festival and Dewsbury. An appearance at The Oval, for Cambridgeshire against Surrey, for the first time since 1862, would have to wait until the following season.

A shadow was cast over the season in July by the death of George Tarrant of pleurisy at the young age of thirty-one. Thomas was entrusted with the administration of the benefit proceeds:

> Burial of George Tarrant. Last Thursday afternoon in the presence of a great number of people, this well-known cricketer was consigned to his last home. He lies within few yards of the celebrated 'Billy Buttress'.

Tarrant was followed to the grave by those of his brother professionals who could attend, and there is no doubt that if Thomas Hayward, Bob Carpenter and J Smith had attended the funeral there would have been many more present. About a dozen relations comprised the chief mourners and these were followed by Mr Inspector Robinson, Dan Hayward, Walter Watts, J Fordham, C Newman, H Dakin and others.

The service was impressively read by Rev JJ Scott of Trinity College, the clerk being Mr Robert Ringwood, one of the best cricketers that Cambridge ever produced.[151]

The late G Tarrant. At a meeting of the committee formed in 1869 to give the late George Tarrant a benefit, held on Monday evening at The Prince Regent Inn, it was resolved 'that the balance sheet be published, and the money in hand be handed over to Thomas Hayward to be given by him to the widow of George Tarrant at his discretion – and that an effort be made to procure subscriptions towards purchasing a small annuity for the widow.'[152]

The three mentioned for missing the funeral were with the All-England Eleven in the north of England at the time, travelling in the latter part of the week between Middlesbrough and Sheffield.

The hatchet now buried, Carpenter and Hayward as in former times made an impression on The Oval in the Surrey v Cambridgeshire clash in 1871. Dan umpired, Carpenter had runs. So did Thomas, 33 and 40 and drew praise for the elegance and effectiveness of his batting.

The balance between Gentlemen and Players and between North and South was beginning to shift, however, thanks in the main to the presence in the Gentlemen and South teams of WG Grace who compiled a number of match-influencing scores. He got 268 in the second innings – compensating for his duck in the first at The Oval and 217 for the Gentlemen at Hove, again following a first innings duck. Hayward accounted for ID Walker and GF Grace but could make no impression against 'The Champion', although it was noted that 'Hayward is also entitled to honourable mention, his batting being not only effective but elegant as ever.'[153]

Against the infant United North of England Eleven in the only first-class match ever played on the delightfully named Back o' the Bank ground in Bolton, the All-England Eleven crushed their opponents, bowling them out for 27 in the second innings to triumph by an innings and 21. Earlier Carpenter and Hayward had again made an impression on the local media:

> Hayward came next and the two Cambridge cracks played the best innings we have yet seen on the Bolton Ground, Hayward particularly excellent.[154]

> Thomas Hayward was the next to appear and in the course of a few minutes McIntyre was neatly taken at point. Bob Carpenter now faced Thomas and to the practised eye it soon became apparent that the two local celebrities intended, by the most careful play, doing their utmost to prevent their opponents pulling off the match. Hence, for something like two hours was witnessed an admirable specimen of cricket of the almost purely defensive kind. The consequence was that runs were made tardily. Bowling changes were rung frequently and no fewer than seven of the field took a turn with the leather, but all to no purpose. It was as fine a piece of generalship on the part of the Eleven as could be witnessed and the sequel will presently demonstrate that the tactics succeeded. Ultimately the spell was broken and Bob was caught at square-leg, after putting together 27.[155]

Thomas played his final first-class matches in 1872, one for the North, one for the United North. He was on the losing side in both, thanks in the first case to another century by WG Grace, already on the way to the landmark which was to challenge Thomas's nephew.

For one born and reared in Cambridgeshire the distribution of the venues on which Thomas played his first-class cricket may seem erratic – 31 at Lord's, 20 at The Oval, 14 at Fenner's and five on Parker's Piece. However, Lord's and The Oval are where most of the first-class cricket was played. It would have been more at Surrey's headquarters, but for the great North-South schism which divided the professional game in the 1860s; Fenner's was gradually eclipsing Parker's Piece as the venue for such county cricket as was in existence at the time. In bowling terms Thomas did better at Lord's than the other two venues (sixty-three wickets at 12.11 as against thirty-eight at 18.96 at Fenner's and forty-two at 21.07 at The Oval) while in batting the reverse was the case, 944 at 17.81 at Lord's (this notwith-standing his career-best 132), 1142 at 34.6 at The Oval and 799 at 44.38 at Fenner's – variations caused possibly by the lower quality pitches at Lord's and lower quality student cricket at Fenner's.

17

MINOR MATCHES AND
ALL-ENGLAND 1864-74

Back in England, after eight months away in Australia, the relentless but lucrative treadmill of All-England and occasional other minor matches continued.

Well known enough to boost local attendances, Thomas attracted a sizeable crowd to Richmond for the United England Eleven match against twenty-two locals in 1864, but some resentment was caused by his questioning of his dismissal and, along with Carpenter, his failure to show up at all on the final day:

> T Hayward faced Mr Hales, amidst cheers, and soon made some splendid cuts and leg hits in his own style; after scoring 12, however, he was bowled by Mr Hales amidst the cheers of the ground. He did not like it, and complained that the ground brought the ball into his wicket; to us, however, it seemed as fair a bowl out as could be.
>
> Some dissatisfaction was expressed at the absence of Hayward and Carpenter on the third day and although we can make all allowances for their wish to have a day at their homes in Cambridgeshire, yet we must remark that their conduct was rather a slight upon the club, to say nothing of a breach of contract.[156]

At the end of the season, the pair added a bit of spice to the Married v Single match in Cambridge, as well as providing a masterclass in batting technique:

Married v Single. R Carpenter and T Hayward kindly consented to play, thereby giving great interest to the match, Carpenter on the part of the Single and Hayward for the Married.

A lesson might be learnt by all amateurs who saw the innings of Messrs Hayward and Carpenter, that 'skying' is by no means the only way to make the ball travel a long distance but that drives and leg hits for four or five runs may be obtained without the ball rising 2 feet above the ground. It ought to be remarked that the inequality of the game was in great measure due to the splendid bowling of Mr T Hayward on the part of the Married.[157]

Thomas continued to play a full role in the All-England matches in 1865 against such diverse opposition as Longsight, Yorkshire, Dewsbury and District, Earlsheaton, Harrogate and District, and Sixteen Gentlemen of the North 'for the benefit of the Yorkshire players who have been excluded from the county matches on Bramall Lane during the past season'.[158]

Thomas's calling and running between the wickets was not his strong point and many years later in a 'talk' with Old Ebor, William Oscroft's recollections are recorded:

A curious incident occurred just before I went in to bat in this match. Parr called me aside and said 'Oscroft, if you are in when Thomas Hayward comes in, mind he doesn't run you out'. I was still in when Thomas comes in, and splendid cricket did he play. After making a fine cut straight to a fielder, Thomas shouted at me, 'Come on.' I replied 'No – go back' but long before he reached the crease his wicket was down and he had to retire. I was top scorer with 52 not out. While I was fielding next day a gentleman whom I did not know called to me and said, 'Here, Oscoft, here's a sovereign for your fine innings yesterday.' I learnt afterwards that Parr and Hayward were staying with a gentleman overnight, and after dinner the question of top scorer was discussed. Hayward said he would lay 5 to 1 against any individual member of the team being top scorer barring himself, and one of the company took the odds to two sovereigns. This may have been the gentleman who gave me the sovereign, though I never knew.[159]

There had been controversy before the season started about the All-England Eleven fixture list. The match with Orsett, in which Thomas did not play but Daniel did, provoked some criticism of George Parr in that it clashed with the North v South match at Lord's. The criticism reverts to a time when professional cricketers were viewed as hired labourers or performing animals and failed to recognise that they have a choice as to where to sell their talent. It is a pro-establishment, pro-gentleman amateur view, one of Disraeli's two nations scornfully commenting on the motivation and life style of the other, but does have a point in recognising that money is the motivating factor:

The MCC has a match North v South at Lord's on June 12; George Parr has made an engagement for his eleven at Orsett on the same day. If this be correct it is, I suppose, a continuation of the North v South grievance of last year. Hitherto certain players have refused to play only at the Oval; now, it seems, they are about to make themselves, if possible, more absurd and refuse to play at time- honoured Lord's. The question that suggests itself is this: how much longer are cricket-loving Englishmen to endure the mortification of seeing the best matches spoilt because 'a parcel of cantankerous fellows' (as I once heard a Surrey gentleman call them) happen to think that there has not been sufficient honor paid them at certain places or by certain individuals? 'We decline playing at the Oval at present' say the Cambridge trio. No reason is given to the public. Probably they have no better reason to give than that the Surrey gentlemen thought fit to draw the line for talent money at 50 and did not give it for 49 or 48. It is within the limits of probability that they may never be invited to play at the Oval again. For two years past the Surrey v England match has been spoilt by G Parr's fixing a match All-England Eleven v Twenty-two for the same day somewhere.

And now it seems that the North v South match is to be subjected to the same indignity. Who is Parr that he presumes to interfere with the arrangements of these gentlemen who support our national game? In olden times a player was told when and where he would be wanted – he was not asked to play as a favour. Now we have the unseemly spectacle of players refusing to play in legitimate matches because they are engaged in 'itinerant exhibitions' for 'gate-money', and because certain gentlemen having treated them with very great kindness thought proper to draw a limit to their generosity. The old players may well say that cricket is not what it was. It is the story of the bull and the frog over again. The frog tried his best to get as big as the bull, and so do certain players try to overtop the gentlemen; but, like the frog, they must come to grief in the end. No doubt G Parr is the author of a great deal of this and possibly he and his followers may think it very fine to be independent of the Surrey and other clubs; but they will find that such ill-bred and uncricketlike opposition will do them harm in the end, and that, when their playing days are over, they will be remembered as disagreeable bouncing fellows who tried their hardest to ruin the noblest of our national pastimes.[160]

All very well to see the role of the professionals as providing entertainment for the gentlemen, but at the end of the day, where would the game be without the players?

In mid-April 1866, Thomas made an appearance as a 'given man' for the Huntingdonshire Militia Officers against Huntingdonshire at Hinchingbrooke Park and came close to winning the match on his own. He had a modest nine in the first innings in a total of 58, then bowled through the county's first innings of 82, taking a minimum five wickets (it may have been six or seven – the scorecard is incomplete). 29 not out batting at number three in an all-out innings of 47 followed, then another four wickets (maybe five) as the county lost seven wickets scraping the 24 required to win.

Later that year when the weather had improved a little even in the north of England, Hayward and Oscroft produced some impressive batting against the Sheffield Shrewsbury Club at Bramall Lane: 'After dinner Oscroft and Hayward gave the spectators a treat. The hitting was brilliant and the defence admirable. To enumerate all their hits would take up too much space.'[161]

Richard Daft recalls the match against Radcliffe-on-Trent and the captain's anxiety in the early stages of it as follows:

When the All-England played Eighteen of Radcliffe-on-Trent in 1870, the former went in to bat first, and several wickets fell rather quickly, my own among others. Hayward, Carpenter and a few more had not arrived, and George Parr, our captain, was afraid they would have to forfeit their innings, as it looked as though the rest of the wickets might fall before the absentees arrived. I can see poor George now as he kept looking expectantly down the road which led to the ground, along which the players had to come. The train was late, which made him still more uneasy, and caused him to have the luncheon arranged to take place earlier than had been first intended. At last, however, the missing players arrived, and singularity enough they stayed at the wickets all that day and the next, and it was not till twelve o'clock on the third day that the All-England innings came to a close for a total of between five and six hundred runs.[162]

Carpenter had 174 and Hayward 118. They added 305 together for the fifth wicket, the first certain instance of a partnership of over 300 according to Rowland Bowen. Parr was 79 not out and the total was 504. However, it was pre-declaration days and the innings was not concluded until the third morning, so there was precious little time to bowl out the opposition twice. They did it once, for 123, but there was no opportunity for a follow on and the match was left drawn.

In August 1871, Hayward and Carpenter were back in their home town, but this time in the away dressing room at Fenner's, playing for the All-England Eleven against a combined Twenty-two of the Town and the University Long Vacation Club. On this occasion, however, it was a backs-to-the wall job to avoid defeat with no opportunity to demonstrate the flamboyance shown at Bolton and elsewhere. They saved the match, Thomas not out at the end, but the scoring rate would have been more appropriate for a single wicket match.

Thomas continued to play for the All-England Eleven until July 1874, a season which also included trips to Edinburgh and Dublin, as well as more local ones in Wakefield, Leicester and Rochdale. His final match was not inappropriately for the All-England Eleven against Cambridge Town on Parker's Piece:

Hayward 'the Cambridge Cricketer' made a stand with Wild, scoring rather slowly till luncheon. No great hits were made during the morning's play, singles being chiefly scored. After Luncheon Wild and Hayward completed their innings of 39 and 37 respectively. Hayward compiling his with a five, two threes, nine twos. He was caught at long-leg off Askew.[163]

The All-England Eleven won by an innings and 15 runs, so the team with which he ended his career and represented for much of it beat the team with which he started it on what was effectively his home ground. It was an appropriate end.

18

Single wicket

We learn from the spirited cricket chronicler on The Sporting Life that Mr Jackson the owner of Saunterer, has backed Hayward and Carpenter for a single wicket match, £200 a side against the three Toms of Stockton – Darnton, Hornby and Robinson to play at Sheffield on Sept 26.[164]

As in Thomas's father's day, these matches were no end of season jollies, but serious cricket played now for much bigger sums of money in front of large attendances, albeit at a slow pace with few risks taken as there were few wickets to lose, often no more than one. It is also an indication of Thomas's connection with the racing and gambling fraternity which would doubtless earn him a few 'tips' and access to information when the racecourse rather than the cricket field occupied his attention.

Thus, at the end of the 1861 season a well-attended and lucrative single wicket match took place, the Cambridge two against the three Toms of Stockton-on-Tees. Many years later in 1926 Richard Daft reminisced about it, as well as his own participation in such a contest when, not for the first time, the fast bowling of his Nottinghamshire teammate, John Jackson, was the difference between the sides:

Old cricketers well remember the excitement there was when the two Cambridge players, Carpenter and Hayward, were matched against 'The Three Toms' of Stockton-on-Tees, Darnton, Robinson and Hornby, for £200 a side. Here, too, the Cambridge men were victorious, as they were later on when the number of their opponents was increased to five, and Tarrant was added to themselves. This addition, in my opinion, made the game more in favour of Hayward and Carpenter than before, as although it gave them two extra opponents to contend with, still it put in their hands exactly what they lacked for a single-wicket match, viz a magnificent straight fast bowler, who was as likely as not to knock up some runs too.

Daft was absolutely correct. The return match was played at Stockton, the Cambridgeshire Three again beating the Stockton Five. William Caffyn was later to recall:

In 1861 Hayward and Carpenter were backed by Mr Jackson, the owner of the famous race-horse Blair Atholm, to play the three 'Toms' of Stockton – Thomas Robinson, Thomas Darnton, and Thomas Hornby – at single wicket for £200. The Cambridge pair were victorious. Later on the two, with Tarrant added, were matched to play the three Stockton players, with Halton and George Atkinson added. The stakes were doubled and the match played at Sheffield, and once more the Cambridge men were the conquerors. The celebrated trio were, however, defeated by Richard Daft, John Jackson and Alfred Clarke at Nottingham twelve months later.[165]

Professional in terms of both finance and attitude, for the 1861 match against the three Toms, the Cambridge pair took the opportunity of practising and familiarising themselves with the ground the previous afternoon, enlisting the help of John Jackson. Even that attracted the attention of the press:

Yesterday afternoon Hayward and Carpenter, accompanied by Jackson of the All-England Eleven, made themselves acquainted with the ground on which the match is to be contested. By having a lengthened practice, Carpenter batted considerably the best of the two, he repulsing for a long period the determined balls of Jackson and Hayward. The latter, during his practice, was several times bowled.[166]

Only the area in front of the wicket was used. No runs could be scored behind the wicket and the batsman could not be out stumped or caught behind the wicket. The following gives a flavour of the interest taken and the detailed almost ball-by-ball reporting. The spectators included Francis Fenner, Daniel Hayward, John Lillywhite and Julius Caesar:

> Hayward's first run was made by a drive off the seventeenth ball bowled, he cut the twenty-fifth ball before the stump for another single; the thirty-fifth, forty-sixth, fifty-second, fifty-seventh and sixtieth he drove each for a single, and the sixty-sixth was a rare fine hit, just shaving the boundary stump, under the umpire's leg, down to the wall for a two. Robinson bowled a wide the next ball. The eighty-sixth and eighty-seventh balls Hayward drove each for a single, one to the off and the other on; another wide was then bowled and another drive for a single made when Robinson gave up bowling having then bowled ninety-two balls (two wides) for 13 runs. Darnton then had a try and from the ninth, tenth and eleventh balls he bowled Hayward made a single; in all Darnton bowled fifty-eight balls for 7 runs, but seeing he was unable to make any impression on the magnificent defence of Hayward he cried 'enough' and turned the leather over to Robinson, who bowled very well indeed, but the eighth and twenty-second balls he bowled were drove each for a single. From the twenty-sixth Hayward made a fine drive which failed to reach the wall by a foot or so but he ran two for it nevertheless and the thirty-fifth ball he finally drove on the onside down to the wall for another two; two more singles (both drives) were scored from the following nineteen balls bowled, when two o'clock and dinner had come.[167]

The 'Two' won the match by 55 runs, largely due to Tom's second innings score of 55, but they had to sort out the fielding position – not easy with only one fielder.

> At first Carpenter was placed to the 'off' where only one run could be got while the longer side was left open or to be covered by the bowler. This little mistake was soon remedied by Carpenter fielding 'on' leaving the narrower side to the bowler.[168]

The game started on a Thursday and continued on the Friday but rain prevented any action on the Saturday. The match was finally concluded on the following Monday, still with a large and appreciative audience.

In 1862, when 'the Two' were joined by Tarrant, the re-match was played in difficult conditions. There were interruptions for bad light caused by smoke from the adjacent furnaces:

> The light was bad enough per se, the ground being in close proximity to several large factories, the density of the atmosphere every now and then, when fresh coals were heaped on the furnaces, was such as to completely envelope it in black smoke and the play had to be suspended until the obstruction had cleared away.

And horses were frightened by the noise generated when Carpenter was run out:

> On Saturday morning, Carpenter resumed his station at the wicket exactly at twelve o'clock and one hour afterwards had got one run when all hands left the ground for refreshments.
>
> When Carpenter was run out at the realisation of this important event, the noise and uproar was so tremendous that it frightened a pair of horses attached to an omnibus that was on the ground and away they galloped pell-mell twice around the ground – about a quarter of a mile – the whole crowd following. Halton and Fred Lillywhite (umpire) tried to climb on from behind. Fred fell on the grass but Halton got hold of the reins and pulled the horses up.

The final reckoning was as follows:

Cambridge Three

R Carpenter	b Atkinson 0	run out 5
G Tarrant	b Atkinson 0	b Atkinson 3
T Hayward	c&b Atkinson 5	b Atkinson 10
Extras	w 4, nb 4 = 8	w 6, nb 4 = 10
Total	**13**	**28**

Stockton

W Halton	c&b Tarrant 5	run out 1
T Robinson	c&b Tarrant 2	c&b Tarrant 0
T Hornby	b Hayward 2	b Tarrant 3
T Darnton	c Carpenter b Tarrant 2	b Tarrant 0
G Atkinson	c&b Hayward 3	b Tarrant 1
Total	**14**	**5**

Bowling
Tarrant 1st inn 211 balls for 11 runs, 2nd inn 176 balls for 5 runs
Hayward 1st inn 81 balls for 3 runs, 2nd inn 34 balls for 0 runs

The matches were hard fought with few concessions:

Darnton batting 'took a severe blow on the leg'. The Three refused to let him have a runner. He appealed to the umpires who declined to interfere. Law 31 says 'No substitute shall in any case be allowed to stand out or run between wickets for another person without the consent of the opposite party.' The 'Three' therefore adhered strictly to the law. They did however let him retire.[169]

Not long afterwards, thanks to the influence of the betting fraternity – in this case the big players, like racehorse owners and the aristocracy – the stakes were being upped to levels out of reach of the man on the Clapham omnibus:

At Newmarket the other day, in one of the principal betting-houses, Mr Jackson, the well-known sporting man, offered to back Thomas Hayward and Bob Carpenter to play a Single Wicket match for £5,000 against any two cricketers in England. The Earl of Stamford at once said 'And I will go in £6,000 with you, Jackson.' This challenge has now been duly announced in Bell's Life. Soon after the recent Single Wicket match which terminated at Sheffield the other day in which Hayward and Carpenter beat three 'Great Northerns' the fact was made known in America, the Americans having evinced a great wish to hear how the match finished. This Single Wicket contest has made a great stir throughout the length and breadth of the cricket world and Cambridge in particular may well be proud of two such players. The £400 played for at Sheffield was at once handed over to the victors; and presents of all shapes and sizes have since poured in upon them. On Sunday afternoon a special train from Manchester to Newmarket stopped at the Cambridge platform. Hayward and Carpenter were at the station and were recognised by some Manchester men, one of whom sprang from a carriage and gave them £5 and another gentleman handed them £2. We understand also that it is intended to 'make up a purse' at Cambridge to present to these two conquering heroes.[170]

Richard Daft recalls another match:

> Another well-remembered match was one in which Jackson, Alfred Clarke and myself beat Hayward, Carpenter and Tarrant. Here is the record of the contest:
>
> Three of Notts v Three of Cambridge, played at Trent Bridge July 4th 1862.
>
> Cambridge. T Hayward c and b Jackson 1, G Tarrant b Jackson 0, R Carpenter b Jackson 0, Total 1
>
> Notts. J Jackson b Tarrant 1, R Daft c and b Carpenter 11, A Clarke c and b Tarrant 0. Total 12.[171]

John Major's *More than a Game* has a list of single wicket matches which stops at 1848. There was, however, a lot of it about long after that, much of it perhaps unrecorded and unpublished. The scorebook for the Cambridgeshire v Nottinghamshire match at Old Trafford in 1865 has the details of a single wicket match played after the main match written in the corner and there were several in lieu of 'fill up' matches on the Australasian tour of 1864. At the conclusion of the Ballarat match in January, EM Grace and George Tarrant took on Eight Victorians and won 20-9. Even more creditable was Tarrant's performance against Eleven at Ararat:

> After the match Tarrant challenged any eleven residents to single wicket and found an eleven to take up the gauntlet. Tarrant disposed of them in 250 balls for 4 runs and then scored two singles and a two in 73 balls, being at last caught out. The match ended in a tie.
>
> On Saturday evening a dinner was given to the Eleven at the Great Eastern Hotel. Tarrant was presented with a diamond ring by Mr Murray, on behalf of the Ararat cricketers, as a mark of their appreciation of his skill as an all round cricketer.[172]

After the final match in Sydney, local cricketers Laurence and Thompson were lined up to take on Hayward and Tarrant, but the match never came off as the two Englishmen had a boat to catch to Melbourne.

19

CRICKET ON ICE

In January 1867, there was something of a novelty at Swavesey – a cricket match on ice. Skating, both recreational and competitive, was a popular pastime in the Fens, and an opportunity was taken to play a summer game in the depths of an East Anglian winter, albeit with some modifications to the usual Laws and practices. Dan is on record as doing some coaching in the snow, but this venture was different and a bit of prize money was involved, an attraction for some, no doubt.

The match, Eleven of Cambridgeshire, including Tom and Dan Hayward and Robert Carpenter, versus Twenty-two of Swavesey and District, was planned for Wednesday 23 January. However a thaw set in on the Tuesday night and although the match still went ahead there was a layer of melt water on the surface an inch deep. The wickets were pitched at 11 o'clock and drawn between two and three o'clock but the ice was 'in a most unsatisfactory and sloppy state, and much amusement was caused by the players slipping and falling over'. The large number of hit wickets and run outs on the scorecard showed how difficult it was to keep a footing. The Eleven, who batted first and scored 128, dismissed the Twenty-two for 92.[173]

But in 1870 conditions were much improved:

The Mere fen at Swavesey, about eleven miles distant from Cambridge, being flooded and frozen, was on Monday crowded with spectators, a very large number of whom were members of the University who travelled by special trains. The programme for the day what is certainly

THE ELEVEN.

J. Smith, hit wicket	0
J. Fordham, run out	6
F. Pryor, b Masterson	16
D. Hayward, hit wicket	19
G. Tarrant, run out	2
R. Carpenter, b Masterson	57
T. Hayward, b Masterson	2
G. Thompson, run out	20
J. Smith, b Bennett	0
— Watts, l-b-w, b Bennett	1
— Pike, not out	5
	126

THE TWENTY-TWO.

D. Gunnell, b Pryor	4
K. Whitaker, run out	5
R. Marsh, run out	17
— Waldock, b Pryor	14
E. R. Odams, run out	8
W. Newman, run out	6
— Carter, b Pryor	3
— Phillips, b Pryor	2
G. Masterson, b Pryor	0
H. Hills, hit wicket	4
— Barker, b Carpenter	2
— Armstrong, b Pryor	3
— Warren, b Carpenter	1
— Fyson, run out	0
G. Mantle, run out	5
D. Bennett, b Pryor	2
J. Linton, Esq., b Carpenter	0
— Wisbey, hit wicket	10
C. Cox, b Pryor	9
— Barnard, b Carpenter	0
J. Hills, run out	2
J. Hodson, not out	0
No balls	1
	92

The 1867 cricket on ice match, as recorded in the Cambridge Chronicle and University Journal.

a great novelty – viz a cricket match on the ice and a skating match for money prizes. In the cricket match, eleven members of the All-England and of the University were pitted against sixteen of the neighbourhood of Swavesey with several members of the University. The wickets were pitched at 12.30 and R Carpenter, the captain of the Englanders, won the toss and placed the sixteen in first. Their innings lasted an hour and a half, in which time they managed to trundle together 125, of which number Mr C Baker made 77. Batsman, bowlers and fielders all wore skating patterns and the ice was as smooth as glass. Shortly before two o'clock the eleven were put on their defence and in about an hour had made 280 runs for the loss of eight wickets. T Hayward played some good all round cricket and carried out his bat for 52, including five fours, four threes and five twos.[174]

The stumps had to be fixed in two blocks of wood, which were steadied by clods of earth, but some latitude had to be allowed the defenders of the wickets as it was impossible to mark the ground out in the orthodox fashion.[175]

Running – or rather skating – between the wickets was obviously still a hazardous business. Five of the sixteen wickets to fall were run out.

Thomas was not the only Hayward to excel in the snow. One of the coldest winters on record occurred in 1878-79. Temperatures remained below zero from the beginning of December until the middle of February. Shortly before Christmas 1878, a student from Peterhouse challenged Bob Carpenter to raise a side to play the University over three days. All the players would wear skates and play for two hours each day. Cambridge Town went in to bat first and put on 193 for nine on the first day. The following day Carpenter and Dan Hayward added 132 more runs to the total and the innings closed on 326. They might have scored even more had not Dan lost his footing. He fell over and was bowled by a full toss.

Batting first when the ice was fresh and smooth gave the Town a big advantage. By the time the University team came to bat the ice was roughed up and rutted. It made fielding difficult but batting more so. At the end of the second day the students had scored 61 for one and on the third day they increased this score to 274 when the two captains agreed on a draw.

Although ice cricket was played in many parts of the country in that winter, the high scores reached in this particular game were considered exceptional.

20

ADDICTION AND LIQUIDATION

Outstanding cricketer that he was, there are some aspects of Thomas's character that are distinctly unappealing. Along with his fellow professionals, he showed a certain arrogance, perhaps justifiably in view of his place in the cricketing hierarchy, but maybe not when it spills over into questioning umpiring decisions. Off the field, he thought nothing of the discourtesies of arriving late, leaving early or neglecting duties of attendance for University and College cricket, but still expecting to be paid:

> Hayward, Buttress, Tarrant and Carpenter, who were all engaged on the ground, having on one occasion taken what is generally known as 'French leave' and not being re-engaged in consequence. It was even said that they threatened to transfer their services to Oxford when their pay for the time of absence was stopped. Their value, however, to Cambridge cricket had been very great, though they were an expensive luxury and were often absent – on leave – to fulfil first-class engagements elsewhere.[176]

Rev RS Holmes has an interesting tale of how Thomas's ignorance of the law then prevailing cost him his wicket on one occasion:

> I recently came across a capital story. It happened thirty or more years ago. Surrey were playing Cambridgeshire. Tom Hayward was batting and the last ball sent down in the day ought to have been fatal to him, but the bowler did not appeal for lbw. In the course of the evening Hayward twitted him for the oversight, and the matter dropped. Next morning, and before a ball was bowled, the bowler said 'How's that'

referring to the previous evening's incident. Umpire who had overheard Hayward's cynical remark ruled him out, and out he had to go, much to his chagrin. Of course, such a decision could not be given now-a-days, for an appeal may not be made after any cessation of play. In those days the exception was before the delivery of the next ball.[177]

Thomas was in the vanguard of the North-South schism of the 1860s when what had once been friendly on-field sporting rivalry spilled over and became vicious off-field antagonism and hostility.

Thomas Hayward liked money. He made lots of it on account of his cricketing abilities from overseas tours to North America and Australia and from single wicket matches and those against the odds. Why then was he subject to liquidation and bankruptcy orders and ended his life penniless? The answer seems to be that he loved money so much that he did his best to make more of it and, as many addictive gamblers do, ended up not by enriching himself, but by donating to the betting and gaming industry. It is known that through his single wicket activities which attracted betting – often by the players themselves, sometimes on themselves and, it is fair to speculate on occasions against themselves – he had access to inside information which he doubtless found useful on occasions, but seems ultimately to have led to his financial downfall.

Building and friendly societies were very much part of the Victorian financial scene; thrift and saving were encouraged. Temperance societies denounced alcohol and nonconformist churches preached against the evils of gambling. Such sermons went largely unheeded by the professional cricket fraternity, for whom there was limited support from the Cricketers' Fund Friendly Society and later the Marylebone Cricketers' Professional Fund. Many, however, disregarded the lessons and ended their lives in poverty and in debt. Early in the century, Wordsworth had written of laying waste our powers with 'getting and spending' which for professional cricketers was very much the way of life.

Haygarth refers to Thomas's keeping the All-England ale stores in 1875. He was, however, into the licensed trade in or before about

1870 and it turned out to be something of a trouble spot: 'Mary Phillips was charged by PC Muncey with being drunk in Petty-Cury the preceding evening. She was turned out of Mr Hayward's public house and then refused to go home.'[178]

His brother had taken over the Prince Regent in 1869, so in both cases it was preparation for life after cricket. Dan lived much longer and made a success of it – within six years Thomas was in his grave, but the evidence is that even if Thomas had matched Dan's longevity his financial circumstances would have been no better. While Dan devoted himself to the business, extending it and living 'over the shop', Thomas was something of an absentee landlord, continuing to live in Burleigh Street. He died virtually penniless and his widow and children were dependent on the efforts of Dan and his contemporaries.

There is an unsavoury tale of Thomas bringing one of his colleagues into court for failing to hand over what were perceived to be winnings from backing a first-placed horse in the Royal Hunt Cup at Ascot when he had made no financial contribution to the stake. It was a no brainer for the jury. Having not parted with any cash, there was no way he could have any claim against the defendant:

Before W H Cooke Esq Judge. T Hayward v W Hodson.

The plaintiff is Tom Hayward, an innkeeper of Cambridge and the well-known cricketer – one of the 'All-England Eleven' and the defendant is William Hodson, landlord of the White Hart Hotel, Ely. The claim was for £25 arising out of a betting transaction.

He said I was at Ascot the day the Royal Hunt Cup was run for. I met Mr Hodson on the course; we were personally known to each other. We talked about which was to win. I said 'Ripponden', he replied 'No, I am backing Theodorus'. I said 'You go to the lists and put on a fiver for me – £2 at twenty-five to one and the other £3 at six to one for a place'. Hodson took a £5 pound note from his purse to do as I said. I gave him no money. Hodson went to the lists and came back to me, showing me two tickets, saying he had got £50 to £2 to win, £18 to £3 for a place. Ripponden won. The next day he said to me 'I have got some money for you, but a pretty thing has happened to me. I have been welshed out of £25.' He paid me £35 saying he could not give me more but would send a cheque for £8 when he got home. I said 'Hodson, I told you a good thing and you are not satisfied with it, and you want to keep part of my money.' I afterwards received a cheque for £8. I told him I wanted another 'pony' when he said he had been welshed.

Cross-examined: I took £100 to Ascot with me. Hodson was to bet for me on commission but not a word was said about it. I did not expect to pay him anything.

The Judge: Am I to understand, then, that persons who bet on commission do not get a percentage?

Witness: I did not offer him anything nor did I offer the £5 to bet for me.

George Mordecai: I am a retired innkeeper, living in Park Street, Cambridge. I went to Ascot with Hayward. I saw Hodson on the course. He said 'Tell Hayward I have taken two twenty-five to two and eighteen to three for a place for his horse.'

Witness (continued). I play at loo. I love a game of loo. I played with Hayward coming from Ascot in the railway carriage. I let Hayward have the £100 for Ascot in Bank of England notes.

This was the case for the plaintiff.

Mr Wilkin (Hodson's Counsel) addressing the jury on the merits of the case, commenting with great severity upon the conduct of the plaintiff, whom he accused of trumping up the claim for £25. He then called the defendant.

William Hodson: I am landlord of the White Hart, Ely. I met Hayward at Ascot. He asked me to lay out a pound or two upon Ripponden for the Royal Hunt Cup. He gave me no money. I had only known him for about a year. I went to the lists, came back and said to him 'I have taken 25 to 1 to win and 18 to 3 for a place. I showed him the two tickets. He said Never mind the tickets'. I wanted my £4 which I had parted with. He never offered me a penny. He said 'Go and put another pound on to win.' We were three quarters of a mile from the lists. I did not like it but went away thinking I was wrong to part with £4 for a comparative stranger. I did not put another pound on. I looked for Hayward to tell him so but could not find him. I, however, saw his friend Mordecai and said 'I can't see Hayward and I therefore declare the bet on to you. I have taken 25 to 1 for winning and 18 to 3 for a place.' I only made one bet taking 25 to 1. I paid Hayward £35 the next day and on my return to Ely I forwarded a cheque for £8 making £43. I am not a commission agent and merely went into the lists to bet for Hayward with my own money. I never breathed a word to Hayward about being welshed. I paid him all I received and a pretty return I have got for it.

The jury, after a minute's deliberation, returned a verdict for the defendant.[179]

These are not small sums of money and it is easy to see how substantial earnings from cricket could be frittered away in irresponsible gambling.

When applying for liquidation of his assets, he did his best to minimise them and therefore the sums to be received by his creditors by disposing of as much as possible in advance of the liquidation sale:

Cambridge County Court. Before E Beales Esq Judge.

The following application occupied the attention of the court for several hours on Friday last re Thomas Hayward's liquidation.

Mr Graham appeared on behalf of Mr CF Jarrold, the Trustee under the liquidation of Mr Thomas Hayward formerly a cricketer and recently a publican of Petty Cury and Clarendon-street, and made an application to have a bill of sale given by the bankrupt to Mr G Low set aside as void.

Mr Cockerell (instructed by Messrs Foster and Lawrence) appeared on behalf of Mr Low to oppose the application.

The whole of the facts relied upon by either side were contained in various affidavits, from the frequent references to which it seems that in August 1874 Low made an advance of something like £140 to Hayward, who agreed to give him as security a bill of sale on his goods and household furniture. The goods were valued by Mr Octavius Parker at upwards of £200 and by some means or other the amount at which the goods were so valued was stated in the bill of sale to be the consideration; but this was alleged to be an error. The bill was kept in existence, without being put into force, until November 4th of the present year, when it was found that part of the things had been removed from the premises in Clarendon-street, and ultimately it was discovered that they had been taken to a house in Kingston-street, in the occupation of Mr Wm Carpenter,[180] who stated that he had purchased them for £100. In the meantime, two days after the seizure of the goods in Petty Cury and Clarendon-street viz on November 8th, Hayward filed his petition for liquidation. The holder of the bill of sale, having reason to believe that

Carpenter's statement was incorrect, also seized the goods in Kingston-street.

The legal arguments for and against the application were urged with great clearness and force by Mr Graham and Mr Cockerell and ultimately His Honour refused the application, subject to his reference to a case or two that Mr Graham quoted, saying that if he thought it necessary to alter his decision he would give notice to the Registrar by Monday Dec 27th.[181]

The issue remained unresolved in Thomas's lifetime. He died of consumption the following year:

Death of Thomas Hayward, the cricketer. This once famous batsman died on July 21st at Cambridge. Deceased will be remembered by crickters as forming one of the celebrated trio – Hayward, Carpenter and Tarrant – who some eight or ten years ago took a prominent part in all the great cricket contests of the country. Hayward besides being a graceful and brilliant performer with the willow was also an excellent field. After his retirement from the cricket field he commenced business at Cambridge but was not successful. The cause of his death was consumption and he leaves a widow and large family.[182]

The funeral of T Hayward. All that is mortal of poor Tom Hayward was on Tuesday afternoon consigned to the tomb at the Cambridge cemetery, Mill-road. There were not many spectators of the mournful ceremony present but the whole of the family of the deceased including his brother Dan occupied the mourning coaches. Among those present at the grave-side we noticed R Carpenter, W Watts, F Prior, Newman and other well-known handlers of the willow.[183]

The *London Gazette* appealed for any creditors to make themselves known:

The Bankruptcy Act 1869. In the county court of Cambridgeshire at Cambridge.

In the matter of a special resolution for Liquidation by Arrangement of the affairs of Thomas Hayward, late of No 13 Clarendon-street in the borough of Cambridge, formerly carrying on a business as a wine and spirit merchant at No 38 Petty Cury, in the said borough of Cambridge, now deceased.[184]

The creditors of the above-named Thomas Hayward who have not already proved their debts are required, on or before the 28th day of February 1877 to send their names and addresses and the particulars of their debts or claims to me, the undersigned Charles Frederick Jarrold, Saint Andrews-street in the borough of Cambridge, solicitor, the trustee under the liquidation, or in default thereof they will be excluded from the benefit of the Dividend proposed to be declared – dated this 26th day of January 1877.[185]

Thomas and Dan had not been particularly close since about 1860. There is no suggestion that there was any family fall out, but the brothers had different lifestyles and different interests. Nonetheless, Daniel was at the forefront of the arrangements to ensure that Lizzie and the children were not left destitute as a result of the bankruptcy of husband and father. There was no longer a breadwinner, but much of what might have been used to purchase bread had found its way in to bookmakers' coffers.

Pensions for widows and dependents of deceased cricketers were some way into the future and Daniel, Bob Carpenter and their colleagues did what was usual at the time and arranged a benefit match under the management of a committee comprising the two of them plus John Perkins of Downing College and Robert Masterton as secretary. The occasion seems to have been a success, in financial terms especially:

A Benefit match for the widow and family of Tom Hayward, the celebrated All-England cricketer has been arranged between the Town and County of Cambridge to be played on the University ground on Friday and Saturday this week. Carpenter has consented to play in the match for the benefit of the family of his late compeer. A large fund has also been raised by public subscription.[186]

Town v County of Cambridge. This match for the benefit of the widow and family of the late Thomas Hayward was played on the University ground on Friday and Saturday last. The weather was all that could be desired. There was a large attendance each day and we hope the gate money will be a substantial addition to the subscription list. The benefit has been under the management of a committee who have worked energetically to make it a success and we understand that something over a hundred pounds has been subscribed.[187]

Bob Carpenter played for the Town and the umpires and scorer gave their services free of charge.

The *Leeds Times* had commented on there being 'little means left in bereavement' for the widow and seven girls, a sad observation considering the extent of his earnings and gifts from the game which had passed into the coffers of the betting and gaming industry.[188] Lizzie, described as a dressmaker in the census twenty years earlier, used the money to set herself up as a lodging housekeeper in Little St Mary's Terrace.

21

DEATH OF DAN

Dan's commercial activities continued for the remainder of his life but unlike his brother, whose activities were of a seedier nature and crammed into a shorter life, he seems to have remained a popular and well respected figure to the end of his days. He is buried, like other members of his family, in Mill Road cemetery, not inappropriately the site of the Cambridge University cricket ground in pre-Fenner's days. The local press reported on his death and funeral:

Death of Mr Dan Hayward. Member of a Cricketing Family.

We regret to record the death of Mr Daniel Hayward, sen who passed away at a quarter to nine o'clock on Monday morning. Mr Hayward, who was 77 years of age, had been ailing for some time past and had been confined to his bed for the last five months. His death took place at the Prince Regent, Regent Street, Cambridge, of which house Mr Hayward had been the landlord for the past 42 years, having entered into occupation on June 24th 1868.

Dan Hayward, as he was familiarly known to cricket-lovers of half a century ago, was a member of the family whose name will always be famous in cricketing annals. He was a brother of Tom Hayward, the famous All-England cricketer of the fifties and sixties, and was the father of the present Tom Hayward, the well-known Surrey and All-England batsman. His other sons include Dan Hayward, the present university custodian of Fenner's and Frank Hayward, who frequently appears in local cricket. Arthur Hayward, another son, died a few years ago.

In his early youth Dan Hayward was a cricketer of more than ordinary ability, but his achievements seem to have been outshone by the more lasting brilliancy of the batting of his older brother Tom.[189] He was, however, a wicketkeeper whose form was sufficient to gain him a place in 'some of the great matches' to quote Haygarth's *Cricket Scores and Biographies* a continuation of Lillywhite's book of the same name.

The funeral took place very quietly on Thursday afternoon. The first part of the service was held in the chapel at the Mill Road Cemetery, and was conducted by the Rev James Morgan who also officiated at the graveside.

The chief mourners were: 1st carriage: Mr DM Hayward and Mr TW Hayward (sons), Mrs Stubbings and Miss A Hayward (daughters). 2nd carriage: Mr F Hayward (son), Mrs DM Hayward and Mrs A Hayward (daughters-in-law) and Mr EE Stubbings (son-in-law). 3rd carriage: Mr R Hayward and Mr T Hayward (grandchildren) and Mr W Brockett (nephew). 4th carriage: Mr W Pont (nephew) and Mrs Pont and Mr RH Shunt.

The wreaths sent included the following:

In loving memory of our dear father, from his sorrowing son Dan, Pollie and Hilda.

In ever loving memory of our dear father from his sorrowing children, Alice, Tom and Frank.

In remembrance from Mrs Arthur Hayward and children - Reg, May and Tom, with deepest sympathy.

With deepest sympathy from the ground staff 'Fenners'.

With deepest sympathy from the Surrey XI.

The coffin was of polished oak, with brass fittings, the inscription being: 'Daniel Hayward, died May 30th 1910, aged 77 years.'[190]

By the end of his life, Dan had accumulated a very healthy sum from which his family was to benefit:

The will of Mr Daniel Hayward, of Cambridge, formerly a famous cricketer, and father of Mr Thomas W Hayward, the well-known Surrey cricketer of the present day, has just been proved.

His estate is valued at £6382. He kept the Prince Regent Inn, and was also a cricket and football outfitter. Half of his business he bequeathed to his son Frank, and a quarter each to his sons Daniel Martin and Thomas Walter. He also left £1,000 to his son Frank, moneys at the bank to his son Thomas, £1,000 each to his two daughters, £500 to his son Daniel, and £200 each to his three grandchildren, and the residue of his estate to his five children.[191]

Daniel's grave at Mill Road cemetery in Cambridge - resting place of several members of the family.

Unlike his sister-in-law and nieces who were dependent on the proceeds of a benefit match after their father had died a bankrupt, Daniel's immediate family did well out of his will. His wife Emma had predeceased him in 1903, eldest son Arthur in 1905 leaving just over £1,000; the other five children received significant sums of money plus, in the case of his sons, Daniel, Thomas and Frank, shares in the business he had headed for forty-two years, selling intoxicating liquors and hiring and selling tents, accommodation, food and sports equipment.

Frank and Daniel Martin both benefited from a profitable business and on their deaths, in 1929 and 1953, left similar sums to those of their father. None had lived anywhere other than Cambridge. The three grandchildren mentioned in the will are two surviving sons and daughter of the deceased Arthur. Laura Ann, his widow, survived more than forty years, dying in 1956.[192]

The other son, Thomas Walter, had taken off in a different direction – to The Oval.

Part Three

TOM

(1871-1939)

22

A CRICKETING PEDIGREE

Tom's first recorded appearance is on the 1871 Census of Population, simply listed as 'Infant – 4 days'. He did not even have a name. He did, however, have an outstanding cricketing pedigree.

Tom grew up in a family of cricketers. His father had played his last first-class game in 1869 but was still umpiring games in the 1870s. His eldest brother, Arthur, was born in 1864; Daniel Martin a year later. A third brother, Frank, was born when Tom was ten years old. They all played for local clubs in Cambridge. Even his older sister Emma had married a cricketer, Ernest Stubbings, a university servant who played local cricket and often appeared in the charity matches organised later by his brother-in-law.

Arthur had been considered good enough in 1882 to play for Twenty-two Colts of England (the sole representative from what was by this time a much weaker Cambridgeshire) against MCC and Ground at Lord's. Eligibility for selection depended on not having played at Lord's before. His team did well enough, recovering from a first innings of 78 in which no one made double figures, to bowl out MCC for 40 then post 120 in the second innings and win by 72 runs. His own contribution to the success, however, was negligible. He opened and made a pair, dismissed by Morley in both innings, and never played there again.[1]

Away from the hallowed precincts of St John's Wood, Arthur was no mean club cricketer. He played a full part in the social aspects of club cricket, acting as one of the stewards at the Rose Cricket

Club ball held at the Guildhall at the end of 1889. Along with his two younger brothers he agreed to play for the Rose Cricket Club, though with flexible loyalties, also for the Cassandra.[2] Two half centuries within days of each other, one for each club, were a reflection of his ability at this level.

> Some capital batting was witnessed on the Piece on Tuesday, when the Cassandra met Sudbury for the first time this season. For the home team EJ Diver (64) and Arthur Hayward (75) rendered yeoman service. The match ended in a draw.

> Arthur Hayward (51), WJ Overstall (38) and H Addison (26) were the principal scorers for the Rose on Saturday against the United College Servants.[3]

Club cricket in Cambridgeshire could be controversial. In 1890, the Rose Club wanted a match to be replayed when the opposition refused to continue after 7 o'clock even when the umpires decided they should. Rose needed only 36 runs to win:

> They had ten minutes batting and in that time the two Haywards (Arthur and Tom) knocked off ten of the required number. They then applied to the umpires for a quarter of an hour's extension of time, which, after consultation was granted. Shelford thereupon refused to continue the game and left the field. The protest was discussed at great length and finally a resolution disallowing it was carried by a large majority.[4]

The Association was right; Rose and the umpires wrong. The rules of the competition provided that an extension of playing time was permitted only to achieve a result on the first innings. In this case that had already been done, so the Rose were out of the cup.

Arthur played only one Minor Counties Championship match – against Norfolk at Fenner's in 1895, batting at number three with Daniel Martin being played as an opening bowler and middle-order batsman – plus a couple of non-Championship matches and a few club matches.

The weather on Wednesday was fine but the wicket was in the bowlers' favour ... Half the wickets were down for 24, Hayter and Dan Hayward were now together. Dan got a couple with his second ball and soon after hit a boundary with a good drive. Four more runs were added when Hayter was bowled. At 39 Dan had a narrow escape of being run out; the wicket-keeper failed to take the return. The half century had just been passed when Hayward was dismissed by a splendid catch. He had played excellent cricket; his 17 – the highest score – was made up of a single, three twos, two threes and a four ... Cambridge returned to their task of avoiding an innings defeat, being 105 behind. Hill and Robertson were playing with fair confidence. When the former failed to keep one of Morley's deliveries away, Arthur Hayward joined Robertson and the cricket became more interesting.[5]

Arthur died at the young age of forty. In the family tradition of gardening and groundsmanship, he had been in charge of the grounds at Christ's and Sydney Sussex Colleges.[6]

Daniel Martin played no first-class cricket but was good enough to represent Cambridgeshire in the early years of their resurrection as a minor county and to play in sixty-five matches in the Minor Counties Championship between 1895 and 1906. As a twenty-one year old in 1887, he played for the Colts of the North against their southern counterparts at Lord's, batted middle order and took a wicket in each innings. Subsequently he played in a number of non-Championship matches for the county, including in most years the annual fixture against MCC at Lord's. He also played for a Minor Counties representative side against MCC at Lord's in 1899, took three wickets and, batting at number ten, had a half century to take his team beyond 400 on the way to a nine wicket win. In 1903, in a twelve-a-side match playing for Kimbolton, he had the rare distinction of taking 'all eleven' with the surreal bowling figures of 10-4-6-11.

Daniel was also coach at Corpus Christi College where his best known pupil had been Ranjitsinhji, who at the time had a fault in his technique of moving out of line rather than getting behind the ball. As a remedy, Daniel nailed Ranji's boot to the ground. While obviously restricting the ability to move to and play on the off side, the stratagem seems to have worked. Within three years Ranji was playing for England, not without controversy, but that was nothing to do with his ability or technique:

> The person who gave Ranjitsinhji most help, with coaching and net practice, was Daniel's third son, also called Dan who was the professional at Corpus Christi College. He was also one of two bowlers available for hire by members of the Cambridgeshire Club which had recently been re-formed as a 'second-class' county in June 1891. Ranjitsinhji, impatient to learn, had been among the first to enrol with the new club along with his friend Ramsinhji. It is important, however, not to misinterpret Dan Hayward's influence on Ranji: he did nothing more than to help make the most of what was already there.

> When Dan Hayward began coaching him, the most serious fault with his game was that he would often step out of the line of the ball. As a fast delivery came towards him, his first impulse was to move out of the way. This was fraught with danger; not only would the stumps be exposed but the stroke attempted would not be played with vertical bat, which was therefore less likely to meet its target. Unusually his movement was not towards square-leg, but towards point. He himself was to confess in possibly the first interview he ever gave, published in The Cricket Field for 2 June 1892, that in the end, during a net at Fenners, the university cricket ground, one of the professionals, Jack Sharpe, had exclaimed to him in frustration, 'Look here, you know, sir, if you can't keep those legs of yours still, I shall have to peg them down.'

> And that had proved to be the solution: if Ranjitsinhji could not remain in the path of the ball of his own accord, he would have to be made to do so until he could unaided. Ranji was later to admit in The Jubilee Book of Cricket: 'I had to have my right leg pegged down almost every time I practised during my first two years at serious cricket.' Although it was probably Sharpe's comment that inspired the idea, it is almost impossible to imagine this embarrassing exercise ever taking place during university nets; the likelihood is, therefore, that it happened only in the less public sessions he enjoyed with Dan Hayward. According to Wild, Ranji was certainly coached by Hayward with his right leg pegged down, and Wild actually attributes the idea to Hayward, rather than Sharpe. The circumstantial evidence is that it happened on Parker's Piece in the spring of 1892.[7]

There is an argument that the stratagem was the origin of Ranji's iconic leg glance:

Ranji's spectacular debut for Sussex was but the beginning. He did not make quite so many runs in any subsequent match, but he had a brilliant season, and long before it was ended it had been brought home to cricketers that a new star of the first magnitude had risen. He took remarkable liberties with Mold, flicking his fastest balls to the leg boundary. This was the famous Ranjitsinhji leg glance, a stroke that was all his own. It was said that he had developed it at Cambridge under restrictions imposed by Dan Hayward, Tom's brother, who pegged his right foot to the turf in practice to stop him running away from the ball. Unable to move his right foot, and refusing to be confined to defence, Ranji deflected the ball to leg with a twist of the body and a flick of the wrists. It was a stroke that could only be brought off by a man of exceptional quickness of eye and flexibility of movement, especially when played against fast bowling.[8]

Ranjitsinhji would never have seen Daniel's uncle Thomas Hayward play, but there must have been something in the Hayward genes which had filtered through to his nephews. When in later years Ranji had made it to international level, William Wright in 'Chats on the Cricket Field' detected a resemblance: 'Ranjitshinhji's play on the leg side reminds me more of the late Tom Hayward than anyone else. Hayward, like him, was very quick on his legs, had a splendid figure and was very graceful in all his movements.'[9]

Aside from cricket, Daniel Martin had also inherited gardening and groundsmanship skills from his father and grandfather and from 1890 was the Curator of Parker's Piece, though the appointment took a year to finalise and was not without controversy and bureaucratic local authority circumlocution, with some of the council failing to understand that re-turfing had to be halted in frosty conditions. Dan later became groundsman at Corpus Christi College and, from 1908, groundsman at Fenner's, replacing a long-serving pensioned octogenarian:

Walter Watts, who has been custodian of the Cambridge University Cricket and Athletic Ground for forty-seven years and who is in his eighty-first year, has been pensioned from Lady Day next. Dan Hayward, the Cambridge County cricketer and brother of Tom Hayward has been appointed his successor.[10]

Younger brother Frank, ten years Tom's junior, played around a dozen Minor Counties Championship matches between 1905 and 1911, his final match when still aged under thirty, after which his heavy involvement in the businesses inherited from his father restricted his opportunities.

As adept with broomsticks as bats, Frank and his colleagues swept all aside in a convincing victory over opponents whose sporting skills lay elsewhere:

Teams representative of the Rodney Cricket Club and Aurora Boat Clubs brought off the annual encounter with broomsticks on Parker's Piece yesterday afternoon. Mainly through contributions of 46, 30 and 23 by HA Hancock, F Hayward and EE Stubbings respectively, the cricketers won by 157 runs to 93.[11]

Frank's local cricket was for the Rodney Club for which in 1901 he scored 317 runs at 21.63 and took 37 wickets at 12.13.[12] In the same season he played in the Cambridgeshire Cup final with a little individual success, but his team was heavily defeated, its two innings of 136 and 86, getting nowhere near the Old Perseians' 311.[13] He also played football for St Mary's and later for the Formica Club, an offshoot of the Rodney Cricket Club, the red, green and white colours of which it adopted.[14] He was elected vice-captain.[15]

On occasions three or four brothers played together in the same match:

The third match on Parker's Piece on Saturday and the one that excited the greatest interest and attracted the largest number of spectators was that between the Rose and Anchor. The former club had got together a warm team including the three Haywards (Tom, Arthur and Dan). For the winners A Hayward and R Stearn made a most useful stand, the third wicket falling with the score at 109. The remaining seven wickets only put on 14 runs.[16]

In the benefit match played for Jack Hobbs' widowed mother and family in 1902, Tom brought a team from Surrey and all four brothers took part, the other three in the opposing Cambridge side. It was an indication of the willingness with which professional players made an effort to turn out for benefit and charity matches:

> Saturday's cricket match on Parker's Piece, organised for the benefit of the widow and twelve children of the late John Cooper Hobbs, who was for many years the well known and greatly respected groundsman to Jesus College, was a splendid success from every point of view. The weather gave no cause for anxiety at any time during the day, the crowd on Parker's Piece was the largest that has been seen for many a day, the cricket was of a most interesting and exhilarating character and the collection was, as far as can be ascertained, a record for a local cricket match. The one great feature of the event, however, which stood out from all the others, was the splendid way in which all concerned worked together.
>
> Four of the Surrey men – Richardson, Lockwood, Brockwell and Stedman – had not arrived, having been hampered by the fog in getting across London, and their places in the field were taken by substitutes … Tom got to within 27 of his three figures when, in running out, he misjudged a delivery from his elder brother and was bowled.[17]

Inevitably, clubs sought to strengthen their membership and, as competitive sportsmen, the Haywards wished to play at the highest level of which they were capable. It was inevitable too, in the way of the parish-pump mentality of club cricket throughout the ages, that there were whinges about stronger clubs 'poaching' players from the weaker ones. In 1891 for instance, 'It is rumoured that the Cassandra intend to further strengthen their ranks by the inclusion of Arthur Hayward. If this is true we must protest against such a proceeding. Last year they took Coulson and Whibley away from the Camden and Daniel Hayward from the Rose and this year they have robbed the CEYMS of FT Church. What encouragement is there for the weaker clubs with this sort of thing going on?'[18]

In 1891, Tom played for Cambridgeshire against Leicestershire Club and Ground at Fenner's. Brother Daniel Martin also played and, in a match in which no innings reached three figures, the brothers top-scored. Tom opened and made 33, Daniel Martin in the middle order had 23 not out and starred with the ball, taking thirteen wickets for 58 in the match. Ranjitsinhji also played, registering a duck in the first innings, but steering Cambridgeshire to a seven wicket win in the second.

Thomas Walter, as the four-day-old baby had later been named, sometimes in his late teens assisted his older brothers with their caretaking and groundsman duties. Indeed, the duties sometimes involved a bit more than that:

> Theft from the Corpus Christi ground. Two youths, named George Frederick Cowell and Alfred Baines, were charged with breaking into the pavilion on the Corpus College Ground, and stealing therefrom a quantity of brandy, two dozen bottles of lemonade and two footballs valued at 15s. The prisoners pleaded guilty. From the evidence it appeared that the pavilion was locked up on Saturday afternoon by Thomas Walter Hayward and when visited on Monday morning, about nine o'clock, by Daniel Hayward, the caretaker, it was found that it had been broken into, entrance having been gained by forcing the window.[19]

As a cricketer, as his grandfather, father and uncle had done, Tom showed early promise. At seventeen, under the auspices of the Cambridgeshire Association playing for the First Eleven against the Next Sixteen, he batted at number seven, made 23 and had a wicket and a catch.[20]

Most of his early club cricket was for Cambridge YMCA, but at a time when club membership was more flexible, he also played for a number of other clubs, including the Rose. It was not long before he attracted the attention of Surrey and as the result of a trial match at the end of the 1890 season was engaged at The Oval for the 1891 season.

Unlike the two previous generations of Haywards, first-class cricket for Cambridgeshire or its antecedants, Cambridge Town and Cambridge Town and County, was not an option for Tom. Cambridgeshire was re-engineered in 1891 but as a minor county and he was too good to spend his career at that level, so Tom took himself off to the venue shunned for a time by his uncle, the Kennington Oval, and settled into the two year residential period required since the rules on county qualification by birth and residence had been tightened in 1873.

In a match for Surrey Club and Ground against Norwood in July 1891, Tom had three catches, then batting at number three had 37 not out in an eight wicket win. The Club and Ground side, as was not unusual at the time, batted on after winning the single innings match by eight wickets. The same season, opening the innings, he was within two runs of a century for the Club and Ground against Wimbledon.[21] Later he had 11 not out against Clapham Wanderers and 44 against Streatham, and back in Cambridgeshire in August for Papworth Hall had thirteen wickets in three matches.[22] The local press in Cambridge continued to take an interest in his progress:

> Success of a local cricketer. Cambridge cricketers will be pleased to hear that Tom Hayward, son of Mr Dan Hayward of Regent-street, Cambridge, has made a successful debut with Surrey Club and Ground. Playing for the Surrey colts on Wednesday against Honor Oak he compiled 75 runs in the first innings without giving a chance and in the second innings he was not out 10.[23]

At the end of the season Tom returned to Cambridge to play for the newly reconstituted county side against Leicestershire Club and Ground at Fenner's. He had a few runs, as did Ranjitsinhji, but the star of the occasion was his elder brother Daniel Martin with thirteen wickets in the match.

The following season saw a number of appearances for the Surrey Club and Ground, and centuries against Crystal Palace and Brixton

Wanderers. He helped his grandfather's old team, Mitcham, to a crushing win over the South Saxons at St Leonard's with 77 as an opening batsman and then six wickets in the first innings and five in the second:[24]

> Success of young Tom Hayward. Playing for the Surrey Club and Ground against Crystal Palace at Kennington Oval on Wednesday, Tom Hayward, son of Mr Dan Hayward, the well known cricketing outfitter of Regent-street, compiled a score of 164. He was at the wicket three hours and fifteen minutes. He gave a chance in the slips when he had made 22, but apart from this it was a fine display of batting. His principal figures were three 6's (hit out of the ground) two 5's, fourteen 4's, four 3's and five 2's.[25]

For Surrey, 1892 had been a highly satisfactory season:

> The presentation of their Annual Report affords your Committee the opportunity of again congratulating the members on the brilliant success of the County eleven. Sixteen first class matches were played, of which thirteen were won, one drawn, and two lost. This record placed Surrey for the sixth year in succession at the head of County cricket.[26]

Tom had not directly been part of that, but was in the right place to absorb the atmosphere and confidence of the country's most successful county club and his apprenticeship and residential qualification period now complete, he was on his way, on the threshold of one of the most brilliant careers in the history of the game.

23

THE OVAL 1893-95

Tom was now equipped to begin a career in first-class cricket of over 700 matches which was to last more than two decades, take him several times to the headquarters of every county on the first-class circuit, many outgrounds as well, to South Africa, and three times to Australia.

The 1893 season and the arrival of Hayward on the first-class scene, following the completion of his two-year residential qualification and success in second eleven and Club and Ground matches, was eagerly anticipated:

> To those more particularly concerned in the well-being of Surrey cricket, it will be of interest to know that Monday and Tuesday next will be devoted to test practice at the Oval. It may be news, too, to some that Hayward, a nephew of the famous cricketer, Tom of that name, of Cambridgeshire fame, who has shown great promise during the last two seasons at the Oval, will be qualified this year by residence. Though born in Cambridge he harks back at no remote date to Surrey. Two generations ago the family were really Surrey. More than that his grandfather actually played for the county.[27]

His Cambridge connection was not severed, however. Along with four other Surrey professionals (Lockwood, Sharpe, Watts and Richardson), Tom was engaged as a bowler at Fenner's, though how much time any of them were able to spend on the university ground once the first-class season had started is perhaps a debatable point.[28]

He started well, scoring a century in a non-first-class match against Leicestershire, opening the innings and sharing a half century partnership with Walter Read and following it with a century one with Maurice Read:

Hayward is a capital find. I hope we shall see his famous uncle over again in him; never was there a more stylish and effective bat than Tom Hayward.

Surrey v Leics. The principal stand was by Read and Hayward at the end of the day. Going in first he (Hayward) had scored 100 out of 299 runs. From the first he played correct as well as attractive cricket, and his innings, which lasted just under two hours and a half, was one of exceptional promise. It is said that he gave a chance at the wicket when he had got six, and certainly he made two hits afterwards either of which might have been fatal. Still he played all the different bowling with judgement and confidence and his performance was the more meritorious as he had hardly thoroughly recovered from an attack of influenza and was obviously very tired towards the finish.[29]

Their ten wickets victory being largely due to the batting of young Hayward, who signalised his second appearance for his adopted county by playing a splendid innings of 100. He went in first and was out fifth at 229, his score, which included eighteen 4's, five 3's and two 2's, being obtained in two hours and thirty-five minutes. He gave two chances, but these were small blemishes in an innings which made a profound impression upon all good judges who saw it.[30]

28 in the single innings Surrey needed to crush Essex by an innings and 190 runs in another non-Championship match followed before the team moved on to yet another at Derby where 'Though Abel and Henderson both failed, Mr Shuter, Hayward, Mr Read and Baldwin all scored freely off the Derbyshire bowlers.'[31]

That brought him to his first-class debut at Trent Bridge where he did well enough, but it was not an over-distinguished performance: 8, 16 and one for 4 in a match which Surrey won by seven wickets.

However, after a run of low scores when he failed to pass twenty in half a dozen first-class fixtures, he was relegated to the second eleven for matches against Yorkshire Second Eleven and Hertford-shire. He returned at the end of July to score a half century against the Australians before his maiden century against Kent and a stylish performance in the return match against Nottinghamshire at The Oval, having already impressed knowledgeable cricket writer Rev RS Holmes and the experienced Richard Daft:

> I am very glad of Hayward's success, for I have twice seen him this year. At Trent Bridge Daft and myself were watching him, not knowing who he was. Said my friend 'that youngster plays the game thoroughly; he has the making of a great batsman; his style is admirable, and every stroke is skilful.' He was delighted to learn he was the nephew of his old chum Tom Hayward.[32]

Tom's 112 against Kent at The Oval brought compliments, al-though the writer's view that he qualified for his county cap reflects an opinion rather than a fact. He was not formally awarded it until the following season:

> Young Tom Hayward, who has qualified so thoroughly for his Surrey cap by his exceptionally fine batting during the last week at the Oval, is, as I think I have said before, a son of the veteran Dan Hayward, of the old Cambridgeshire eleven, and nephew of the grand old cricketer whose name he bears. Though the young Surrey cricketer was born at Cambridge, the Hayward's two generations back were Surrey people. They hailed from Mitcham and his grandfather in his time actually played for Surrey. Young Tom, who was born on March 19, 1871, be-gan real work as a cricketer as a member of the Young Men's Christian Association CC at Cambridge. His first score of any note was for that club in a Cup tie, against the United College Servants, on which oc-casion he scored 91. He also did good service for the Rose Club, and it was from it that he received the testimonial which led to his engage-ment at the Oval, at the commencement of the season of 1891.[33]

On what must have been a pitch of questionable quality at Grace Road, with 3 and 0, he did not come near a reprise of his earlier century, but nor did anyone else, there being no double-figure scores in Surrey's first innings total of 34 and only two in Leicestershire's reply of 43. Surrey were out again by the end of the first day and Leicestershire struggled their way to a five wicket win next day. Had man of the match awards existed at the time, the one for this match would have gone to Arthur Pougher with the best batting and bowling in each of the four innings, 10 and 24 not out, five for 15 and six for 26.

In the return match against Derbyshire 'Hayward showed sound and attractive cricket, and his 49 was a thoroughly good innings'.[34] His maiden first-class century came in August against Kent:

> The best feature of the match was the batting of Hayward. Going in first on the Thursday evening, he was at the wickets during a part of the whole three days, his score of 112 being obtained in as nearly as possible five hours, and so far as we saw, his only serious mistake was a palpable chance at slip in the early part of his innings.[35]

Although he had recorded the first of his eventual 104 centuries, a batting average of just over 18 was not an outstanding start; better times lay ahead. He was, however, by now well established as a first eleven player and turned out alongside some distinguished names for Walter Read's Eleven against WG Grace's Eleven in the end of season jolly at Reigate Priory.

Presciently, *Wisden* had no doubts about the young man's future:

> In Hayward and Street the Committee introduced into the eleven two young batsmen who have done big things for the Club and Ground. Whether Street will develop into a first-rate player is open to question, but as to Hayward's future we have the utmost confidence. Not for a long time have we seen any young professional batsman with so sound, graceful, and finished a method. In his second match he scored 100 against Leicestershire, but subsequent ill-success caused him to be left out of the team, and it seemed as though his chance had gone for the year. However, he had another opportunity afforded in the second match against the Australians, and his fine play contributed in no small degree to the victory of his side. He afterwards played a splendid innings of 112 against Kent, and maintained his place in the side for the rest of the season. We do not wish to seem over-sanguine, but we shall

be greatly disappointed if he does not in the future obtain a very high position.[36]

Matches against counties previously not considered first-class, namely Derbyshire, Essex, Hampshire, Leicestershire and Warwickshire, became so in 1894, although they were not admitted to the County Championship until the following year. The result was that Surrey now had twenty-six first-class matches rather than nineteen. Hayward, not omitted from the team at all this year, had a much more prolific season, playing twenty-six first-class matches (not quite the same twenty-six that Surrey played; he had an appearance in the South v North representative match) and scored 884 runs at an average of 26.79. He had no scores between 50 and 100, but centuries against Somerset and Kent, both at The Oval, helped boost the average to some way above that of the previous season and earned him the distinction of being awarded his county cap and, on the national scene, being nominated one of *Wisden*'s Five Young Batsmen of the Year in the distinguished company of Archie MacLaren, CB Fry, Billy Brockwell and John Brown. Under a new captain, Kingsmill Key, and with an attack spearheaded by Tom Richardson, Surrey regained the Championship they had surrendered to Yorkshire the previous season, winning thirteen and tying one of their sixteen matches.

Eleven of the matches were won by an innings, as was that against the South Africans, a fixture not given first-class status – almost certainly correctly, as at this stage in their history the tourists were very much on a steep upward learning curve, although nonsensically three huge defeats on their own soil were subsequently given the status of Test matches.

After a shaky start to the season, Hayward settled into a groove which again won him compliments from the Almanack:

During the first half of the season, Hayward was far from realising the hopes formed of him, but he came on wonderfully as the season advanced, his scores of 113 against Somerset, and 142 against Kent, being sufficient in themselves to prove that no mistake had been made in proclaiming him a first-class batsman.[37]

Hayward's 142 was in all respects admirable. He was at the wickets about four hours and twenty minutes. This is the highest innings Hayward has played in first-class cricket and his fourth of a hundred or more.[38]

The local press took a civic pride in the fortunes of the local boy made good:

Tom Hayward of Cambridge who played a magnificent innings of 113 for Surrey against Somerset on Friday says he is not troubled at all with nerves. He was first tried at the Oval at the end of 1890 and had the good luck to come off at once. Two years of probation followed during which he was qualifying for Surrey. His first county match was against

The 1894 Surrey team, the season during which Tom earned his county cap.
Back: JM Read, T Richardson, GW Ayres, FE Smith.
Middle: H Wood, WH Lockwood, KJ Key (capt), W Brockwell, WW Read.
Front: TW Hayward, R Abel, AE Street.

Warwickshire but he was unsuccessful. In his next match, however, against Leicestershire he scored a hundred.[39]

By 1895 Tom was now a key member of Surrey's batting line up and making a useful contribution as a change bowler. He played a major role in Surrey's topping the now-expanded Championship for the fifth time in six seasons. He had three centuries and over a thousand first class runs in the season. Between then and his retirement two decades later, this was a barrier he would never fail to cross in a domestic season.

Against Warwickshire, 'Hayward, who was in an hour and twenty minutes, showed as good cricket as any on the side for his 55.'

Ranjitsinhji had recently scored his maiden century and having been coached by Daniel Martin and faced Tom as a ground bowler, expressed his appreciation in a manner which few would have the means to do:

> Next, perhaps to the batsman himself, Hayward, the Surrey cricketer, has perhaps the most substantial reason for remembering KS Ranjitsinhji's successful introduction to Sussex cricket. Hayward had been bowling to the Indian Prince up at Cambridge early in the season, and indeed, has taken an active part in his practice during a great part of his residence at the University. As a mark of his appreciation Ranjitsinhji promised the Surrey player a diamond ring when he got his first hundred in an important match. Hayward had not long to wait, it need hardly be added. In fact the first innings the Cantab played was his 150 for Sussex v MCC and Ground at Lord's.[40]

Coincidentally Surrey's next fixture was against Cambridge University, though without the Indian prince who had now left (rather than graduated) and was carving out a cricketing career with Sussex:

> At the end of the day Hayward, with one life, and Street put on runs quickly, so that when play ceased the total was 500, with only seven batsmen out. On Saturday morning the three outstanding wickets added 43, so that the innings closed for 543. Hayward, who had with Street put on 91, was not out at the finish. He was in an hour and forty minutes for his 81, a bright display of free and stylish batting.

It was unfortunate for Hayward last Saturday morning that he could find no one to stay sufficiently long with him to enable him to add one more record to Surrey's credit, that of being the third batsman in an innings to score a century for the county. His play was so free and confident that there is little doubt that he would have achieved this feat if he had had a worthy partner. Though three centuries have never been made for or against Surrey at the Oval, yet in the match Australia v England in August 1884 three centuries were scored by the Australians.[41]

Tom then played in Walter Read's Testimonial match against an England side: 'The Surrey eleven was the best available, Maurice Read standing down for Hayward, who had batted so well in Surrey's last match.'[42] Notwithstanding that, the England side was stronger and won the match by an innings and 75 runs, Hayward contributing just 14 and 9 and bowling two wicketless overs. Then against Nottinghamshire at Trent Bridge, although making only four, he evoked the admiration of one of the locals, a friend of Rev RS Holmes: 'My dear Sir, Surrey possess genius. Look at Hayward, he didn't score many, but he played two rising balls with an absolutely vertical bat, the top of which was just about on the level with his nose – a perfect stroke.'[43]

Then, after a century against Gloucestershire, his bowling (18.1-7-39-5) played a part in an innings victory over Lancashire:

The fact that Mr Grace had during the month of May completed a thousand runs in first-class matches and had, moreover, assisted his county in gaining three brilliant victories, invested the Surrey and Gloucestershire match with far more interest than it had excited for many seasons, and in the course of the two days over which it extended more than 19,000 people paid for admission ... Far and away the best feature of their batting was the splendid innings of 123 played by Hayward. He was at the wicket just under three hours.[44]

Hayward's bowling success in that innings put all the regular bowlers into the shade; without his five wickets Surrey might easily have been defrauded of victory.[45]

Having made a substantial contribution with his batting to the innings victory against Gloucestershire and with his bowling to one by a similar margin at Old Trafford, Hayward and his Surrey colleagues then crossed the Pennines to Bradford where a century against Yorkshire followed, described in the media as 'an admirable innings' which, combined with 'some superb bowling by Richardson gave Surrey in this match a brilliant victory by eight wickets.' Hayward's 108, said *Cricket*, 'was quite free from fault and might be pronounced his best display during the season.'[46]

Between the Gloucestershire and Lancashire matches, there had been a nine-wicket, two-day win against Somerset at The Oval, part of a purple patch that led to a Championship winning season.

Following the back-to-back wins against the red and white rose counties, the team headed back south, pausing for just two days at Grace Road to demolish Leicestershire by an innings and 91 runs. No significant contribution with the bat from Hayward this time, but an idiosyncratic bit of bowling: three wickets in six balls across two innings producing figures of 0.3-0-0-1 and 0.3-0-0-2.

Then another century, 111 against Middlesex, supplemented by match figures of seven for 50, contributed to a victory by ten wickets:

> Another hundred to Hayward, his third this month. He is his uncle over again: not so brilliant, but just as sound and reliable, whilst he promises to be every whit as handy with the bat.[47]

That performance brought to an end June, a month that saw a run of seven consecutive victories; three by an innings, two by nine wickets and one by eight. In all of them Tom had played a significant part, either with the bat or the ball, or both, registering three centuries and capturing eighteen wickets at a cost of just under ten runs each.

He then went through his thousand for the season against Kent – 'Hayward had made 76 in two hours and a quarter and completed his 1,000 in first-class cricket this year' –before concluding with an appearance for the long-defunct but temporarily resurrected United South of England Eleven against Swansea at St Helen's, taking eight of the seventeen wickets in the first innings and four in the second.[48] He had also played in the first two of his Gentlemen v Players matches, one at Lord's and one at The Oval, played back to back in the same week. Tom made two half centuries, losing his wicket to CB Fry on three occasions, and following in his uncle's footsteps, being run out for a duck in the other.

Wisden's summary the following year conceded he was not at his best on slow pitches, but was nevertheless developing a reputation as one of the country's most reliable batsmen:

> The slow wickets told heavily against Hayward, but during the month of June he was unquestionably one of the best bats in England, scoring three innings of over a hundred for Surrey and fully justifying his selection for the Players at Lord's. His style remains as perfect as ever, and though his play on bad wickets was disappointing, we see no case to recall a single word of what we have previously written in Wisden in his praise. We look upon him and Holland as the most likely men for the next few years to keep up the reputation of Surrey batting.[49]

Life in London was not all beer and skittles. Tom had to get to grips both with the capital city and becoming a well-known figure. His grandfather, father and uncle had had their share of court appearances and this year Tom followed suit, not for financial reasons or activities of dubious legality, but as a victim of petty but well-planned crime:

> A well known cricketer robbed. At the Lambeth Police Court yesterday, Arthur William Shaw, aged twenty-four, who described himself as a warehouseman, was charged on remand before Mr Paul Taylor with obtaining by means of false pretences a silver watch and gold chain, a Georgian sovereign, a silver sovereign purse containing £5 and a suit of clothes, the property of Thomas Hayward, a professional cricketer, who plays for Surrey. At the first hearing, Mrs Mabel Cairns of Trigon-road, Clapham, said that the prisoner called at her house on the 12th ult. and said he had come from the Oval from Mr Hayward who lodged with the witness, for his clothes. Mr Hayward was playing at the Oval

that day. Believing the man's story she gave him Mr Hayward's clothes, together with the other articles enumerated in the charge. When Mr Hayward returned home he found he had been robbed. Mr Hayward afterward showed her a photograph of a group of men, and she picked a man out from it. She believed that the prisoner was the man to whom she gave the clothes etc. The prisoner denied all knowledge of robbery and Mr Jones, who now appeared for the defence said he would be able to show conclusively that this was a case of mistaken identity. Mr Paul Taylor thought it would be better that the case should be heard by Mr Denman, before whom it originally came, and again remanded the prisoner.[50]

24

South Africa 1895/96

Tom had done enough in the first three domestic seasons of his first-class career to be invited to join Lord Hawke's tour to the Cape, an opportunity to exchange the worst of the winter for a bit of southern hemisphere sunshine, albeit in a country on the verge of war. He was one of four professionals in a predominantly amateur party:

> The members of Lord Hawke's team for South Africa, except the captain and Sir TC O'Brien, who sail in the Moor a week later, leave Southampton in the Union SS Guelph on Saturday next. The team consists of Lord Hawke, Sir T C O'Brien, Messrs CW Wright, SMJ Woods, HT Hewett, AJL Hill, CB Fry, C Heseltine, AM Miller, HR Bromley-Davenport, Hayward, Butt, Tyler and Lohmann.[51]

The political background of the impending Boer War and the Jameson Raid was a more difficult challenge than the battles on the cricket field. Over the years there have been debates as to whether sport and politics should or do mix. The pages of the press found no difficulty in reporting them side by side. It was scarcely a peaceful co-existence, but the front page of the *Cape Argus* on 16 January 1896, alongside reports of armed raids, arson and general unrest, had an adjacent column which began laconically, 'The English team resumed their second innings this morning, and closed their innings at 268 for eight wickets. The chief scorers were Hewitt, 36; Fry, 49; Hayward, 42; Lohmann 14; O'Brien 22; Hill (not out) 58; Wright (not out) 17.'

One match in Johannesburg was cancelled because of what *Cricket* euphemistically called 'disturbed times' and the Wanderers Hall performed a tripartite function of mortuary, hospital and cricket pavilion.[52] Parts of the tour were rescheduled. A train on which the team was travelling was held up by armed border guards at Vereeniging on the frontier of the Transvaal Republic. A thorough search and the levying of duties ensued and they were nonplussed to discover that what was suspected to be a weapon was in fact a cylindrical toothbrush. Nevertheless the tour was completed, despite the complications of the English-Afrikaner relationship and the colour question. Apartheid was already in place. It was not called that at the time and was based on convention rather than legislation, but it added another dimension to a political situation which confused Edgar Wallace, a medical orderly and later a journalist in the country:

> Home politics, I understand… There were two parties in England – Conservative and Liberals. If the Liberals came in you had Home Rule [in Ireland], and if the Conservatives came in you didn't … in South Africa politics were racial. On the one hand you had the psalm-singing, coffee-drinking Dutch, on the other hand the true-born Englishman with his inalienable right to do as he damn pleased in any country at any time.[53]

And that, with Lord Hawke and his amateur majority, is how the team got through the tour, pacifying the border guards by presenting them with a couple of cricket bats.

There had been two earlier tours to South Africa, both privately arranged, one under Major Warton in 1888/89 and one under Walter Read in 1891/92. Three matches, subsequently deemed to be Test matches, had been played and all won by large margins by the tourists, the locals having no answer to the bowling of Johnny Briggs and later John Ferris. The gulf between the two teams was of such proportions as to render the three further Test matches on the 1895/96 tour to be farcical and a number of Test career statistics are unrealistically distorted. In the first Test in Port Elizabeth, South Africa were bowled out for 30 and George Lohmann ended the series with a bowling average of 5.8. Hayward had a century in the second Test at the Wanderers and picked up a handful of the wickets that Lohmann did not get.

It might have been assumed that, as had been the case on Tom's uncle's tour to Australia thirty years earlier when EM Grace (the only amateur) mucked in with the professionals' activities, the social distinctions between amateur and professional might have been sunk in an attempt at some kind of team spirit. Not a bit of it. The professionals in Tom's party stayed at separate hotels, attended separate functions and continued to be regarded as social inferiors. In Pietermaritzburg, Lord Hawke stayed at Government House, the other amateurs with the Seventh Hussars and the professionals were left to find their own accommodation. The patronising attitude of amateurs towards professionals was epitomised by Lord Hawke when he expressed the view that he liked the country, representing as it did the attitudes and trappings of empire, but thought the professionals might find it rather dull and boring.[54]

Outside the Test matches there were only two other eleven-a-side matches, one a one-day one-innings fill up after an untypical and unexpected defeat in two days by Fifteen of Western Province (though in mitigation, three players had travelled separately and an accident to their steamer meant that they had not arrived in time). Western Province won that one by one wicket – though *Lillywhite's* gives the result as a draw – with Tom missing a run out and Tyler dropping a catch with the last pair at the crease.

In the other eleven-a-side match, designated first-class and played just before the third Test, Tom had 83 against Western Province, giving him a final first-class average for the tour of 46.16. In all matches, he had 31.46 and twenty-two wickets at 9.09. Perhaps his outstanding rescue act, like the boy on the burning deck whence all but he had fled, was against Twenty-two of King Williamstown, who put up a far better performance than the 'national' side. Tom made 84 not out of a total of 109, Henry Butt at number ten (Lord Hawke was absent ill) had 11, no one else more than five.

Tom returned to Surrey a fully-fledged international cricketer and a wiser man, appreciating there were conflicts in the world rather more serious than those which took place at the Kennington Oval and on Parker's Piece.

25

PLAYER POWER 1896

Plenty of water had flowed under the bridge since Tom's uncle and his colleagues had been spectacularly welcomed to the Antipodes in 1864/65. The inaugural Test match, retrospectively designated as such, had been played at Melbourne in 1878 and, four years later, a *Sporting Times* mock obituary had resulted in the creation of the Ashes. International cricket was now regularly part of the summer programme, interspersed with tours to the southern hemisphere as regular series between England and Australia took centre-stage in the programmes of both countries. At this time, however, English teams touring overseas were still privately organised and, for home Test matches, the Gentlemen v Players tradition of the host venue selecting the team was maintained. Consequently, Tom was included in the team for the first Test at Lord's, omitted for the second at Old Trafford and recalled for what turned out to be the decider in the three-match 1896 series at The Oval.

Lohmann and Richardson created havoc in Australia's first innings at Lord's, bowling them out before lunch on the first day. Hayward, as *Cricket* pointed out, was one of half a dozen who had not previously played in Anglo-Australian Tests. He did not let the side down, running out of partners at number seven in the first innings and recording a few at number three in the second as England chased the handful of runs required to win. Furthermore, he had bowled a few overs at first change after Richardson and Lohmann had failed to repeat their first innings devastation, faced with a double-century partnership by Gregory and Trott.

Tom then became one of a group of five players who created a sensation in the cricket world by declining to play in the third Test unless the fee was increased from £10 to £20. Their grievances were threefold: firstly, the discrepancy between the professionals' pay and the amateurs' expenses (especially those of WG Grace, despite the club's denial); secondly, the discrepancy between their Test match fee and what the Australians were making from the tour; thirdly, the sums Surrey were making from gate receipts. Negotiations continued by telegram from Leyton where, the week before the match, Surrey were being beaten by an innings, and on the morning of the match.

The press took a detailed interest. At a time when the power of organised labour was increasing, various organisations and movements highlighted the void between what Disraeli had called 'two nations', and a decade before football had overtaken cricket as 'the people's game', this was news.

Grace enjoyed what Gideon Haigh has succinctly described as the privileges of amateurism and the profits of professionalism.[55] Nowhere was this anomaly mentioned as part of the 'demand', but it was an implicit factor in the case of the 'Oval Five'. The Oval, in an example of spin that has continued over three centuries, formally denied that Grace received anything beyond legitimate expenses. There were those, including the strikers and a not inconsiderable section of the general public, who suspected otherwise.

Tom was the youngest of the quintet and had less experience of international cricket but, having had almost four seasons as a professional plus a two-year qualifying period and with a family cricketing pedigree and four Test matches already on his CV, found no difficulty in identifying with the cause.

The attempt at player power failed with the surrender of Abel, Hayward and Richardson to the Surrey committee on the morning of the match. For different reasons, Lohmann and Gunn held out. Ultimately the rebels recognised the might of the committee and the authority of Charles Alcock and that their continued employment and potential future benefits and testimonials depended on appropriate deference. In a way it was the boot on the other foot of his uncle's experience in Melbourne over thirty years earlier, when the Australians had held out for pay equivalent to that of the Englishmen. They had simply been replaced. In the case of Lohmann and Gunn, the same happened here. Had the other three held out, they too would have been replaced and maybe never have played Test cricket again. Hayward had more to lose than the others. He was at the beginning of his international career, the others at or near the end. Nonetheless it could be argued that they had lost the battle but won the war. Shortly afterwards, the fee for playing in a Test match was doubled to £20.[56]

The *Sheffield Daily Telegraph*, from a county not generally associated with unequivocal support for its southern rivals but one always likely to sympathise with workers against employers, summed up the position:

> The Surrey executive have done the right thing in re-admitting Abel, Hayward and Richardson to the All-England Eleven against Australia. An English team with Surrey left out could scarcely be called representative, although the men who took the places of the dissatisfied professionals were by no means feeble substitutes, having proved themselves admirable exponents of high-class cricket on many a hard-fought field. Still, when the three players so promptly put themselves at the disposal of the committee, it was wise to show that official resentment was not irreconcilable with making the interests of English cricket the first and paramount consideration. The unfortunate disagreement has attracted widespread attention, the feeling excited being precisely what we anticipated. The five professionals are regarded as having a thoroughly good case, the only objection being to the inopportune moment taken for pressing it. Unpleasant as the incident has been, it will probably be fruitful of good results, and bring about a reconsideration of the whole question of remunerating the men who live by the game. It is high time for this to be done.
>
> A professional cricketer's life, from the popular point of view, is a merry one. He plays a game in which he delights, and gets £5 a match with £1 more when his side are the victors. Then, if the batsman makes

fifty runs he gets one sovereign 'talent money' and another sovereign for every additional fifty he puts on. That is the pleasant side of the picture. Now for the other. Out of the £ 5 or £6 per match the player has to pay his own expenses – railway fare, hotel bill, luncheon on the field etc.

The servant is worthy of his hire, whether he be British or Colonial born; and the great gulf at present fixed between the pay of English and Australian players is altogether indefensible.[57]

Notwithstanding the acrimonious background, the match provided an opportunity for Hayward to team up with his former pupil Ranjitsinhji. Tom had played his first Test in England at Lord's then missed out at Old Trafford. There Ranji, despite the controversy about whether as an Indian he should have been selected at all, marked his debut with an undefeated century which, along with outstanding bowling by Tom Richardson, almost won the match for England after they followed on. Now for the first time they were on the same side and though neither made much of a contribution, they must have been gratified to have been on the same winning team in a winning series.

On the domestic scene, having led the Championship most of the season, Surrey faltered towards the end and surrendered the title to Lancashire:

The eleven it is to be regretted failed to maintain the high position the county had occupied for some years past, the brilliant promise of the first half of the season being followed by disappointing and uneven play in the later matches. Altogether thirty matches were played, of which seventeen were won, three drawn and ten lost.[58]

Despite all that, Tom's performances continued to impress – five centuries including one for the Players and an early season double century at Derby. His ninety-one wickets (eighty-one of them in the Championship) demonstrated his potential as all-rounder, though not many years ahead he would abandon his bowling (and indeed fielding) to focus entirely on his batting:

Hayward, though he stands second on the list [to Abel] is some distance below Abel in batting, but he proved himself by many degrees the finest all-round cricketer in the eleven, scoring 1182 runs with an average of 37 and taking 81 wickets for less than 15 runs each. From the time he first found a place in the Surrey eleven, we have always had the highest opinion of Hayward's capabilities, and we confess to feel more than ordinary satisfaction at the progress he has made. He had the distinction of being chosen for England against Australia both at Lord's and the Oval, and though it was not his good fortune to do anything remarkable on either occasion, there can be no question that on his form he was fully worthy of his place. Considering that he is too young to have any recollection of his uncle – the famous Tom Hayward of the 1860s – it is strange that he should most closely resemble him as a cricketer, in something like the same beautiful form, and being also a medium pace right-handed bowler.[59]

His seven for 83 against Gloucestershire helped his team to a ten wicket win and his six for 24 against Lancashire almost produced an unexpected victory. Lancashire, needing 60 to win in the fourth innings, collapsed to 30 for six, the last four wickets falling at the same total before Archie MacLaren who had opened and batted through, and Johnny Briggs pulled it round.

26

THE BOWLER 1897

George Lohmann had spearheaded Surrey's bowling from the mid-1880s until 1892 when the breakdown in his health led to a two-year convalescence in South Africa. He missed the 1893 and 1894 seasons, when his mantle fell on Tom Richardson and Bill Lockwood. Lohmann returned to county cricket in 1895 and was still good enough to be selected for England in 1896 and to lead the players' strike, but his rift with the club and final departure in 1897 meant the bowling resources were weakened and provided an opportunity for Tom Hayward to develop as an all-rounder. It was a role he embraced and in 1897 he did the double of a thousand runs and a hundred wickets:

> [Richardson] was fortunate in having two capital supporters through the summer in Hayward and Lees, and for just a week or so Brockwell gave excellent help.
>
> When it became known that owing to differences between himself and the committee, George Lohmann was not going to play for Surrey, the question of the team's bowling became a serious matter. Hayward had of course in 1896 proved himself very good, but it was certain that if he had to share the bowling with Richardson, his batting would suffer. Even as it turned out these fears were to some extent realised, for finely as he played, Hayward never made a hundred after the first match.[60]

The thousand runs was par for the course, but the hundred wickets was unique. When Richardson was rested against Oxford

University, Hayward took full advantage and, with seven in each innings, produced his career-best match figures:

> Surrey gave a rest to Richardson, but Hayward bowled so well at the outset that the absence of the famous professional did not look like causing the county uneasiness ... For Surrey, the hero of the game was Hayward, who scored 46 runs in the two innings and took 14 wickets at a cost of 103 runs.[61]

> Oxford put themselves out of the running by collapsing in the first innings when the wicket was at its worst, against the bowling of Hayward and Hayes. Hayward had for the two innings the fine analysis of 14 wickets for 103 runs, but except that Hayes came with a rush when he was put on at the end of the first innings, the other Surrey bowlers did not in the least distinguish themselves. It looks more than ever as if Surrey would have to rely almost entirely on Hayward and Richardson as a rule which is not quite as promising a look out as could be wished.[62]

Against Leicestershire at Grace Road, Tom bowled through the innings with Richardson to dismiss Leicestershire twice, coincidentally for the same total, 35, still their lowest score against Surrey:

> Hayward bowled finely and took seven wickets for 43 runs, but, exceptional as was his success, it was quite overshadowed by that of Richardson.[63]

> A Match Finished in a Day. On a wicket which helped the bowlers immensely a county like Leicestershire, weakened as it was by the absence of Pougher had practically no chance whatever against Surrey. It often happens that Richardson cannot get a foothold when rain has been having its way for some time, but on the day of this match everything was in his favour, and he was not slow to take advantage of his opportunities. Hayward was also in very great form, and it was found unnecessary to change either of the two bowlers in either innings against Leicestershire.[64]

Hayward had five for 23 and two for 20, Richardson five for 6 and seven for 14. Later in the season against Lancashire at Old Trafford:

The tail could do nothing against Hayward and Richardson who, except for one over, were unchanged. In the follow on, several men made a great effort to save the innings defeat, but Richardson and Hayward again proved themselves equal to the occasion.[65]

As Surrey completed the double over the Red Rose county in August, while his batting could by no means be disregarded, Tom's four wickets (including JT Tyldesley in both innings) played an important role in a six-wicket victory:

It was a brilliant win for the Surrey eleven – all the more creditable for the fact that the match was not played under conditions calculated to show them at their best. The chief honours of the victory rested with Richardson, Hayward and Mr Jephson. Richardson took eleven wickets and Hayward and Jephson obtained between them 178 runs out of the 303 scored for Surrey from the bat. Moreover Hayward took four wickets.[66]

Earlier, in July, his bowling for the Players at Lord's had been impressive:

It looked as if a long score was going to be made, but the batting broke down, Hayward was the cause of the change in the fortunes of the game for when he went on he managed to stick up the batsmen considerably and got rid of Mr Dixon, KS Ranjitsinhji, Mr Jackson and Mr Jessop for 43 runs – a great bowling feat.[67]

The turning point in favour of the Players being the remarkable bowling of Hayward, who, in addition to dismissing Dixon, sent back Jackson, Ranjitsinhji and Jessop, hitting the wicket on each occasion.[68]

Writing some time later about what was his first Gentlemen v Players match, Gilbert Jessop points to the difficulties of facing Hayward's bowling:

Although Tom Richardson bowled finely, as he did in these matches, the bowler who did the most damage in the first innings was Tom Hayward. On account of his greater fame as a batsman one is rather

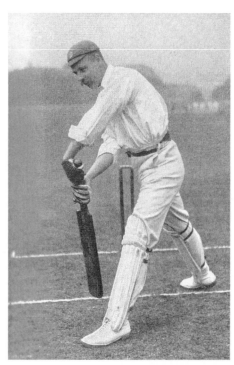

Tom demonstrates the correct way to play a forward drive, captured in The Jubilee Book of Cricket *by KS Ranjitsinhji.*

apt to forget what a good bowler Hayward was. His 'nip' off the pitch on a wicket even a trifle worn was as quick as almost any bowler against whom I have played. Moreover he had an awkward kind of delivery, which made him rather difficult to see. As he bowled from the extreme width of the crease, he came in at you at a difficult angle. That is from a hitter's point of view. Of all bowlers Tom Hayward was my greatest bug bear. He was what may be called a 'flat-catching' bowler. He looked so much simpler than he really was. Overconfidence rather than diffidence of my ability to cope with him usually upset my apple-cart for I never could rid myself of the conviction that in almost every ball there lurked a half-volley.[69]

The following month Surrey played Essex at Leyton and, according to *Cricket*, 'From the beginning of the game the wicket was just a little tricky – just tricky enough to give experienced bowlers like Richardson and Hayward a great advantage.'[70]

Not until the next decade was Tom's fielding to decline. At this stage it was a third string to his all-round bow. Against Yorkshire at The Oval, 'The Yorkshire captain was out when well set and likely to make a long score, to a truly remarkable catch at third man by Hayward, who seemed to have no chance whatever of getting to the ball.'[71]

As a result of bowling more than 800 overs in the season (with 700-plus for Surrey), Tom's batting declined. His only century came against Leicestershire in the first match of the season. It was, said *Cricket*, 'a masterly innings':[72]

> In Surrey's innings, Abel and Hayward put on 172 runs together in an hour and fifty minutes for the second wicket. Abel was batting three hours for his 144, and scarcely made a bad stroke. Hayward – also seen at his best – made his runs in something over two hours and a half.[73]

Despite a lack of triple-figure scores, Stuart Surridge's Patent Rapid Driver was now being advertised as 'used by Abel and Hayward', a partnership that may have improved sales.[74]

Never again that season was Hayward seen at his best as a batsman and never again in his career was his bowling to form a significant part of the Hayward package. The pendulum had already begun to swing against his bowling in the next match against Essex when 'Surrey had the task of fielding on the first day and found that their bowling depended a little too much on Richardson and Hayward'. That was not wrong. Hayward bowled thirty-nine overs and had three for 104, Richardson thirty-six overs and four for 92. When it came to batting, Hayward's innings of 66 was 'soundly played but somewhat fortunate'.[75]

However, he had done enough with the bat during the season to be first to the 'double', on the only occasion he achieved it:

> During the Kent match, Hayward who had some time previously made his thousand runs brought his total of wickets to a hundred, thus being the first cricketer to accomplish both feats this season.[76]

Towards the end of the season Tom dislocated a finger in attempting a catch, causing him to miss Surrey's last two matches and, it could be argued, Surrey to miss out on the Championship. The timing was unfortunate. His opening blast of three for 11 in five overs had helped reduce Somerset to 21 for six. He took no further part in the match with either bat or ball as the Cidermen recovered to win a match reduced to two days by 66 runs:

> The championship slipped out of Surrey's hands just when it seemed fairly in their grasp, but for all that they enjoyed, in 1897, a most brilliant season. The altogether unexpected defeat suffered at the hands of Somerset at the end of August, was of course a bitter disappointment, the more so as it was partially brought about by an accident to Hayward during the early stages of game.[77]

He did not bat in the match, nor indeed again that season. He was listed in the South team to play the North at the Hastings Festival, but his injury compelled him to withdraw.

Regardless of the imbalance between batting and bowling this season and notwithstanding his solitary century, *Cricket* was keen to point to an improvement in consistency and his season's batting average:

> Hayward has been much more consistent. His only century was made in his first innings of the season; but 23 of his other 38 innings are of over 20, and eight of the 23 over 50. His average of exactly 38 is the best he has yet achieved; and it is a notable fact that he has made a step forward each year, progressing from 18 in 1893 to 25 in 1894, 29 in 1895 and 34 in 1896 to 38 this year. As a bowler too he has made marked progress, and is now really first class.[78]

27

AUSTRALIA 1897/98

To speak the plain truth there has not for a very long time been anything so disappointing in English cricket, as the tour of Mr Stoddart's
team in Australia last winter ... Hayward [as a bowler] had only one day
of success ... Hayward, as a batsman, made a bad start but played very
finely indeed as soon as he had accustomed himself to the great pace
of the wickets.[79]

So opined *Wisden,* sagely and sadly. There have been a number
of other series – home and away – of which the same might be said,
but it is difficult to argue against the Almanack's comments. After
the falsest of false dawns with a win in the opening Test match,
Stoddart's team suffered heavy defeats in all of the remaining ones,
Richardson was never the same bowler again and the travelling, the
heavy programme and the heat resulted in thirteen jaded tourists,
Hayward among them, returning to England somewhere between
burnout and breakdown. Tom's bowling never reached the same
heights as in 1897 and, with one very obvious exception, his batting
the following season veered away from the excellent standards he
had set in earlier years.

Three days after landing in Australia the tourists found themselves in the field at the Adelaide Oval. It was scarcely the ideal
period of acclimatisation. There was, however, huge interest among
the hosts and large crowds came along to watch the net sessions with
particular interest in the curiosity that was an Indian prince. Was his
reputation justified?

The Indian Prince played his first cricket on Australian soil at the nets at the city Oval on Monday morning. A large crowd visited the ground to see the brilliant young Cantabrigian stretch his muscles. The prince opened his practice by wheeling up some medium pace balls to his captain with a little work on them.

Storer and Hayward, Stoddart and Wainwright took the creases first. Two pitches were used, but the lookers-on evinced but little interest in their batting. At noon, however, the prince put on his pads, and took Stoddart's place at the wickets. The batting of Ranji showed that he is all that his admirers claim him to be. The trundlers were Hayward, Richardson, Jack Hearne and Briggs so that the prince was treated to plenty of variety.[80]

There was also praise for and optimism about Hayward's likely contribution to the tour, not entirely justified in the early stages, but becoming more so as he took time to adjust to Australian conditions.

If selecting a man now for the best average, Hayward would be my choice. He is a professional who knows his business, and a more gentlemanly fellow never played cricket. He knows what he is being paid for and does it to the best of his ability in a most determined way. For style as a bat nobody can surpass him; in fact, he is like Ranji and plays 'perfect cricket'. He is a fast scorer. As a bowler, he is medium to slow; keeps a good length and breaks both ways. He is sure to be a great favourite amongst the public.[81]

In Sydney too, the arrival of Ranjitsinhji was anticipated with enthusiasm, diluted a little when he appeared dressed in the western-style team 'uniform', part of a group which, even in a country, less class conscious than the one which they had left, as far as hotel accommodation was concerned, maintained the rigid distinction between gentlemen and players.

Mr Stoddart and his twelve merry men from England are in Sydney at last. They steamed into Redfern railway station at a few minutes past midday in a special train made up of a locomotive, brake van and luxurious sleeping car. A tremendous crowd had gathered to welcome them, and to see the wonderful Ranji with their own eyes. The window shutters of the Pullman car were down, and a full minute elapsed before the genial faces of the cricketers were seen. The form of Ranjitsinhji was waited in palpitating expectation. At last a slim figure of medium height was espied and a cheer went up. Those who had conjured up a regal being, black as the ace of spades, with a wonderful headgear and other queer Oriental garments must have felt disappointed with the actual Ranji. He was wearing a straw hat with the team's colours on the band and in his well-cut suit of dark blue serge he looked every inch an English gentleman. The other members of the combination wore light suits and straw hats. The amateur members of the team were driven to the Australia Hotel and the professionals to Roberts, Grange and Market Streets.[82]

'Ranji' was to make an impression off the field as well as on it, contributing to the press anecdotes about the outward journey, the thrill of the team at attending the Melbourne Cup and trenchant thoughts about the quality of player accommodation and the Adelaide Oval outfield, as well as not being backward in coming forward with unequivocal views on a topic which has kept legislators occupied in three centuries, the use of the elbow in the bowling action.

From Naples to Port Said the passage was a smooth one and the different members of the team thoroughly enjoyed themselves. From there to Colombo, however, a heavy sea seemed to affect Storer, Hirst, Board, Wainwright and myself in varying degrees. From Ceylon to Albany changeable weather was experienced, and the only excitement during this part of the voyage was the introduction of ladies cricket matches. The ladies showed great keenness for the game and in their spare moments practised assiduously ... To the new members of this team the differences existing between the English and Australian grounds, both as regards the pavilion and ground itself were clearly noticeable. The rather primitive conveniences in the dressing room of the players and the members enclosure were a keen disappointment to us. So also was the general outlook of the ground, apart from the wicket. The ground appeared very hard and bare of grass and on the rough side, much reminding of one of the cricket fields of the North of England where football plays an important part during seven months of the year.

But coming to the wicket the disadvantages of the Adelaide Oval ceased and in this respect it would compare favourably with any other cricket ground in the old country.

This match was made memorable by the fact that a bowler of a very superior class was, for the first time in Australia 'no-balled' for unfair bowling. I cannot but admire the pluck and judgment of the umpire who 'no-balled' him.

I wish it clearly to be understood, before making any further criticism that I don't in any way accuse Jones of throwing deliberately; that is to say of throwing knowing himself to be throwing when he was supposed to be bowling; but at the same time I cannot help thinking that his action is still such that were I to practice or cultivate it, I would have no hesitation in believing myself to be throwing.

But any person unprejudiced would see that the actions of Jones or Fry constitute in every sense a throw inasmuch as they use not only the wrist and shoulder but also the elbow which plays an important, if not the leading, part in imparting the pace and projecting the ball.

I, for one, think the cricket communities in all countries owe a debt of gratitude to Phillips for having partly smoothed the way for other umpires to treat such unfair actions in the way that they deserve.[83]

The vicissitudes of the media as well as the fluctuating fortunes of the game, in particular those of Tom Hayward's batting as he became acclimatised to Australian conditions are illustrated in the following extracts, admittedly from different newspapers, but on consecutive days:

Hayward came out with the reputation of being the best all-round man of the lot but his doings have caused nothing but disappointment. Whenever he has been tried his bowling has not possessed any sting on Australian wickets and his batting has been of a most mediocre character. His one decent score was at Glen Innes, where he accounted for a century, but in the important matches his figures were: 6, 7, 5, 9 and 18 not out. He made 31 at Brisbane and this lifts his average to 15.2.[84]

The stand made by Hayward, ably supported by Wainwright, virtually saved the Englishmen from making a score of probably under three figures for the first time this tour ... Hayward made a most favourable impression as a sound, vigorous batsman.[85]

There was controversy about delaying the start of the opening Test in Sydney because of a very wet outfield, a decision taken by the ground authorities with no consultation with players or umpires. It was assumed that the decision would favour the Australians. It didn't. England won their only Test of the series and Hayward, after his hesitant start was now fully acclimatised for the matches which mattered:

> Hayward is to be warmly congratulated on his very fine effort. There were many good judges who prophesied for him a career in this country something akin to that of Brockwell's but this may only be premature, and it is hoped, for Hayward's sake, that it is so. Now that he has made a start there is no reason why he should not perform as well as he does in the old country. He played better yesterday than he has yet done. There was none of that hesitation about his strokes which was apparent in some of his innings, notably the one at Brisbane. He got the ball on the full face of the bat and he never hesitated about leaving his crease. He played M'Kibbin better yesterday than he has done before.[86]

The cricketers continued to have their tribulations, both on and off the field. The fourth Test in Melbourne was played partly in thick smoke emanating from the bush fires burning outside the city and at the end of series presentations, after the official niceties, the captain was not slow to contrast the civility characterising relationships between the players with the 'ockerism' demonstrated by some sections of the Australian public. He had had his watch and chain stolen during a fracas in Brisbane and although through the generosity of his hosts he had had it replaced, the treatment to which he and his team had been subjected by a part of the public – and press – continued to rankle.

> At the close of the cricket match, a presentation was made on behalf of the trustees of the Sydney cricket ground, to Mr AE Stoddart, in recognition of his services to cricket in the colonies. Mr Stoddart was unostentatiously 'relieved' of his watch and chain while playing in Brisbane, and it was decided, as an appropriate testimonial, to present him with a gold chronometer, gold chain and sovereign purse. Mr Stoddart replied in an appreciatively worded speech of thanks and his health was drunk with enthusiasm.

Mr Stoddart then said that, as this was the last occasion of the rival teams meeting, it was his duty to thank the trustees of the Sydney cricket ground for a most enjoyable tour. The pleasure and the comfort of his team had been most carefully studied, and they were grateful for it. But he had something rather unpleasant to say, because he thought it his duty to say it. He felt it absolutely his duty to make reference to insults which had been poured on himself and his team as they journeyed through the country. They had been insulted, hissed, hooted and howled at by a certain section of the crowd. Another grievance was against a certain section of the press which had been equally insulting, and had never lost an opportunity of treating the team with ridicule. The crowd had gone out of its way to insult them; and he could not see what they had done to incur all that. This matter had been on his mind for some time, and he had determined to mention it.

Referring to the cricket Mr Stoddart said his team could bear their defeat as they had been beaten by a better side and by sportsmen. He had never played against a nicer lot of fellows and his team had great regard for their opponents.[87]

From an individual point of view, Hayward's batting on tour had not been the worst: he played in all five Tests averaging 37, with a highest innings of 72 in the first. His average in other first-class matches was just under 40.

Nor did he let up in minor matches. The bowling tended to be shared around and he did his bit, opening the bowling against Northern Districts of New South Wales and dismissing the first four batsmen. On the batting front, from various positions in the order, he had 108 not out against Glen Innes, 68 against Toowoomba, 45 against Bendigo, 49 against Western Districts of Victoria, before coming down to earth with a duck against Australian Universities.

28

MAGIC MONTH 1898-1901

1898 was far from Tom's greatest season, the post-traumatic stress of an Australian tour having kicked in. The effect of his bowling was to reduce it to ineffectiveness:

> Hayward fell a long way below the standard reached in the previous year... In 1897 Hayward did first-rate work for his county, taking ninety-one wickets at an average cost of little more than nineteen runs each, but last season he was hopelessly ineffective, securing only twenty seven wickets, and these at an average cost of 36 runs each.[88]

But for one very exceptional innings, his Championship batting average for the season would have been 36, rather than the eventual 47 to which it was boosted by his career-best, and Surrey's second highest at this stage, 315 not out against Lancashire at The Oval. It fell short of Walter Read's 338 against Oxford University ten years earlier but was a masterclass in technique and stamina. It included the addition of a hundred runs before lunch on the second morning:

> Hayward stands second only to Abel in the averages, but finely as he often played, he owes his position in great measure to his 315, not out, against Lancashire – the highest innings of the season in first-class matches.[89]

> Jephson helped Hayward to put on 175, the score at the close being 361 for five wickets, Hayward not out 163. On the following day Hayward had the satisfaction of carrying out his bat for 315, the highest individual score of the season, and with one exception the highest ever

hit for Surrey. He batted for six hours and three-quarters and hit two 5's, thirty-seven 4's, seven 3's, twenty-nine 2's and seventy-eight singles. He had some luck but his driving on the off side was exceptionally fine. It was not until half-past three that the innings closed for 634 – the highest of all their scores – the delay in finishing the innings probably costing Surrey a victory.[90]

He later had support from Len Braund, who played a few matches with Surrey over this and the preceding two seasons before switching his allegiance to Somerset. 204 was added for the eighth wicket.

The innings brought Tom a collection of over £7 plus a few shillings and an odd halfpenny. The latter he donated to Johnny Briggs who had bowled at him for much of his innings, his reward, in addition to the halfpenny being the final three Surrey wickets, but innings figures of 56-8-142-3 must have made him welcome the opportunity to put his feet up. As often happens when there are huge scores there was insufficient time for a definite result (at this time declarations were permitted only on the final day) and Lancashire had no problems in salvaging the draw.[91]

There was a suggestion in Committee that subscriptions be received towards a presentation but there are no further references and nothing seems to have come of it.[92] Maybe the Committee took the view that he had done well enough already.

Tom had a few other impressive innings that season, including centuries against Nottinghamshire:

Not much more than an hour's play was possible at Trent Bridge in the match between Notts and Surrey, and in that time the visitors' score was increased from 111 for one wicket to 201 for five. This admitted of Hayward completing his century. On the opening day he had made 66 not out; yesterday he was not dismissed until he had carried his score to 126. It was not quite a faultless innings but Hayward displayed great patience and skill and he was batting just under three hours.[93]

Against Kent:

For this satisfactory result of their labours the visitors had mainly to thank Hayward, who played splendid cricket for 101. Going in third wicket down at 84, just before mid-day, he was not dismissed until a quarter to four, when, with the score at 239, he was seventh man out. In little more than three hours of actual cricket he had made the large proportion of 101 out of 156, giving no chance and hitting eleven 4's, three 3's and nine 2's. His innings, indeed, showed him at his best.[94]

During the winter Tom continued the family interest in and proficiency at billiards, narrowly losing a match to a distinguished local player, the final outcome of which was a tribute to the handicappers:

At the Criterion, Market passage on Thursday night a most interesting billiard match was brought off between Mr W Thurston, the well-known amateur and Mr Tom Hayward, the popular Surrey cricketer. It was a good all-round game and the finish was particularly fine.

Thurston 1,000 points, Hayward (received 400) 987.

The scratch man had an uphill task but he showed good form and well deserved his victory. On the other hand Mr Hayward did not give up and his fine effort at the finish was a feature of the game. The game occupied about three hours and a quarter.[95]

1899 was the season of the first five-match Test series against Australia in England. The advent of the Board of Control in 1898 and of a selection committee ensured a consistency not always present when the arrangement was that the host venue was responsible for selecting the team. Consequently, Hayward was selected for all five matches. Ahead of that, however, he had the opportunity of having an early look at the tourists, for the South of England at Crystal Palace:

[Fry] and Hayward came together when the score was 20 and raised it to 134 before they were parted ... Hayward fell for a successful innings of 50; he had batted very steadily and well for a couple of hours, but made one over memorable to Noble by hitting the Australian for three fours. It was a fine catch which disposed of him.[96]

The following week, Surrey played the Australians at The Oval and came unstuck by an innings and 71 runs, bowled out for 64 in their second innings. Wearing an England shirt against the same opposition, Tom did not have the most satisfactory of starts to the Test series:

> At 116 four wickets were down – and Hayward came in. This was decidedly unpleasant but worse was to follow, for Hayward placed the ball to leg and started to run. Darling fielded, and returned with great despatch and Hayward in trying to get back fell. He stretched out and stuck his fingers over the crease, but already Kelly had broken the wicket.[97]

Once that indignity was behind him, this was by some distance his best season in Test cricket. He scored two of his three Test centuries; one at Old Trafford, one on his home patch of Kennington Oval. These were three-day Test matches, four of which were drawn, Australia taking the series courtesy of a ten-wicket win at Lord's. It was a series which saw the departure of WG Grace, the arrival of Wilfred Rhodes and, for the visitors, the Test debut of Victor Trumper. England tried a variety of opening partnerships of which the final one of FS Jackson and Hayward was the most successful, so successful in fact that it gave England's innings in The Oval Test a platform of 186, a record opening partnership at the time for Anglo-Australian Tests. Hayward's 137 was his highest Test innings and followed immediately on his 130 at Old Trafford.

Tom's contribution to the draw in the first Test at Trent Bridge was measured in time at the crease, rather than runs scored. Along with his former protégé Ranji, he stayed at the crease long enough to prevent an Australian victory which looked likely when Joe Darling declared Australia's second innings closed, leaving England 290 to win, but Australia did not have enough time to bowl them out in an eventual ninety-nine overs. At 19 for four the draw looked unlikely:

> The most noticeable points in the innings were the catch by Hayward to dispose of Iredale ... It may be pretty safely said that no two batsmen

were ever placed in a more trying position at this moment than Hayward and Ranjitsinhji ... The Australians were now playing up for all they were worth. Everyone knows that in similar circumstances bowlers are fifty per cent above their usual form, while the field are capable of doing the most brilliant things. So Ranjitsinhji and Hayward prepared to hold the fort. Hayward did not lose his nerve when the turning point of the innings came and he was missed at short leg, he played exactly the right sort of cricket that was required. Runs were of no value whatever, and no effort was made by either batsman to do anything in the way of quick scoring. But time went by and the danger seemed to be almost past, when Hayward was at last out about an hour before time ... Ranjitsinhji carried his bat for a superb innings of 93; he might have made his hundred, but he could take no risks.[98]

In Cambridge, the press stressed the local angle:

The England cricket team at Trent Bridge in 1899, Tom's best season with the international side.
Back: Dick Barlow (umpire), Tom Hayward, George Hirst, Billy Gunn, JT Hearne (12th man), Bill Storer, Bill Brockwell, VA Titchmarsh (umpire).
Middle: CB Fry, KS Ranjitsinhji, WG Grace (capt), Stanley Jackson.
Front: Wilfred Rhodes, Johnny Tyldesley.

Cambridge to the rescue. Cambridge, in the persons of Ranjitsinhji and Tom Hayward, was able to turn a game that seemed quite hopeless for England into a drawn event. Those who gave up all hope for England had left out of the reckoning the staying power of Ranjitsinhji and Hayward.[99]

At Lord's, where he had 77 in the second innings:

Hayward and Jackson made things look a little better, but just before the time for drawing stumps Jackson was easily caught and bowled on playing forward to Trumble ... Hayward batted well, but when he had made a single he was palpably missed by the wicket-keeper standing up to Jones. MacLaren joined Hayward, and so long as these two batsmen stayed together, there was still a chance of England making something like a fight. Indeed, things were looking comparatively cheerful when 150 went up without further loss. However, on Laver being tried Hayward, Tyldesley and Jessop were caught in quick succession, and ... the match was as good as over.[100]

At Headingley where he had an invaluable 40 not out, 'Hayward's innings, though marred by two chances, was in the main, a fine exhibition of defence'.[101]

Six wickets for 119 – in the absence of Briggs it was practically seven for 119 – a very different thing from four for 119 and there were now only Hayward and Lilley who could possibly be depended on to make any runs. It was indeed a time to test the mettle of a man. Hayward and Lillee were however equal to the occasion. They defied the attack of the Australians for an hour and forty minutes during which they brought the total up by about a hundred. Both men played wonderfully good cricket, and although Hayward was missed once or twice, it must not be forgotten that the wicket was entirely in the favour of the bowlers.[102]

Then, more spectacularly, at Old Trafford:

Hayward's innings of 130 was in every way magnificent. Rarely or never in the whole series of England and Australia matches in this country has a more remarkable display of batting been given. Up to lunch time he took an hour and a half to make 20 runs, but so completely did the character of his cricket change when things were going better for his side that after the interval he added 110 runs in rather less than two hours and three-quarters.[103]

One hardly dared to hope that Hayward, who in each of the England v Australia matches has had to go in when his side was in great straits, would for the fourth time in succession rise superior to all difficulties. But there was no nervousness about him and no excitement – his first business was to keep up his wicket and trust to something happening later in the innings, and for three-quarters of an hour he let the bowlers do their worst, making only eight runs. After lunch Hayward went on with his innings in his obstinate way, and the Australian bowlers must soon have come to realise that if they got him out at all it would be through accident.[104]

The follow-up century at The Oval came in for even more praise and earned him a ground collection of £131. He was clearly in good nick, having had a huge double century against Yorkshire two days before, his innings eventually ended on that occasion by FS Jackson, the man with whom he now shared the crease. The opening partnership of Hayward and Jackson was an adventurous choice but, in view of England's early innings collapses in the preceding matches series, it was fully justified. Only on one occasion – Fry and Grace at Trent Bridge – had the opening partnership exceeded 30. The tactical change had worked.

It was rather a curious order, for there were regular first men in MacLaren, Fry and Jones, yet none of them were given the opening honour. It was left to Jackson, who has been doing so well for Yorkshire and Hayward, who got his eye in to such a tune on Saturday, to begin the innings in this fateful match.[105]

Hayward's play in the Test matches was the feature of the whole season. At the Oval for the first time in the five games he had the opportunity of starting his innings when the side were not in difficulties, and nothing could well have been finer than his batting. Risking nothing at the start of the match he took nearly two hours and a half to get his first fifty, doubled his score in an hour and twenty-five minutes and wound up making his last 37 runs in forty minutes. Above everything else his innings was remarkable for the perfection of his placing in front of short leg. Watching the game with the utmost closeness, he only made three strokes that could be described as dangerous.[106]

The innings attracted compliments from across the border:

England v Australia at Oval. Record stand by Jackson and Hayward.

The cricket was of a very high class, Jackson and Hayward batting with great skill, while the bowling maintained its accuracy. Another lovely stroke to the off boundary by Jackson from Noble brought forth cheers, and then in successive overs from Jones, Hayward absolutely blocked a ball from Jones and sent it to the off boundary and turned a shortish ball beautifully to leg for 4; so the game soon became bright, and what was looked upon as an experiment in putting in Jackson and Hayward first, promised to be attended with the happiest result. One hundred without a wicket was a splendid start for England, and the spectators were in high good humour, the many incidents of the play keeping them full of life.

Except for the brief period when Jackson was so much in trouble with McLeod's bowling the batting of the two Englishmen had been beyond praise and their wonderful start aroused a general feeling of confidence as to the ability of the representatives of England again putting their rivals in the position of having to play an uphill game.

At Manchester four weeks ago, Hayward made 130, a fact it would hardly be necessary to mention but that by this second three figure innings Hayward accomplished a feat without parallel in Test matches in England, no one else having played two three figure innings in these contests in one season, so Hayward occupies a position by himself in the history of cricket.

During the four hours and a half Hayward was at the wicket he had played grandly, making few faulty strokes and giving nothing like a chance. In his 137 were twenty 4's, five 3's and eleven 2's.[107]

Once again, the Cambridge media stressed his local background and drew attention to a well-merited collection:

Handsome collection for Hayward. The Australian captain recently expressed his opinion that Tom Hayward was the greatest batsman in the world at the present time. The batting of the old Cambridge YMCA boy on Monday was not calculated to cause the skipper to alter his opinion, and Hayward's scores this season in the Test matches are as follows: 0 and 28 (Nottingham) 1 and 77 (Lord's) 40 not out (Leeds) 130 (Manchester) and 137 (Oval) average 69. In recognition of the professional's share in the record first wicket stand yesterday. Mr MacLaren authorised a collection on the ground which realised the handsome sum of £131 3s 6d which was handed to Hayward.[108]

Even before his back-to-back centuries, 'Pavilion Gossip' in *Cricket* was singing Hayward's praises as the man to get his country out of a crisis:

If ever a man has conclusively shown that he is the man for a crisis it is Hayward. There used to be a theory that Hayward was a good-wicket player, and that he made his runs when everything was going well with his side. But he has lately had such a trial as can rarely have fallen to any other batsman in the course of the history of the game. In the first England v Australia match at Nottingham he had to go in when England were fighting for existence in the second innings. Four wickets down for 19 runs and about two hours and three quarters remained to play, Hayward kept in until a draw was nearly a certainty. In the second match at Lord's with his side in a hopeless position, he played so splendidly in a partnership with MacLaren that when he was out at last a draw seemed quite possible. Again in the third match, at Leeds, he had to bat under circumstances which were almost more disheartening than the others, and again he triumphed.[109]

Between the Headingley and Old Trafford Tests, the third and fourth respectively, he featured in the Gentlemen v Players matches at The Oval and Lord's. His 77 north of the river could not help the professionals avoid a heavy defeat by an innings and 59 runs, reversing the previous week's result in Kennington when Tom had contributed 134 not out to a total of 647 and victory by an innings and 36. 'From first to last,' said *Wisden*, 'he played beautiful cricket.'[110] The Cambridge media again made much of the local connection, its match report lapsing into the hyperbolic: 'Yesterday Tom Hayward, though in great form, played his best innings of the season. It was a wonderful innings, quite worthy of the most polished batsman that ever lived.'[111]

On the domestic scene, despite the shaky start against the tourists, for Hayward and Surrey it was a golden summer. Surrey, in Kingsmill Key's final season as captain, won the Championship for the first time since 1895. In addition to his two Test centuries, Tom had five more, four for Surrey and one for the Players. He shared a partnership of 344 with Bobby Abel against Somerset en route to Surrey's 811, still a record team total. Abel went on to 357, still Surrey's highest individual innings.[112]

Within three months of their partnership against Somerset, Abel and Hayward went one better and added 448 for the fourth wicket against Yorkshire, then a record for that wicket in English first-class cricket and still the record for any wicket for Surrey. Tom's contribution was 273, which remains the record for an individual innings for Surrey against Yorkshire.[113]

While, in response to Yorkshire's 704, 'Abel and Hayward with nothing but a draw to play for, staying together for six hours and a half adding 448 runs for Surrey's fourth wicket.'[114] Tedious in the extreme no doubt for those interested in results rather than statistics, but they did the job. There had been controversy earlier in the innings when Yorkshire were of the opinion that Hayward had been bowled – but the umpire wasn't and that was the deciding factor:

The question of whether Hayward was bowled in the match between Surrey and Yorkshire on Friday evening when he had made 63 has given rise to much discussion. The umpire at the bowler's end is positive that the ball did not hit the wicket until it rebounded off the wicket-keeper. Hayward is equally positive that he was not bowled – and no one will dispute that he is a good sportsman. On the other hand most of the Yorkshiremen and some of the onlookers who were in a good position to see are convinced that the bails were off before the ball reached the wicket-keeper. There cannot be much doubt that the umpire at the bowler's end was actually in the best position to see what happened, while it is very seldom that a batsman does not know when he is bowled.[115]

No video replays then. We shall never know.

At Taunton, following his centuries against Yorkshire then Australia at The Oval, Tom brought up his third in just over a week: 'Hayward played his third consecutive innings of three figures. He batted very finely.'[116]

Back on his old hunting ground in Cambridge on a rain-affected pitch, he was in form with the ball, eleven wickets in the match, seven for 20 in the first innings, without assistance from the field, six bowled, one lbw, as the university plunged to 60 all out:

> On a wicket seriously affected by rain in the early part of the week, Cambridge had no chance against Surrey, the county winning the match at half-past six on the second afternoon by 271 runs. Hayward's bowling contributed far more than anything to this overwhelming victory. On the first day he was irresistible, bowling in a style that he never approached during the remainder of the season.[117]

He passed 2,000 runs for the first time in his career, going on to 2,647 and going through the 10,000 barrier in seven domestic and two overseas seasons. He did a bit of bowling, but without approaching the levels of 1896 and 1897, had sixty-seven first-class wickets, including (emulating his uncle's performance of three decades earlier) two hat-tricks, one against Gloucestershire at The Oval in May and the following month against Derbyshire at Chesterfield. Those who chased leather round The Oval as he compiled his 273, which included forty-three fours might just have given his season their county's highest accolade of 'not bad'.

Surrey were certainly weaker when he was absent:

> 'Referring to the result of the match at Southampton, a contemporary says:
> 'Although due allowance may be made for the fact that Brockwell, Hayward and Richardson were not playing, no effort should be made to explain away Surrey's defeat.' Quite so. The mere mention of the three names is sufficient for all practical purposes.
> It's not of much importance
> That Richardson should play;
> And as for Tommy Hayward –

He's just as well away;
While Brockwell is a person
Who's not worth counting in,
So it's wrong to make excuses
If you happen not to win.[118]

The obstinacy exhibited in the Test matches was also in evidence in county cricket. Immediately after the Headingley Test, Tom found himself in a similar situation for his county against Essex:

Three of the best wickets down for 21! Needless to say that the Essex men now played up for all they were worth, but they had two cool hands to contend with in Lockwood and Hayward, the latter having recently had sufficient experience of going in when his side was in a hole to last him a life-time. Long before the Essex bowlers had succeeded in getting another wicket they had learned to appreciate how stubborn can be the resistance of Hayward when he makes up his mind to stay.[119]

Hayward was self-evidently a difficult man to remove from the crease. WH Patterson of Kent had a controversial way of doing it, but the tactics would now be illegal and even at the time were considered to be against the spirit of the game. The Oval crowd certainly thought so:

At the Oval on Tuesday, in the second innings of Surrey, a section of the crowd expressed disapproval in no half-hearted manner at the action of Mr WH Patterson in bowling the ball very high in the air so as to fall vertically on the wicket. As the bowler was quite within his rights, the remarks made by the crowd when Hayward, in playing a ball which came high up at his face, stepped back on his wicket were quite uncalled for.[120]

The remarks were from FS Ashley-Cooper; from a Surrey source they may well have been more critical. His disapproval of the actions of the Surrey crowd, however, did not cloud his judgment on Hayward's season overall, his success in international, domestic and representative cricket justifying praise which verged on hyperbole:

Hayward has been making such fine scores of late that on his present form he is the best batsman in the world. Of his three scores, his 137 against Australia was probably the best, considering the bowling it was made against; but only of slightly less merit was his huge score against Yorkshire. Hirst and Hayward certainly deserve the congratulations of cricket enthusiasts, for to score three separate centuries in successive innings is a marvellous performance, even in a great run-getting year … Nobody will deny that the finest professional batsman of the year was Hayward, who scored runs on all kinds of wickets against all kinds of bowling.[121]

Notwithstanding Ashley-Cooper's comments, Tom revealed to Digby Jephson in a newspaper interview at the end of his career that his best innings in England was his rescue act of 130 at Old Trafford, and that MacLaren was the best captain under whom he played:

'What was the best innings you ever played in England?'
    'The hundred I made at Old Trafford against Australia.'
    'Who was the best captain you played under?' And the answer to this question came like a flash, 'AC MacLaren,' and I heartily endorsed the answer.[122]

At twenty-eight, supremely fit in mind and body notwithstanding a touch of sunstroke picked up at the unlikely venue of Old Trafford, Hayward had now played a major role in rescuing England, Surrey and the Players when others had failed and put the team into difficulties.[123] The question arises as to whether, displaying the obduracy of an opening batsman by having all the strokes but being judicious about when to use them, he could not do a job as opening batsman and obviate those difficulties in the first place. His opening partnership of 185 with FS Jackson would seem to provide the answer to that one, but it was not until 1903 that he was used as a regular opener for Surrey when the Abel-Brockwell duopoly had run its course. England saw the light a bit earlier than that and, after his success at The Oval used him in that capacity, especially in Australia. His partners, however, were a succession of amateurs: MacLaren, Warner, Fry and AO Jones (the exceptions were Rhodes and Hobbs). Batting was for the amateurs, bowling for the professionals. Hayward and (later) Hobbs were in the vanguard of changing that balance and establishing the credentials of the high quality professional batsman.

Tom had yet another century, against Warwickshire at The Oval, before winding down at the Hastings Festival with a Home Counties team who played the Rest of England and – a blast from the past – playing with Abel, Digby Jephson and Harold Pretty in a single wicket match against a Dover Eleven.[124]

Notwithstanding Tom's relatively little bowling after 1897, in 1900 he was again appointed as a bowler at Fenner's, along with several others, providing high quality practice for the undergraduates and encouraging Ranjitsinhji to be back in town for pre-season preparation:

> Fenner's ground will be opened for practice April 19. The following bowlers have been engaged. Tom Hayward (Surrey) Clarke (Surrey) Woodcock (Leicester) Jack Sharp and W Attewell (Notts) Burn (Essex) L Braund (Somerset) Peppal (Gloucs) O'Connor, Coote, G Watts, Bowyer, Hurry and Edwards (Cambridgeshire) and Biral (Uppingham).[125]

> Prince Ranjitsinhji has commenced practice at Cambridge for the coming season, and was present on the Trinity College Cricket Ground yesterday, indulging in net practice. Tom Hayward, the Surrey professional, with W Bryan and J O'Connor, Cambridgeshire professionals were bowling for him.[126]

The following month, however, it was not his second string as a net bowler but his forte as a batsman which caused him to hit the headlines:

> Tom Hayward yesterday accomplished the feat of scoring a thousand runs in first-class cricket before the end of May. Last week he went off considerably but contributions of 40 and 140 against Sussex left him within 18 of the requisite number. Yesterday he was sent in first against Gloucestershire and he compiled a masterly 92 before being dismissed.[127]

Only eight men in the history of the game have scored a thousand first-class runs before the end of May, Bradman having done it twice, Graeme Hick the most recent in 1988. Tom was the second to reach the milestone (the first being WG Grace five years earlier), albeit with the advantage of a 16 April start and a bit of batting order adjustment as he approached the target, but nonetheless a target most batsmen come nowhere near – and with 1,074 he still has the highest aggregate. He started the season with five centuries in his first seven innings, with half centuries in the other two. He then wobbled with three single figure scores before bouncing back with 40 and 146 in a match spanning 28 to 30 May, and being allowed to open the innings in the time remaining on 31 May, 92 against Gloucestershire to take him over the line and beyond.

It was a special record and, although it was some way in the future, one of his other records (a century of centuries) might have been achieved a year earlier, had he not run out of partners when on 99 at Leyton.

Surrey were nowhere near repeating their Championship success of the previous season, but after the start Tom had, it was no surprise that he exceeded (though only just) his first-class aggregate for the previous season.

It was supremely ironic that the club and the ground which had been the subject of his uncle's vicarious antagonism in the great schism of the 1860s should become something close to the south London temple in which he was worshipped for a quarter of a century and, in the case of the Cambridge protégé he was responsible for introducing, well beyond that.

Notwithstanding his national and international prestige, Tom never forgot 'the base degrees by which he did ascend' and continued his habit of taking a team to Cambridge for the purposes of charity and/or the benefit of one of his fellow professionals:

A match was played at Cambridge for the benefit of J O'Connor, between sides captained respectively by Tom Hayward and Mr Whibley, the game producing some fine batting by Hayward, Ranjitsinhji and AJ Rich.

Hayward's Eleven went in first and scored 220 for six wickets, the innings then being declared closed. Hayward contributed 93, his score including sixteen fours. Whibley's Eleven, thanks to the splendid play of Ranjitsinhji and Rich subsequently hit off the required runs for the loss of two batsmen in an hour and three quarters and won the match by eight wickets. Ranjitsinhji played an innings of 122, which included eighteen 4's and Rich made 109, his chief strokes being fifteen 4's.[128]

It was in the 1901 season that Tom achieved his best innings bowling figures with eight for 89 at Edgbaston. Surrey had led by 93 on the first innings and Hayward, brought on after short spells from Brockwell, Lockwood and Lees, cleaned up, leaving Surrey 126 to win. Having reached 81 for four, they then collapsed and failed to get them.

There were no Test matches that year, but in domestic cricket he continued to impress with the bat, as reflected in his Championship batting average which another single would have brought to 60 for the season. He had two centuries early on, but after that failed to 'convert' any of the twenty innings of over 50.

His specialism continued to be digging the team out of trouble, beginning early in the season against Gloucestershire, following 158 the previous week against Derbyshire:

> The Surrey innings began in a startling manner, three wickets being down for 21. It was almost a toss up whether Hayward was not stumped off [Lane] soon afterwards, but from this moment there was no further uneasiness for the welfare of Surrey, Abel and Hayward playing the bowling in a masterly manner. When stumps were drawn Abel was not out 76 and Hayward not out 53. Hayward went on as steadily and methodically as ever. Hayward's 181 was put together in five hours.[129]

He was unable to emulate his thousand runs in May, but he hit the target by early June, beating Bobby Abel to the landmark by a few minutes:

When Surrey went in a second time, Abel required 67 and Hayward 66 to complete their thousand runs for the season. Abel had a short start, but Hayward made the necessary runs a few minutes before his partner, the two men being the first to reach their thousandth run this year.

They were probably more concerned with their innings in the context of the match, rather than individual landmarks, Surrey being in a tricky position at Bradford:

There was only one chance of saving the match: it was that Abel and Hayward should both come off. They began their partnership with the utmost care and deliberation, and gradually played themselves in until they were masters of the situation. They never made a false stroke or a mistake of any kind, and when at last Hayward got his leg in front of the wicket they had brought the score to 169, their partnership producing 135 in two hours and a quarter. Their cricket can only be described as perfect.[130]

However, his batting was not immune from criticism:

Hayward does not seem to be able to hurry; he can hold on tenaciously, but he has his limits. He was particularly slow during the latter part of his innings, not being able to get comfortably settled or to get any command over the bowling.[131]

This particular match, against Middlesex at Lord's, was eventually drawn with Middlesex 295 for seven, pursuing a fourth-innings target of 371. It brought Tom 91 and 83 so, if he was aware of the criticism at all, he was impervious to it, probably believing that answers could best be made with the bat.

The criticism was continued in a review of the season, albeit in a toned-down version and with mitigating circumstances built in:

Throughout the season Hayward has played the steadiest and most painstaking of games and at no time, even in his biggest innings, has he made his runs at a fast rate, but it must be remembered that over and over again he has had to bat when Surrey seemed in a desperate position, and that by his steadiness he has done much to retrieve the fortunes of the side. In the latter part of the season Hayward did not make as many fine scores as usual, but he would still be chosen in the best England eleven.[132]

Other out-of-season comments were kinder, concentrating more on mannerisms than technique and performance:

Hayward, on his outward journey, wags his head in an alarming manner and when homeward bound, especially after a good innings, he runs half-way from the wickets to the pavilion. The remainder he walks slowly, fanning himself with his bat.[133]

At the end of the 1901 season, a charity match was played for the benefit of Addenbrooke's Hospital. Even on the brink of his second Australian tour, Tom did not take much persuading:

Parker's Piece Cambridge was the venue of an unusually interesting cricket match on Wednesday. The weather was of a most delightful character and large numbers of people turned out to witness the game. This was not at all surprising for several well known first-class county professionals were advertised to appear, while the proceeds of the match were for a deserving cause viz Addenbrooke's Hospital. Capital teams had been selected by two veterans H Mason and J Clifton and included Tom Hayward (Surrey) and W Reeves (Essex), 'Tom' making his last appearance in England previous to departing for Australia.[134]

Tom and Dan were in Mason's team, Frank in Clifton's.

For the third consecutive season, Tom had a batting average over 50 in first-class matches and was an automatic choice for another tour of Australia, under the leadership of AC MacLaren.

29

Australia again 1901/02

In the summer of 1901, the Surrey Committee received a request from Hayward to go to Australia as a member of AC MacLaren's team and referred it to the Match Committee.[135] It is an indication of the stranglehold county committees held over their professionals at the time – lest it be thought that the granting of such permission was an automatic formality, it needs only to be said that further north, Lord Hawke, who ruled Yorkshire with a rod of iron, declined permission for Rhodes, Hirst and Haigh to go on the grounds that it would reduce their effectiveness for the White Rose county the following season. He had a point, as witnessed by the poor seasons players often had returning from an Australian tour (including Hayward in 1902), but it is an example of parochial interests taking precedence over national ones. The omission of the three Yorkshiremen came in for some savage criticism from the Australian media:

> It is very hard, both on Mr MacLaren and on Australian cricket for a county to tell their players they shall not join a team; especially when they are in their very best form. The players I allude to are the Yorkshire representatives, Wilfred Rhodes, Schofield Haigh and GH Hirst. They were told by Lord Hawke that they should not join the team.[136]

> I do not envy Mr MacLaren the billet he has had of making up his team. I do not say 'choosing' it for, in consequence of the inertness, and almost imbecility of that august silk-stockinged, shiny-hatted, kid-gloved, tan-booted body styled the Marylebone Cricket Club, and the 18 carat selfish stupidity of his lordship yclept Hawke it has been

scraped up, gathered in, found or collected in the best manner possible.[137]

Clearly the Australian media – or parts of it – had not changed since Stoddart's criticism at the end of the previous tour.

In an interview at the beginning of the tour, captain MacLaren, while referring back to a chequered journey out – part enjoyable, part less so – was circumspect about the possibilities of success:

Speaking of the trip the only deviation from the usual order of things was brought about by a raging epidemic of cholera at Naples, which necessitated a call at Castellamare, a port 17½ miles SE of the infected town. The weather was most favourable throughout, and, in addition to other amusements a near-completed cricket scoring book bore silent testimony to the fact that both eye and hand had not been allowed to lose their cunning through inaction. Matches of seven-a-side against passengers and the ship's company were played for the benefit of the Marine charities, the results being almost as monotonous as the regularity with which Mr GS Jessop, the hurricane hitter, insisted on sending balls astray.

My team is, I think, a versatile one, the kind of combination, in fact, which commends itself to the public of course. I might have brought out a stronger following, had the men been available but as it is we are a young and active side, nearly all sound bats and as fine a fielding lot as you could possibly put together. The bowling is our weakest point. In due fairness to my men, when I say our weakest point I mean to imply that it is well up to the English average of the present day but contains nothing startling.[138]

His caution was well justified. It was an inexperienced side, himself and Hayward being the only survivors from Stoddart's 1897/98 tour. The Test series was a huge disappointment for England as they repeated their performance on that tour by winning the first Test and then losing the series 4-1. Apart from his 174 against New South Wales between the second and third Tests when MacLaren and Hayward gave a magnificent display of batting, Tom had a half century in the earlier match against the same state and one against South Australia.[139] 69 in the Sydney Test and 90 at Adelaide gave him a Test average of 33.88 and a tour average in first-class matches of 36.94, a more satisfactory individual performance than that of the team.

There was an expectation among the Australian public that their superiority would win them the Test series, though the opening Test offered a scare for the hosts and a false dawn for England:

> There was an undisguisable expression of satisfaction on the usually placid countenance of the English skipper at his luck in winning the toss. MacLaren had decided to leave out M'Gahey, Garnett and Robson and in taking Tom Hayward in with him to start the batting he hit upon a happy combination as the result proved. Their opening partnership realised 154 runs and might have produced many more. It was singular that such a cool and experienced player as Hayward, after making 60 without once taking the slightest liberty, and when he and his partner had both got the bowling unmistakably under control, should suddenly give way to an impulsive desire to hit recklessly. He certainly threw away an 'even money chance' of reaching three figures, and sacrificed it without the slightest reason. However, while the Surrey crack may be blamed for his one faux pas, he must be credited with having played an innings which should have rendered moral assistance to every batsman who followed him. It was a faultless display until it suicided and up to then thoroughly worthy of one of the greatest names in cricket history.[140]

In the third Test at Adelaide, Hayward's batting was again outstanding, but it failed to contribute to an England win:

> The English innings was opened by MacLaren and Hayward, the Melbourne bowlers, Trumble and M'Leod starting the attack. Neither batsman attempted aggressive cricket and in the first half-hour 23 runs were made. The batsmen went along placidly taking their time. They were still together at the luncheon adjournment, the score being 88, each batsman 43.
>
> The two batsmen continued successfully after luncheon. MacLaren, however, at 51 was bowled by Armstrong with a no-ball; it fairly 'had' the spectators who had not heard the call. One hundred runs went up after 105 minutes' batting. Trumble, Howell and M'Leod were rung in as changes, but the score was taken to 119 before a brilliant bit of

fielding by Trumper got rid of him. The English captain cut one from Trumble, and went for the run hesitatingly but Trumper, fielding at third man returned the ball to Trumble, who dislodged the bails before MacLaren got to the crease; he was easily out. (1-49)

Hayward, who had been scoring faster than MacLaren, had made 79 when the wicket fell. He was joined by Tyldesley. Noble was bowling with Trumble. The latter soon got rid of Tyldesley. He failed to score. (2-160)

Four runs later Hayward ran out to one from Noble and just touched the ball, which rebounded from Kelly's hands on to the wicket and he was run out. The Surrey man was batting 2 hours 50 minutes for 90 and he hit eleven 4's. It is his best innings in Australia this tour.[141]

Between the third and fourth Tests, Tom contributed to a massive 769 and an innings victory against New South Wales, scoring 174 in a record opening partnership with MacLaren:

> The match England v New South Wales was resumed today in the presence of a large crowd and proved to be one of the most remarkable in the history of international cricket, as at the present England's score is four wickets for the enormous total of 650. The score of 314 for the first wicket is a record for Australia in first-class matches. The score also creates a first-wicket record in international contests, the previous best, in which Hayward also had a hand with FS Jackson, being 185 in a test match in England in 1899.[142]

MacLaren had 167, Tyldesley followed up with 142, Quaife chipped in with a half century and Jessop had a typically rapid 87.

Shortly afterwards, the team ran into a spot of political controversy when, with some encouragement from the Australian hierarchy, they declined to play a match against Bathurst whose team was to include a coloured bowler by the name of Jack Marsh, on the grounds of his suspect action. He was eventually withdrawn from the side and the match went ahead in preference to the alternative of a trip into the Blue Mountains. As well as the suspect action, it is difficult to avoid the suspicion of a colour bar against the Aborigine. Nevertheless, two years later on during Pelham Warner's 1903/04 tour under the auspices of MCC, he did play for Bathurst and had a five-for. Maybe he had straightened out his action – or maybe English and Australian administrations were just more tolerant.

In the fourth Test at Sydney:

> Mr MacLaren's team of English cricketers made a good start last Friday, the captain and Tom Hayward putting on 73 before the Cambridge man was bowled for 41. Tyldesley assisted to put on 102 for the second wicket but afterwards the side did badly and were all put out for 317. The Australians did nothing startling with the bat and finished their first venture 18 behind.
>
> Then came the downfall of the Englishmen. Hayward, who had hurt his foot, made only 12, after playing for twenty minutes without scoring. The innings closed for 99 and assisted by their opponents' bad fielding the Australians won easily by seven wickets. They have thus secured the rubber.[143]

MacLaren pulled no punches, saying 'We lost the match through bad cricket'. Nor were the non-first-class matches pushovers. West Maitland, albeit with eighteen players, ended the first day of a two-day match at 424 for eleven, before going on to declare at 558 for fifteen the next day as all of MacLaren's side had a bowl. There was no time for any result other than a draw as Tom opened and helped himself to a half century.

By contrast, in the next match against Glen Innes, the tourists used just two bowlers in the first innings, Quaife and Blythe, and two in the second, Gunn and Blythe. In between Tom's century, a reprise of the previous tour (hit wicket for exactly 100 – deliberate maybe to give someone else a go?) paved the way to a win by an innings and 89 runs. Sydney Barnes played but was used as neither batsman nor bowler, so it may be assumed the match was taken none too seriously.

In a three-day fixture at Bendigo, Tom top-scored with 87, but it did little to compensate for a consecutive poor series result in Australia. MacLaren was the captain Hayward admired the most, but he was unable to acquire a better result against superior opposition.

'Felix', expressing surprise that Hayward was not used more as a bowler, summed up the tour with appropriate recognition of the part played by Tom and his captain:

> Their tour in these parts has been a pleasant one, despite the fact that they lost four out of the five test matches.
>
> It may safely be said that they would have made a much better show but for the regrettable and unfortunate breakdown of Barnes in the third test.
>
> It is very satisfactory to note that throughout Australia our visitors were accorded a splendid welcome by the vast crowds that fringed the fields on which they gave us those admirable displays of batting, bowling and fielding, which will be an abiding and most pleasant memory of the season 1901-2.
>
> In batting, the eminently prominent performer was the captain, AC MacLaren. In first-class matches he is 20 runs per innings ahead of the second man, the redoubtable Surrey crack, Tom Hayward. One of the special features of the tour was the splendid initiatory stands made by this famous pair of batsmen.
>
> When the team landed in Adelaide early in November, AC MacLaren said that in bowling his side was 'a bit weak'. Well, the tour is over now and a glance at the totals made against the Englishmen shows that their bowling did not fail. It was their batting that failed and when MacLaren and Hayward did not make a good start, there was, as a rule, no large total.[144]

Back in his home town at the end of the tour, Tom was honoured with a dinner and illuminated address. Brothers Dan and Frank were there, but his father was too ill to attend. The speech in Tom's honour tediously covered his statistical achievements and at times lapsed into the platitudinous but was well-intentioned and exhibited civic pride in 'one of their own'.

> They had met, not simply or mainly as cricketers to do honour to a great cricketer, but as Cambridge men to do honour to a real good fellow, who was one of themselves. The deeds of his uncle in the past and his father – with whom, he was sure, they felt in complete sympathy in the reason for his not being there – and to whom they all wished to send a message of sympathy through their guest – showed that it ran in the

Illuminated manuscript presented to Tom on his return from the unsuccessful 1901/02 tour of Australia.

family ... The characteristics of a great cricketer were patience, control over his temper, unselfishness, good humour and a healthy suspicion of those whose profession it was to stand still and tell them why they had made a mess of things. Tom was the best example of all those and he had the authority of one who was perhaps the best living authority – he meant Prince Ranjitsinhji – that Tom, at the wickets was a perfect model of style.

So, they all said to him 'Tom, good luck to you; hard wickets, plenty of centuries, top of the averages and winning stroke in all the Test matches.'

The toast was received with musical honours and with the utmost enthusiasm, after which an illuminated address, the work of Mr William Offord (one of Mr Hayward's most sincere admirers) enclosed in a black and gold frame, was handed by Mr Green to the guest of the evening.

The cheering was of a vociferous nature when Mr Hayward rose to respond and it was some minutes before he could be heard. In suitable words he thanked all for the kind reception they had given him. He said the flattering remarks of Mr Green had made him more nervous than playing in front of 40,000 people. As to their cricket in Australia they had had a very pleasant time. There was only one thing to regret, and that was that they lost four test matches out of the five, but he thought all would agree that they had very bad luck, because of the best bowlers getting injured. He thought England could recover her laurels lost over in the colonies.[145]

On the latter point he was correct, but not in the forthcoming summer, a series in which he would play very little part, but on the next tour to Australia in 1903/04.

30

ALL THAT GLISTERS 1902-03

Even superstars are allowed the occasional poor season. For Hayward this came in 1902 – the opening of the 'Golden Age' was not as golden as it might have been:

> The great disappointment was Hayward. He did not get into form until the season was nearly half over and though he wound up with an aggregate of 1079 runs in county matches his record was, for him, a very poor one. Moreover it must be said that in fielding he was often slack. It struck one that he would have benefited by being a stone or more lighter in weight, everybody remarking that he had not anything like the alertness that distinguished him in his early years in the Surrey eleven. Judging him by his best scores last summer there is no reason to think that his falling off as a batsman will be more than temporary but he must look to his fielding.[146]

It was also his benefit season and, as he had off-the-field activities to think about as well, it is possible that at times his mind might not have been right for batting. He was in his tenth year which was about par for the course, the Committee having given a positive response the previous summer to a request that the benefit be granted and in the spring that he be allowed the Yorkshire fixture – more lucrative than most – for his benefit match.[147] A circular was sent to members with the report and balance sheet. It was well supported:

> It was thoroughly satisfactory to find such an excellent attendance at the Oval yesterday for the first day's play in this match, which is set aside for the benefit of the popular Surrey professional Tom Hayward,

the son and grandson of cricketers who have played for Surrey, and a nephew of one who, by many, was considered the greatest cricketer of his day, Hayward the elder. Fully fifteen thousand witnessed the play which throughout the day was of an interesting character.[148]

A very important benefit match, that in which Tom Hayward is receiving his well-merited reward for some ten years splendid service to Surrey is meeting with excellent support at Kennington Oval.[149]

He had 95 in the match, a rare spell with the ball which brought him two wickets, and a couple of catches.

At the end of the season, it was agreed 'that Hayward be engaged for next summer his benefit having ended the agreement made with him on July 28th 1898 as per minutes of Match Committee of that date. It was decided to recommend that he receive a sum of Sixty pounds in lieu of winter wages for this winter. The Secretary reported the receipts in Hayward's benefit match £675.2.4 and expenses £144.7.5 leaving balance of £530.4.11 and that subscriptions amounting to £396.12.0 had been received to date.'[150]

Benefit monies did not go to the beneficiary, but were held in trust by the cricket club and were released only when there was a convincing reason – a policy which made some sense, given the profligacy and lack of financial nous of some of the beneficiaries. The following summer he applied for £500 to buy a house in Cambridge.

MacLaren's team had been followed across the oceans by the Australians for another five-match series in England. The tourists took a 2-0 lead after the first two Tests had been heavily rain affected. Hayward's poor form meant he was not selected until the final Test at The Oval. He made 0 and 7 in a match remembered for Gilbert Jessop's second innings century and the legendary, maybe mythical, dialogue between George Hirst and Wilfred Rhodes – 'We'll get 'em in singles' – which enabled England to scrape home by one wicket.

Tom was unstinting in his efforts to raise funds for the widow and twelve orphans of the Hobbs family following the death of the popular Jesus College groundsman:

A Cricket Match will be played on Parker's Piece on Saturday September 27th. The teams will be selected from the following: Hayward Tom Capt, Brockwell, Clode, Hayes, Lockwood, Richardson, Smith, Stedman, JT Hearne (Middx) W Reeves (Essex), Frank Morgan Capt, J Bacon, W Bryan, P Chaloner, J Colville, P French, A Hayward, DM Hayward, F Hayward, R Phillips, A Rich, F Robinson, R Stearn, O Stibbons, H Tebbutt, G Watts. The Town Band have kindly volunteered to play during the afternoon.[151]

Recently Hobbs, the Jesus groundsman at Cambridge died and a benefit match for the widow and twelve children was got up by Tom Hayward. Altogether the nice sum of £170 has been collected. Tom Hayward presented a bat on which were the autographs of the players of the two teams. This was drawn for, the subscriptions being 1s each and the bat realised £12.1s.[152]

The Hobbs benefit fund has been closed. The amount already collected amounted to £170 and there is a further sum of £8 to come in. Bye the bye, I note Tom Hayward, who rendered very material assistance in bringing about such a splendid result, has expressed his willingness to arrange a similar match on Parker's Piece on behalf of some charitable object at the end of future seasons.[153]

The eldest of the twelve Hobbs orphans was to play a major role in the Hayward and Surrey stories.

Forty years on from his uncle's success at the table, Tom marked the end of the close season by following in his footsteps and winning a local billiards tournament with some ease:

Billiards Handicap. On Tuesday evening the final of the billiards handicap, which has been in progress for some weeks past at the Central Conservative Club, took place in the presence of a large gathering. The game was 500 up, the competitors being Mr Frank E Morgan (who owed 100) and Mr Tom Hayward (who owed 20). The Surrey cricketer had matters all his own way and never looking back won with ridiculous ease by 264 points.[154]

For Surrey, if not for Hayward, success on the green fields in 1903 did not match that on the green baize. After Digby Jephson's relinquishing of the captaincy, an erratic and disorganised season followed. Livingstone Walker took over, but with no success as Surrey plunged to eleventh in the Championship table.

It is part of the politics of envy and jealousy that those with lesser or no talent will take opportunities to snipe at and criticise those whose boots they are not fit to lace. Hayward had been the subject of some media criticism for slow scoring in 1901, but now it attracted readers' letters and, in this instance, a reader with a stopwatch. It follows a complaint that contemporary scoreboards with individual batsmen's scores were providing too much information and allowing a batsman to know when he is approaching a milestone:

> One day I timed Hayward at the Oval, and he took longer to pass from 39 to 50 than he had done from 0 to 39. And he had not actually 'dashed at 'em' at any particular period of his innings. After the 50, he certainly ran to somewhere in the 80s at quite a decent rate of scoring, but after once getting into the 90s his pace was funereal in the extreme, and when he had stolen two or three short runs off (what appeared like) the same kind of half-volleys he had been taking 'fours' from twenty minutes earlier – simply pushing them away for stolen singles – it was with very little disappointment. And Hayward, though undoubtedly a bad – very bad – example of this 50 and 100 craze, is by no means singular to it.[155]

Tom and other 'guilty' parties may well have countered that, at whatever speed, they were scoring runs in the middle and were not going to get any more when back in the pavilion.

As if to demonstrate the validity of the old adage that form is temporary but class is permanent, Hayward began the season with 107, as well as a few wickets, and 50, both against London County, at The Oval and Crystal Palace:

> The only Surrey bowler who met with marked success was Hayward, but bowlers were decidedly handicapped by the cold weather … On Tuesday Hayward and Hayes quickly settled down to their work and the Surrey score progressed steadily. Both players exhibited fine cricket, Hayward's display being a very meritorious one considering the earli-

Tom accepts an invitation to play for the Players in 1903.

ness of the season. Several of his strokes were quite reminiscent of the form he showed in 1899 … His capital all-round cricket was quite the most gratifying part of the match from a Surrey point of view. His score of 107 was comprised of two 5s, eleven 4s, eight 2s and thirty seven singles, there not being, curiously enough, any 3s.[156]

He had two further centuries, against Worcestershire and the touring Philadelphians and a dozen more innings between 50 and 100:

Hayward still lacked smartness in the field, but he played many fine innings and had no such run of failure as pursued him in the early part of 1902.[157]

The summer was a wet one and it marked something of a watershed. At around the midpoint of his first-class career and on the eve of his fourth and final overseas tour, Tom abandoned his bowling almost entirely and now became a regular opening batsman, having on several occasions demonstrated his ability to fill that role, not least in the Oval Test four years earlier.

He again captained the Players and put up a bit of resistance in an innings defeat by Yorkshire, making 21 and 15 in all out totals of 84 and 73, being bowled by Hirst in the first innings and Rhodes in the second.

It was a good season, but not an exceptional one:

> Hayward has played in more innings than anybody else, but he has also scored more runs than anybody except Fry, and as usual he owes his position to a series of good innings rather than a few very big ones against weak bowling.[158]

Towards the end he suffered a bit of eye trouble, reducing his effectiveness and causing him to miss a match against Gloucestershire, but he was still selected for a third tour of Australia and would be joined by his Surrey wicketkeeping colleague, Herbert Strudwick. Ric Sissons maintains that the county withdrew their winter pay of £60 and that it was not until 1909 that Surrey agreed to pay their professionals in winter even if they were touring or coaching overseas.[159] That, however, is contradicted by the minutes which record a decision to pay winter wages to Hayward and Strudwick during their trip to Australia.[160]

The end of the season was marked by the usual return to Cambridge where three Hayward brothers including Tom took part in an internal Rodney Club match, but the autumn was tinged with sadness at the death of their mother Emma, who had been an invalid for some time.

31

AND AGAIN 1903/04

As in 1901, Tom preceded his third and final Australian tour with a trip to Cambridge, though on this occasion not to play in a charity match, but one organised by the Rodney Club between two teams drawn from its members. His presence ensured a large attendance:

> The redoubtable Tom Hayward seldom allows a season to pass without taking part in a local match on his native Heath, Parker's Piece. This year he is going out to Australia with the MCC team, but he managed to find time to give the inhabitants of his native town a treat on Saturday. The occasion was a match organised by the Rodney Cricket Club between two teams of its members. The sides were respectively known as 'the President's' and 'the Captain's'. Although the game was hardly so attractive as that played at the end of last season for the benefit of the widow and family of the late Mr John Hobbs, the attendance was by far the largest at any match on the Piece this season.
>
> Frank Hayward upheld the reputation of the Hayward family by playing a splendid innings. He did not receive much assistance, but when set he hit freely all round the wicket. He was still not out with 48 to his credit when, according to arrangements, the innings was declared closed with the score at 141 for eight wickets.
>
> Tom gave a fine exhibition of driving, which was much appreciated. In one over he sent the ball to the boundary four times. Runs came at a great pace until, with 96 on the board Hayward was neatly caught by his brother Frank in the long field. He had made 49 which included seven 4's and the spectators were sorry to see him go. After his dismissal the crowd diminished considerably. Hancock and A Hayward stayed at the wickets until half past five when stumps – and the game – were drawn.[161]

Once in Australia, 'Hayward did not perhaps make so many runs as had been expected, but he played very finely indeed, his best, though not his highest innings being the 91 with which he did so much to win the Test Match at Sydney.'[162] In retrospect, he was to consider that innings his best in Australia (though he understated it as 60) 'because they were wanted'.[163] No further explanation of his attitude to batting is needed.

Against South Australia, 'Hayward played a wonderful innings, of a steady kind, batting for over six hours without giving a chance.'[164]

Warner, who was suffering from a blistered hand and Hayward, only put on 30 runs in the first hour, Hayward being very uncertain and unsteady for a time. At the luncheon hour the score was 45. Afterwards, during the continued partnership of Warner and Hayward, things were a little brighter, and when at last Warner was dismissed for an admirable 65 play had been in progress for two hours and a quarter.[165]

The total at this stage was 122 for one. Tyldesley came and went for a single and Foster became yet another victim of the Hayward blind spot in judging a single, but former Surrey colleague Len Braund stayed with him till 'stumps' when the score was 247 for three and Hayward 126 not out.

With thunder in the air, Braund was out early on the second day, but Hayward battled on to 157. That was followed by 91 not out from Arthur Lilley before MacLaren caused some consternation by declaring the innings closed, an action unfamiliar to the Australians:

The action of the English captain in declaring his innings closed at the tea interval caused much comment. In first class cricket in Australia the closing of an innings is an unknown device, and as a matter of fact it has not been legislated for. The two rules dealing with the follow-on and the declaration of the innings refer distinctly to three-day matches, and cannot be made to apply to the conditions here, where all games are supposed to be played out. The follow-on has been dealt with and a distinct margin of 200 runs agreed upon.[166]

Tom impressed against Victoria:

Tom Hayward's fine batting evoked general admiration after lunch.
He and his captain were very slow in the morning but after dinner
Hayward in particular showed the crowd what a model professional
batsman is like. A thorn in the side of Australian bowlers is good old
Tom, who never bats so well as in Australia. Probably Hayward is the
most popular cricketer ever sent to Australia.[167]

In the match against a Fifteen in Newcastle:

There was a curious contrast in the batting of the Englishmen, Foster
and Hayward knocking up a large score for the first wicket, the former
making his runs much more quickly than his partner, while after lunch
there was a decided breakdown, which was only stopped by some good
play by Braund and Hayward.[168]

This was the first tour under the auspices of MCC rather than a
privately arranged one, though the *Daily Mail*, in the universal tradition of criticising selected teams, suggested it would be better called
an 'MCC Club and Ground' team, rather than 'England'. Despite

Tom (seated left) relaxes in Adelaide Botanic Gardens with friends including
fellow tourists AE Relf, EG Arnold, GH Hirst and AA Lilley.

such misgivings, it could be regarded as a successful one to the extent that England won the series 3-2 to regain the Ashes. For Hayward, too, on his touring swan song, he was able to finish on a strong note, beginning with that innings in Adelaide, averaging 35.66 with the bat in Tests and 58 in all first-class matches.

In the first Test in Sydney, after innings victories over Victoria and New South Wales, his grit and experience took England to a five-wicket win and an ideal start to the series. At 81 for four in the fourth innings, England were still over a hundred short of their target:

> But Hirst then made a much needed stand with Hayward who had been playing an admirable game, and when stumps were drawn the total had been taken to 122 without further loss, and England now only required 72 runs to win with six wickets in hand. Hayward was not out 60 and Hirst not out 21. On the sixth and last day of this memorable match, the issue was not left long in doubt, for the two not outs had practically won the match before they were separated. Hayward just missed the distinction of scoring a hundred runs; his 91 was in every way worthy of a famous cricketer.[169]

Anti-climactically, as Australia had a consolation victory in a dead rubber, Tom finished his overseas Test career with a duck and an 'absent ill', but could look back with satisfaction on a series where, if he had not quite reached the brilliant standards set at home, he could say with some honesty that he had let no one down and finished on the winning side.

His captain, Pelham Warner, was appropriately complimentary about his opening partner, as well as recognising that increased integration off the field between professionals and amateurs contributed to team spirit:

> England has had few better number ones than Hayward. So steady and sure, he has been the rock upon which many a bowler has split. As a player of fast bowling he was in the same class as WG Grace and Ranjitsinhji. I used to go in first with him on this tour, and learnt an enormous amount from watching him bat at such close quarters ... the

team worked together as one man, and were a 'happy family', and that had a great deal to do with the eventual result. For the first time on a tour of this sort amateurs and professionals stayed at the same hotel, and the experiment was a great success. It was felt that we were all one team, and the Captain could look after his men, and attend to any of their wants or desires better far than if we had been separated.[170]

Even on occasions when circumstances necessitated sharing the same hotel it had been the practice for professionals and amateurs to dine at separate tables, so in terms of breaking down class barriers, both in cricket and in society, the relaxing of previous conventions was certainly a step in the right direction.

Tom also played in a few further upcountry matches against the odds in addition to the one in Newcastle, such as Northern Districts of New South Wales, Melbourne Juniors, Bendigo, Ballarat and Bathurst. Although, as on previous and subsequent tours, these matches were not treated flippantly as they were taken seriously by the locals, they did provide an opportunity for anyone not playing in the Test team or looking for match practice to play a bit of cricket away from the glare of the Test arena and maybe hone a few skills. Tom had a Boxing Day century in Bendigo and half centuries against Northern Districts, Newcastle and Bathurst, the latter against Jack Marsh, the Aborigine with the alleged suspect action who was strategically omitted on the previous tour. Test schedules in the twenty-first century provide no such opportunities for fringe players or those out of form.

The end of his third and final and (in terms of team results) most successful tour to Australia was once again marked by the usual civic appreciation in Cambridge, though this time with a silver tea and coffee set rather than another illuminated manuscript, Again there were the traditional platitudes, nostalgia and reminiscences, but again he no doubt appreciated the efforts of his fellow townsfolk

Presentation to Tom Hayward. Tom Hayward was entertained at a smoking concert on Tuesday night at Cambridge, upon the occasion of his return from the Australian tour. Mayor GF Whitmore, President of the Cambridge Cricket Association, took the chair, and in the course of the proceedings presented the famous Surrey cricketer with a silver tea and coffee set, which had been subscribed in restricted sums by a large number of Tom Hayward's admirers in his native town and county.[171]

Public presentation at Cambridge. The presentation took place in the interval and it was made by the Chairman (Major GF Whitmore). He said they had gathered together that night to do honour to one who had done honour to them. They had their old townsman back among them and they were proud of what he had done when away. It was with great gratification that the committee observed how many had gathered to do honour to Hayward. Hayward was known to all Cambridge men, and it was hardly worth while his going through his career. A great many of them had played with him, and he was told that their worthy ex-Mayor was Captain of the YMCA when young Tom used to play for that club. He was sure Mr Young found pleasure in looking back to the time when he captained one of the greatest cricketers that England ever produced.

While they were very proud of their returned townsman, they felt a certain amount of regret that the county of Cambridgeshire should lose his services.

With regard to their guest, he had proved to be one of the best cricketers in England, and in Australia he played better than he did in England. He had asked him why it was that he played better in Australia and he said it was because the light was better.[172]

The appreciation was not restricted to Cambridge:

The management of the Canterbury Theatre of Varieties, London, have decided to present testimonials to the Surrey Cricketers Tom Hayward and Bert Strudwick in appreciation of their brilliant service during the late successful Australian tour.[173]

32

FAILING BETTER 1904-05

The 1904 season was no better for Surrey. They followed Samuel Beckett's dictum, 'Try again. Fail again. Fail better.' They fell no lower in the Championship placings than the previous season but had fewer wins and more defeats. They were unable to find a regular captain (it was of course unthinkable that the appointment might be offered to a professional) and it was late in the season before Lord Dalmeny emerged as a possible candidate. Again they finished eleventh, a disappointing position after the successes of the last decade of the nineteenth century and, at the time, the worst in their history, though there have been a few mediocre seasons since. Notwithstanding the disappointing performance of the team, Hayward, after two relatively thin seasons, exceeded anything he had done previously by scoring eleven centuries on his way to a 3,000-plus run season.

His 188 not out at Canterbury included the addition of a hundred before lunch on the third day which helped Surrey recover from a large first innings defeat but failed to prevent Kent winning the match. He also carried his bat through a completed innings, the second of seven occasions on which he was to do so:

> One feature of Surrey cricket stood out above everything else and must be mentioned separately. We allude, of course, to Hayward's batting. In no way affected by his labours in Australia, Hayward played magnificently all through the season. Taking part in thirty of the thirty-four matches he scored 2,734 runs with the splendid average of 55. Among his many great innings perhaps the best of all were his 188 not out

against Kent at Canterbury, 122 against Lancashire at the Oval, and 116 at Whitsuntide against Notts at Trent Bridge. Against Sussex at Brighton he made 106 and 112, he being the first Surrey batsman to get two 100's in one match in county cricket. Both these innings were remarkable for the pace at which he obtained his first 50 runs. For sheer brilliance, however, nothing he did during the season was more astonishing than his 197 against the South Africans. Rarely or never since he first found a place in the Surrey eleven has he so fully revealed his hitting powers. On nearly all occasions during the summer the mainstay of the eleven, he was as fine a bat last season as when he played his two great innings in the Test matches at Manchester and the Oval in 1899, and to say that is almost to reach the limit of praise.[174]

Just before the beginning of the 1905 season, Tom found himself in an awkward situation. Like his grandfather, father and uncle, he did not manage to avoid the judiciary. On this occasion Tom escaped with an out-of-court settlement and the subject matter was very different from those which had brought the two previous generations before the bench. Amid the anodyne prose of the Surrey CCC committee minutes for 1905 – dealing with finance, commercial contracts and requests to use the premises – there is the following letter, the text of which was reproduced in full:

A letter was read from T Hayward as follows:
91 Regent Street, Cambridge. March 9th 1905. To CW Alcock Esq.
Sir,
My case is settled on one condition that is if I find the money to the amount of £400 and all costs which I should think will come to £650. I am now going to ask you if I could draw on my benefit, of course Sir I can get some money on my property but just now property is very low market and that would mean me losing quite another £100 and I don't want to do that. I don't mind paying the money anyway, I would rather do that than the case should go to Court as the Press would make such a lot of it and I am sure it would affect my cricket for the future. I hope you will help me in my difficulty, as the money is to be paid 7 days from yesterday. Trusting to hear from you shortly.
Yours obediently, (sgd) T Hayward
The Committee recommend that the Trustees sell out as much of Hayward's money as they consider necessary.

It is clear that Tom is anxious for the matter to be kept out of the courts and the newspapers, fearing the publicity. It is equally clear that if it were to go to court he would lose: otherwise why be so blasé about shelling out such a large sum of money to keep it quiet? What is not clear and what cannot be guessed at from the contents of the letter is what exactly he is supposed to have done. The attempt to avoid publicity was not completely successful as the list of cases to be heard in King's Bench was published in many daily newspapers including the *Yorkshire Evening Post* and subsequently picked up by a number of Australian newspapers. These revealed that what was at stake was the issue of a breach of promise of marriage to an Australian lady, hence the Australian interest.

> Cricketer's Love Affair. Tom Hayward sued for Breach of Promise. An amicable settlement probable.
> In the King's Bench Division this morning, before Mr Justice Walton, the action for breach of promise brought by Miss McDiarmid, an Australian lady, against Tom Hayward, the well-known cricketer was mentioned.
> Mr Marshall Hall, KC, said the parties had practically come to a settlement and terms had been drawn up. He asked that the case should stand out of the list for seven days. His lordship agreed and the case stands out accordingly.[175]

> An action for alleged breach of promise to marry, in which the plaintiff is Miss Margaret McDiarmid and the defendant Thomas Walter Hayward, the well-known cricketer, will shortly come on for trial at the English law courts before a judge and a common jury. It is understood that the lady is an Australian and that she claims heavy damages.[176]

> It is stated that an action by an Australian girl for breach of promise of marriage will shortly be decided in England, the defendant being Tom Hayward. It would be remarkable if after defying the break of Noble, the swifts of Cotter and Howell's Yorkers he should succumb to a maiden after all.[177]

Tom's attempts to cover up this story were remarkably successful. The press did not follow up the story and Miss McDiarmid sank back into anonymity.

With that difficult situation out of the way, the 1905 season began on a cold Easter Monday with Hayward leading the side against WG Grace's Gentlemen of England. The match was drawn, a prelude to three Championship wins and a draw against the Australians. Tom was now beginning to feel his age and had provision in his contract that he would not be required to bowl. With the bat, however, he had the distinction of scoring the first run of the season: 'The first run in the first-class season came from the bat of Hayward; it was the result of a hit to cover-point from the third ball of the first over of the match bowled by GW Beldam.'[178] More than two and a half thousand more were to follow.

Surrey's season was much improved as they moved up to fourth in the Championship, not reaching the giddy heights of the 1890s, but a far more satisfactory performance than the previous two seasons when they had finished in the lower reaches. Abel and Richardson were now off the scene, but the appointment of Lord Dalmeny as a regular captain certainly contributed to the improvement, as did the steadiness and consistency of Ernest Hayes in the upper middle order and the advent of the schoolboy wonder Jack Crawford.

On the Test scene, England had retained the Ashes which had been regained on the 1903/04 tour of Australia under Pelham Warner. Now under the captaincy of Stanley Jackson, England won the series 2-0. Hayward played in all five Tests, against just one three years earlier when his form had been below par, but did not reach the three figure mark. His highest was 82 at Old Trafford, though he did have 129 not out in the early season fixture for Surrey against the tourists in addition to his three centuries in the Championship and one for the Players.

While on the county scene, against Sussex at The Oval:

Hayward played a very careful innings, never hurrying himself and hardly making a mistake. He was two hours and a quarter in making his first 50 runs, but his last 76 only took him an hour and twenty-five minutes to put together.[179]

Against Hampshire:

Hayward played another fine innings, in which he showed all his usual resources and skill. His partnership with Baker produced 104 in an hour and a half.[180]

The Test series resumed at Trent Bridge where England were behind on the first innings, but came back to win by 213 runs:

Hayward was 'playing for keeps', never hurrying, never being in difficulties. He and MacLaren put up 145 for the first wicket and when he was out England being in a most satisfactory position, being 120 runs on the board with nine wickets in hand.[181]

In the second Test at Lord's:

No one was surprised when MacLaren and Hayward opened the game with the greatest possible caution, for they had to find out the pace of the wicket, but when they had found it they were obliged to continue to act on the defensive. When the partnership was broken with the total on 59 after lasting for an hour and twenty minutes, Hayward, who was then dismissed lbw, had only scored 16.[182]

Tom found batting against Oxford University at The Oval somewhat easier and was able to score his runs at a greater pace:

But Hayward was in great form, making his runs so much more quickly than usual that in less than an hour he had scored his first fifty. His brilliant innings of 70 included seven 4's.[183]

He was 'rested' for the match against Cambridge University at The Oval ahead of the Headingley Test match, but his appetite for the game was insatiable. He took himself off back to Cambridge where, doubtless much to the consternation of the club cricketers in the opposition he helped the Rodney Club win a second round Cambridgeshire Senior Cup tie:

> On this occasion they had the assistance of Tom Hayward, the Surrey professional who was 'resting' in Cambridge, prior to assisting England against the Australians at Leeds. It is rarely one has the pleasure of seeing Hayward bowl, although he has proved himself a very efficient trundler. The L and NW batsmen found him so and he captured four of their wickets for 46.
>
> The Rodney batsmen collared their opponents' bowling and hit the required number of runs with the loss of one wicket. Tom Hayward was responsible for 49 of these and he might have been batting yet, had it been necessary.[184]

Tom came back for the third Test match, this time to open with CB Fry. His running between the wickets and judgment of a run, inherited from his uncle, came in for comment, but with his new partner he put up some spirited resistance against some negative Australian tactics:

> In the absence of MacLaren, Fry went in first with Hayward, whose judgment in running has never been his strongest point, and there would have been a catastrophe in the first few minutes of the match if Clement Hill, for once in his life, had not fumbled the ball a little … With a lead of 106, England began their second innings with Fry and Hayward. To the surprise of the spectators, the Australians seem to have made up their minds that their best course would be to play for a draw. At any rate, Armstrong began the bowling, and for three hours and a quarter, that is to say, until the day's play ended, he was bowling without a rest, generally wide of the leg stump. On the other hand, McLeod bowled chiefly wide of the off stump. Fry and Hayward made runs very slowly, and the former did not make his second run until he had been at the wickets for thirty-five minutes. The rate of scoring was very slow, and when at last the first wicket fell, Fry being given out, caught at the wicket, eighty runs were up and the game had been in progress for an hour and forty minutes. But although the Australians had succeeded in keeping down the runs, they had not prevented England from placing themselves in a splendid position, thanks to the play of their first two men, and the remaining batsmen were enabled to take risks.[185]

The Australian tactics had worked, however. Despite England being in a 'splendid position', declaring in the second innings with a lead of just over four hundred, Australia managed to hang on for the draw. The steady opening batting of Hayward and Fry had laid the foundations for centuries for Jackson in the first innings and Tyldesley in the second.

In the Gentlemen-Players match at Lord's the following week, Hayward shone again, despite a rain-affected pitch:

> The Players won the toss and batted first on a wicket that had been made soft by the thunderstorms of Sunday. The Players innings was opened by Hayward and Bowley, who batted so well that they took the score to 76 in about an hour before the latter was caught. Hayward by turns was enterprising and cautious in the extreme, but he always seemed to find the bowling easy. Towards the end of his innings he was nearly half-an-hour without making a run, and altogether he was at the wickets for an hour and forty minutes for his 32.

He was more prolific in the second innings:

> Hayward's innings was characteristic of the player; it had hardly a fault and during its progress the bowling was made to look quite simple and easy. Hayward made his runs at a quicker rate than usual, and he was only at the wickets for two hours and forty minutes.[186]

His undefeated 123 contributed to a win by 149 runs.

Surrey struggled against Yorkshire as they and other counties frequently did, but, not for the first or only time, Hayward led the fightback. The match was lost by an innings and 108 runs, but Hayward, almost alone, emerged with credit. In the follow on:

> When stumps were drawn the total was 89 for three wickets, Hayward who had played a most plucky game, being not out 51. Thus Surrey on Saturday required 237 to save the innings defeat. For a time the prospects of Surrey became brighter, for while Hayward was playing a masterly game, Davis hit with great vigour. Between them the two men raised the score from 100 to 150 in less than twenty minutes, the runs

being made off three overs each by Haigh and Ringrose. But the stay of Davis was all too brief and after he was out the only question of interest was whether Hayward would have enough time to make his hundred. He succeeded in accomplishing this feat and was last out after showing almost perfect cricket for three hours and twenty minutes.[187]

It was a useful 'net' for the fourth Test at Old Trafford where Tom's innings of 82 helped lay the foundations for an England victory by an innings and 80 runs, an unassailable 2-0 lead in the five-match series and the retention of the Ashes. His good form continued in the next match as, with new Surrey recruit and opening partner Jack Hobbs, he participated in one of his 162 century partnerships in first-class cricket. After their Manchester defeat, however, the Australians regained some self-respect, winning the match by 22 runs:

Hayward and Hobbs soon settled down and seemed to find no difficulty whatever in the bowling. They had made over a hundred in partnership and there seemed no reason why they should not reach the second hundred, when Hayward, just after making some brilliant hits, was out. He had played a beautiful game for about an hour and three-quarters for his 70.[188]

In the final, drawn Test at The Oval the early dismissals of MacLaren and Tyldesley paved the way for a resumption of his partnership with CB Fry who batted at number four and made a big hundred. Hayward shared a century stand before dislodging a bail when attempting a pull:

In the course of an hour and a half [Fry] and Hayward put on 100 runs, and so easily were both men playing the bowling that there seemed no reason why they should ever get out. But Hayward, in trying to hit a short one from Hopkins to leg, miscalculated his distance from the wicket, with the result that he knocked off a bail. His fine innings lasted for two hours and ten minutes, and once more he showed that he is quite at his best in a great match.[189]

Tom began to suffer with rheumatism towards the end of the season and it restricted his batting and fielding against Gloucestershire, but did not hinder his making a century against Leicestershire, nor his playing in three end-of-season matches, Players of the South v Gentlemen of the South, South of England v Australians and Rest of England v Champion County (Yorkshire) where, without doing anything over-spectacular, he reached double figures in each of five innings. Inevitably there was criticism of his methods, mainly from those who knew little or nothing about the game, but he was vindicated by EHD Sewell who had seen a typical innings of 44 against Northamptonshire:

> The following comments on Hayward's methods as a batsman appeared last week in the *Evening Standard* from the pen of Mr EHD Sewell whose sensible and thoughtful criticisms in that paper have been one of the most interesting features of the season's daily work in the press:
>
> Hayward had made 44 in his usual sound style, and had throughout played the right game in keeping one end up while his partner hit. Some critics I see blamed him for not hitting like Holland did on Monday, but Hayward may, I think, by now be trusted to know which is the proper game to play. Your average critic does not sufficiently realise what it is to field and bowl against Surrey with the discomforting knowledge that Hayward is 'still in'.[190]

The season ended once again with an effort in the direction of charity. For the charity match in aid of Richmond Hospital he presented for sale on the ground a bat with the autographs of the twenty-two players who had taken part in the final Test match of the summer.[191] This year his brother Arthur could not take part as he had died suddenly, aged forty-one, in January.

> The funeral was conducted at Mill-road cemetery on Wednesday afternoon by the Rev FC Fitzpatrick, Dean of Christ Church College and the Rev AE Brown, curate of St Barnabas' church. A large number of cricketers attended. Wreaths were sent, among others, from Camden Cricket Club, the Christ's College Association and Rugby Football club, the Christ's College Cricket Club and the Rodney Cricket Club.[192]

Of Tom's performances in the 1905 season, *Wisden* said, 'Hayward was practically as good as ever, and the fact of his falling below his best records for Surrey may safely be put down to his labours in the five Test matches.

33

ANOTHER CAMBRIDGE MAN

Tom Hayward was, according to Neville Cardus, the boyhood hero of Jack Hobbs.[193] While Cardus's writing is frequently more impressive for the quality of its prose rather than its historical accuracy, on this occasion he is almost certainly correct. The two families were part of the professional cricket, college, Parker's Piece and Fenner's groundsmanship community and Tom played a major part in 1902 in organising the benefit match for Jack's father's widow, the mother of twelve children of whom Jack was the eldest. Furthermore, Jack was twelve years Tom's junior, about the right kind of gap for hero worship in cricket, pop music, business or any other walk of life. What is not in doubt is that Tom Hayward played a large part in Jack Hobbs joining Surrey's professional staff.

Unlike the privileged undergraduates across the road, the developing Jack Hobbs was never formally coached. He learned his cricket from observing the techniques of cricketers on Fenner's, Parker's Piece and the college grounds. Among them was Tom Hayward. Great cricketer that he was, there was a sense in which Hayward was John the Baptist to the Messianic Hobbs. There was a strong professional connection between the families; Tom's elder brother Daniel Martin being groundsman at Fenner's, Jack's father at Jesus College until his death in 1902. Jack had impressed Hayward with a 26 not out against the Surrey team which Tom had brought to Cambridge for the end-of-season charity match in 1901. As a result of that, Hayward invited him to test himself on Parker's Piece against Bill

Reeves of Cambridge and Essex. In his early days, Jack may have regarded Hayward as the master, himself as the pupil. Satisfied as to Hobbs' ability, Tom decided to recommend him to Surrey. Before long, however, as Hayward's career drew to a close, it was Hobbs who became 'The Master'. Before that Hobbs and Hayward enjoyed a productive decade for their adopted county

Leo McKinstry, biographer of Jack Hobbs, has no doubt about Hayward's influence:

> The cricket correspondent and MCC tour manager Colonel Philip Trevor, a man of strong, if sometimes erratic, opinions, once wrote 'It is absolutely certain that without Tom Hayward there would have been no Jack Hobbs'. By this he meant that Hayward, another Cambridge cricketer and the greatest English professional batsman at the turn of the century, was a crucial influence on Hobbs through his example and his 'careful tutelage'. In one respect, Trevor's statement was misleading. Hobbs always maintained that he was a self-made player and fiercely resented any claim that he had been reliant on coaching. 'I am a natural batsman, self-taught,' Hobbs wrote. His own career showed, he said, 'that those who have no great advantages, such as coaching, can hope for success, provided that they possess a certain amount of gumption and natural aptitude and, next, unlimited persistence and perseverance.' The 'popular belief' that Tom Hayward coached him was 'not correct' he concluded.
>
> Yet this should not diminish the importance of Hayward as a key figure in the fulfilment of Hobbs's ambition to make his living from the game. During the 1890s, after he had first won fame at Surrey, Hayward was the hero to nearly all cricket-mad boys in Cambridge. It was an adulation sparked by his local connections to the town.
>
> Hobbs revered Hayward as much as any of his mates did. Whenever Surrey were playing, he used to run to the library to find out from the evening paper how many Hayward had made. Occasionally he had the chance to see Hayward batting against the University at Fenner's, and like so many others, marvelled at his strong defence and off-driving.[194]

Hayward's standing at The Oval was such that he was able to influence the largely amateur-run establishment into giving Hobbs a trial. His views were respected and he had power and gravitas. He seems to have had firm friendships with Digby Jephson and Jack Crawford, but was less tolerant of amateurs of lesser ability. He was an elitist, though a generous one, rather than an egalitarian, but his elite was based on merit, not the inherited amateur-professional, gentleman-player divide:

> There was also a match in which a temporary young amateur took charge of Surrey and sought Hayward's advice on placing his men. He replied wearily, 'I always stand there and the rest just spread out. They'll stop the ball right enough if it comes near them.'[195]

Surrey agreed to the trial (Essex had also had the opportunity to offer a contract to the young man, but did not pursue the possibility) and rarely, if ever, over the next thirty years did they have cause to regret the decision.

> During the winter of 1902/3 he took over his father's job as the groundsman at Jesus and in this capacity he had several long talks about his future with FC Hutt, a college servant, who was also the cricket team scorer and had been his father's closest friend. Hutt resolved to take action. Using his Cambridge connections, he asked Tom Hayward to give Hobbs a trial with a view to Surrey offering him a place on the staff. Hayward agreed and late in 1902, Hobbs was asked to present himself on Parker's Piece where his batsmanship would be tested by Hayward himself and another cricketer from Cambridge, Bill Reeves, who opened the bowling for Essex. Hobbs's feeling that he had made a good impression seemed to be confirmed when Hayward muttered through his thick moustache a casual remark about 'getting a trial at the Oval next April'.
>
> In the spring of 1903 after a long, fretful wait, Hobbs was summoned to see Hayward who told him Surrey wanted him to report to the Oval on 23 April for a trial.
>
> He was the only trialist from his cohort to have been selected. 'I went back to Cambridge and, elated beyond measure, ran off to tell the news to Tom Hayward, who was highly pleased and congratulated me most warmly,' he wrote. Unbeknown to Hobbs, Hayward privately performed another kind deed on his behalf. Still mindful of the tragedy that had befallen the family the previous Autumn, he persuaded Alcock to include in Hobbs's contract an additional bonus of £10 to be paid

Surrey's prolific opening partnership, Hayward and Hobbs, stride to the crease in 1907.

at the end of the 1903 season. It was an act that again displayed both Hayward's influence within the portals of the Oval and the compassion that lurked beneath a sometimes lugubrious exterior.[196]

Even people who have little interest in the game will have heard of Jack Hobbs, along with WG Grace and Sir Donald Bradman, the answer to pub quiz questions, particularly those of a statistical nature, and the first professional cricketer to be knighted for his services to the game at a time before such honours were spread around like sweets at a children's party. However, even those better acquainted with the game's history might not be fully aware of Hayward's influence on 'The Master'. In any age the cream of Hobbs' talent would have risen to the top, but unlike Hayward, Hobbs had no connection with Surrey. Cambridgeshire at the time of its zenith had been regarded as a 'northern' county, convenient for administration and balance, but a geographical anomaly. The midlands did not feature in this north-south categorisation, but with the expansion of the number of first-class counties, first-class cricket was a regular part of the programme at Trent Bridge and would soon become so at Edgbaston and Aylestone Road. When it became apparent that Hobbs' talents would outgrow Cambridgeshire, now resurrected but as a minor county, natural progression might well have dictated a route to England via Nottinghamshire, Warwickshire or Leicestershire. The influence and intervention of Tom Hayward dictated otherwise.

It was perhaps fortunate for Hobbs that on his first-class debut, for Surrey against the Gentlemen of England in April 1905, Hayward, in the absence of any suitable amateurs, was appointed to captain the county. He and Hobbs opened the innings, Hayward making 9, the new boy 18. The partnership realised an unmemorable few runs before Hayward was bowled by George Beldam, but it was a portent of things to come.

Tom and Jack were to become Surrey's most prolific opening partnership until the advent of Andy Sandham, who replaced Hayward as The Master's opening partner. Despite his success as an opening batsman for England, it had taken a while for Surrey to use Tom regularly in the same capacity, there being little sense in breaking up the Brockwell-Abel combination. But on Brockwell's retirement in 1903, the Abel-Hayward partnership took over and it was obvious that on Abel's retirement the following year there should be a seamless progression to the Hobbs-Hayward combination. There was insufficient overlap in their Test careers for them to become a dominant force for England – though they did open together on one occasion in 1909. Hobbs was of course to form legendary opening partnerships for Surrey with Andy Sandham and for England with Yorkshire's Herbert Sutcliffe.

McKinstry comments on the importance for Hobbs, and by implication for English cricket, of those opening stands:

> His alliance with Hobbs at Surrey which lasted until 1914 was the first truly dominant opening partnership in English cricket and he exerted a profound influence on Hobbs's approach to batting. 'I found him a great source of inspiration. He made the bowlers, especially the fast ones, look so simple. It gave me great confidence,' Hobbs told the BBC in 1930. In another interview, Hobbs explained how opening with Hayward taught him how to build an innings. 'After seeing Tom

at the other end I was an experienced player. I learnt to know what balls to leave alone and what to go for. I learnt the scoring strokes to improve and those to drop. Tom was one of the classics, Tom was, and I learnt a lot.'

There was, however, a less admirable aspect to Hayward's batting which Hobbs adopted, and that was his regular use of pads as a second line of defence. Indeed he elevated pad play into an art form, much to the outrage of traditionalists who regarded this development as against the spirit of cricket. Hayward's attitude was summed up by his reproach to the young amateur Surrey batsman Donald Knight, who had been bowled by an off-spinner. 'Oh, where were your legs, sir?'[197]

Curiously, despite the developing affinity between Hayward and Hobbs, the senior man was not invited to the junior's wedding in September 1906, a reflection of Hobbs' diffidence and the height of the pedestal on which he had placed his mentor.

There was some surprise in Cambridge that Hobbs did not ask Tom Hayward but the decision reflected his continuing sense of diffidence towards his mentor, as he explained, 'The fact was that, although I had been associated with him for two cricket seasons, I had not lost that feeling of awe of him. I did not think the wedding would be grand enough for him or that I should be able to accommodate him in the style that his position warranted.'[198]

Hayward was apparently not in the least offended and he generously supplemented Lord Dalmeny's wedding present:

Hobbs, the young Surrey batsman, was married yesterday at Cambridge. Hobbs, whose father was a professor cricketer, learned his cricket at Cambridge, and before qualifying for Surrey, played for Cambridgeshire in the Minor Counties Championship. Lord Dalmeny presented the bridegroom with a cheque and Tom Hayward gave a silver cruet.[199]

34

ANNUS MIRABILIS 1906

1906 was the season in which Yorkshireman George Hirst achieved his famed 'double double' of two thousand runs and two hundred wickets. No longer bowling, Hayward was never going to challenge that, but his batting assumed new heights. With 3,518 first-class runs in the season he established a record that was not to be broken until forty-one years and two world wars had passed and Denis Compton, Bill Edrich and Middlesex dominated the Brylcreem Summer of 1947.

Some saw it coming:

> For years past Hayward has been the backbone of the Surrey team. In the dark days he hit his big scores with almost unfailing regularity, but he was compelled to restrain himself, knowing full well that upon his play might depend the issue of the game. Now, however, with a vastly improved team, he feels more free to adopt his natural tactics. He is neither ultra-careful nor recklessly aggressive, says a southern writer. He is a perfect batsman who recognises the ball that is to be hit and hits it as the ball should be hit.[200]

In a busy season, Tom (or his ghostwriter) found time to reflect on cricket as a career and point to the difficulties of breaking into the professional game:

> Cricket as a career by Tom Hayward. There is always a risk that the steadiest of youngsters may fail. He may be a keen cricketer of great natural abilities, he may be imbued with a determination to succeed

and may make that serious study of the game which is essential to success; yet for all that he may fail in his earlier trials, and having failed may never again be given an opportunity of proving his worth. It would be easy to quote instances of really fine young players who have the makings, both in point of character and skill, of great players, yet have been relegated to obscurity and sickened of their ambition by reason of a sequence of failures under conditions that would try the most iron-nerved and experienced of men, if they were placed in the same position and went in in the knowledge that their cheap dismissal meant failure to go further in their profession, exclusion from the side and hence practically involved the closing of their career.[201]

Tom equalled the record of thirteen first-class centuries in a season, four of them coming in the space of one week. Beginning on Monday 4 June at Trent Bridge he had 144 and 100, then 143 and 125 at Aylestone Road against Leicestershire. Surrey won both matches, by five wickets and 110 runs. A large attendance turned up the following Monday to see Surrey play Sussex, but with the added bonus of seeing Hayward extend his phenomenal run.[202] Although Surrey won the match by 289 runs, he 'failed' with 54 and 69.

Two of his centuries were converted to doubles – 219 against Northamptonshire and 208 against Warwickshire – both at The Oval. And in a season with a superfluity of records and statistics, of his 135 against Leicestershire at The Oval all but ten were scored before lunch: 'As in August he got nearer to the record, conscious of its significance and potential durability a change in his approach to batting from one of stroke-making to 'extreme carefulness' was noted.'[203]

Inevitably there were numerous tributes. The Surrey Yearbook commented that 'The marvellous batting of Tom Hayward was a great feature of the year's cricket.'[204] Another came in the traditional end-of-season charity match on Parker's Piece when Albert Craig, 'the Surrey poet' penned the following lines in a piece entitled 'Our Hero, Red-letter day at Tom Hayward's Happy Home':

Today we gather in the classic quarter,
From county strife we feel a glad release;

Cambridge are proud to meet their honour'd townsman,
Cheers, long and loud, are heard on 'Parker's Piece',
We breathe a prayer, 'God bless the Cambridge lad,
And God preserve for years his honour'd dad.'[205]

Craig died in 1909 so there was little opportunity for Hobbs and his contemporaries to feature, but Hayward has eighteen mentions in his verse. Only WG and Abel have more.

1906 was significant on the field for Tom's record-breaking aggregate, but off it there was speculation that he had deflowered and made pregnant a chambermaid in the employ of his captain, Lord Dalmeny. If that were true it would be part of a good old family tradition, the brides of both his father and grandfather being pregnant on their wedding day.

Richard Usborne wryly proposed a reason why Hayward hit such a prolific vein of form in a 1964 edition of *Wisden Cricket Monthly*: 'In the spring of that year he had got a parlourmaid in Lord Dalmeny's employ in the family way, and her fiancé had threatened to shoot Tom. So he felt safest in the middle of The Oval batting when he wasn't fielding.'[206] The accuracy of Usborne's statement may perhaps be gauged from the fact that earlier in the same piece, the writer refers to his uncle Daniel being considered the best professional batsman in the country in the 1860s. His *father* Daniel was not; his *uncle* Thomas was in the frame. Usborne claimed that he had been told this story by Charles Cobham, a former President of the MCC. It does sound rather like 'locker room talk' or a joke and Tom would probably have shared in the banter.

Once again, as had now become traditional, Hayward concluded the season by taking a full-strength Surrey team to Cambridge:

Tom Hayward is taking a team to Cambridge on the 22nd to play sixteen of the town and his side will be selected from Lord Dalmeny, NA Knox, Carpenter, Hayes, Hobbs, Holland, Lees, Reeves, Smith (WC), Strudwick, Tyldesley, Larry Lynz and Hayward.[207]

As always, it was well supported:

Cartoonist Spy's take on Tom from 1906, putting him in the elite club of Vanity Fair *caricatured cricketers alongside WG, Ranji and Lord Hawke.*

Although Cambridge people are very backward in supporting their county club, or any outdoor event where a gate is charged, they always respond liberally to any charity match at the end of the season. These are now an annual occurrence in which Tom Hayward, who lives at Cambridge, is the pioneer. For tomorrow the famous Surrey cricketer has got together a strong eleven, including Lord Dalmeny, NA Knox and Tyldesley against XVI of Cambridge. The match is for the benefit of the District Nurses Fund, and spectators from all parts of the Eastern counties are expected. Special trains will be run by several companies.[208]

The attendance was reported to be around 10,000, boosted no doubt by Hayward's record year and not far short of what some counties attract in a season of Championship matches nowadays. Tom's brother Dan captained the local side and the Surrey players, particularly Lord Dalmeny, made a special effort to be there:

The Hayward Charity match, which has excited so much interest in Cambridge and district for some long time past, took place on Saturday afternoon and was attended with a measure of success far exceeding the expectations of the most optimistic.

The weather was all that could be desired for the time of year and the crowd attracted was the largest ever seen at a cricket match on Parker's Piece. The spectators were standing several deep round the circle and the general opinion was that there must have been something like 9,000 or 10,000 present.

Tom Hayward brought down a strong team of thirteen, which included Lord Dalmeny the popular Surrey captain who travelled all night from Scotland to take part in the match, members of the Surrey team and the Oval ground staff, W Reeves, the Essex professional and the sporting writer W Lotinga (Larry Lynx) who was formerly up at Cambridge University. They were opposed by a local team of eighteen captained by Dan Hayward, who has in the past rendered invaluable service for Cambridgeshire ... The collection made at the match realised £61.14.6 the largest amount which has been raised at a Hayward Charity match.[209]

Lord Dalmeny's overnight journey from Scotland was a generous gesture and suggests that rumours about his parlourmaid had not soured his relationship with Tom!

35

SENIOR PROFESSIONAL 1907-09

1907 did not have the happiest of starts for Surrey. The leading 'amateur' of former years and current coach, Walter Read, died in January. He was followed in February by Charles Alcock, who had devoted more than half his life to the Secretaryship of Surrey CCC and held the office throughout the time of Tom Hayward's association with it. Tom attended the funeral along with several other current and former players. He and his fellow professionals sent a wreath.

For Tom it was an 'after the Lord Mayor's show' sort of season. He played in all three matches of the first home Test series against South Africa, but made a negligible contribution, his top score in five innings being 24. Other than that, however, without reaching the giddy heights of the previous summer, he still had over 2,000 runs at an average of over 45.

Time's winged chariot was beginning to catch up, however, and he was obliged to miss a few matches with lumbago, though there were insinuations, possibly in the light of off-field events in the previous two seasons, that there might have been other reasons:

Although some ill-informed folk have darkly insinuated that Tom Hayward's non-appearance in the Surrey eleven for the three last matches has been due to other causes than lumbago, there is no foundation for the allegation. In standing out of these three matches Hayward has acted under medical advice and also in the ultimate interest of his county and himself.[210]

There were rumours that he would retire from the game at the end of the season, appropriately and correctly denied. They were seven years premature:

> Persistent rumours have been afloat of late that Tom Hayward, the popular Surrey batsman, intended to retire from County Cricket at the end of the present season – or that, at any rate, he would not play regularly. The report was given publicity again yesterday by one of the morning papers.
>
> There is happily, however, no truth in the rumours. A representative of the Pall Mall Gazette was informed yesterday by Mr W Findlay, Secretary of the Surrey Club, who had just had an interview with Hayward, that there was not a word of truth in any of the stories being circulated.[211]

Now a senior professional, not only with Surrey but in the land, Hayward captained the Players in both their matches that year and his county in his first match of the season when his team beat the Gentlemen of England, led by WG Grace, by nine wickets.

He looked to be in form in the first Championship match of the season, a rain-affected draw at The Oval with Northamptonshire:

> Hayward proved to be in fine form and reached 50 out of 89 in 80 minutes; in all he scored 68 out of 118 in an hour and three-quarters, and hit eight 4's.[212]

Cricket was optimistic about Surrey's prospects for the season, though eventually they did no better than the previous year, finishing fourth behind Nottinghamshire, Worcestershire and Yorkshire:

> Recent events lead one to believe that Surrey will this season enjoy no small measure of success. Although Hayward and Hobbs have been playing together for a couple of seasons only, they have already indulged in a dozen three-figure partnerships for Surrey's first wicket.[213]

Many more were to follow, totalling forty in all.

Tom's good form continued against Essex. On the occasions when he and Hobbs did not launch the Surrey innings with a century partnership he was able to put runs together with the middle order:

> Hayward, although beaten once or twice by the ball, played excellent cricket, and after Marshal was stumped found two useful partners in Holland and Crawford, adding 63 with the former and 86 with the latter. He reached his 50 in 125 minutes, 100 in 195 and altogether scored 161 out of 320 in four hours and a quarter without a mistake of any kind.[214]

Surrey went on to 411 then bowled out Essex for 124 and 125, before going on to beat Hampshire, also by an innings. Then, to prove he was human, Tom came down to earth with a first-ball duck against Derbyshire.

It was this year that a book appeared in his name as Volume 2 Number 17 of Spalding's Athletic Library. At least his name was on the cover and the feature and the ideas were no doubt his own, but the words were contributed by his friend and former captain Digby Jephson. It was well reviewed:

> During our last non-cricket season, Hayward busied himself with putting together his hints on the game, and a very useful little book is the result. Every branch of cricket is dealt with in a thoughtful manner, and the majority of his suggestions are decidedly interesting. For instance, he advises the adoption of a scheme whereby fielding averages may be kept as they are in baseball, for, as he truly remarks, 'The merits of good fielding are not sufficiently recognised. Let a player clearly understand that his good work when chasing the leather weighs as much as his batting score, and we shall soon see a great improvement in our fielding.
>
> The advice tendered by Hayward, as was only to be expected, is very sound, and as he expresses himself clearly he should score heavily with his useful little publication. The volume is profusely illustrated with photographs of Hayward and Strudwick.[215]

Those who knew Hayward, however, and even those who did not, would quickly appreciate that the concluding paragraph reflected neither his approach to life, nor to the game, but were closer to those of his 'ghost':

> Quite what Tom Hayward thought of it all, it is difficult to imagine. Perhaps he only looked at the illustrations, but many must have been the ironic congratulations on his new-found fluency of expression. The Spalding Book of Cricket's final words of advice may well have made the pragmatic Hayward cringe. He would certainly have heard them all before: 'Cricket, in addition to being a pastime, is a creator of character. It teaches patience, perseverance and pluck, three Ps which will carry you well through the trials of life ... One word more, my youthful master. Take for your motto 'Play the Game!' Cricket is a game which, above all others that I know, generates gentlemanly characteristics. It is not wealth that makes a gentleman; it is conduct. So compose yourselves on the cricket field that, whether you win or lose, you will at any rate bring credit to yourself and to the game which you and I love so dearly.'[216]

Tom travelled to Cambridge for the fixture against the University, but stood down from the match, although he doubtless took the opportunity to catch up with friends and family:

> Surrey were without Hayward and Crawford for this match, the former, although present, considering it advisable not to play owing to the cold weather.[217]

The cold weather did not, however, prevent him making a guest appearance:

> During the present week a Summer Sports and Pastimes Exhibition is being held in the Tribune Rendezvous, Bouverie Street EC. On each day at noon the Exhibition is declared open by a gentleman prominently identified with some branch of sport or out-door life. Today the ceremony is to be performed by Mr JA Pease MP and Tom Hayward.[218]

By the end of June the weather had warmed up enough for the sun to shine on a very unusual week when, in four innings across two matches, the pair of Hayward and Hobbs had four century opening partnerships. Ernie Hayes and Alan Marshal, on the card at number three, must have developed a serious bout of pad rash. First against Cambridge University:

> At the Oval this week Hayward and Hobbs accomplished a most exceptional performance of scoring over 100 together for the first wicket in each innings of Surrey against Cambridge University.[219]

Then, in the second half of the same week, across the river at Lord's:

> Hayward and Hobbs, upon facing a total of 457 gave Surrey a splendid start, making over a hundred together for their County's first wicket for the third time in succession during the week. They reached 50 in thirty-five minutes, and it was not until 147 had been made that Hobbs was out lbw for a capital 70. Upon Crawford joining Hayward some very attractive cricket was seen. Hayward remained until 312 when having scored 119 in two hundred and thirty-five minutes without giving a chance he was out to a fine catch by MacGregor on the leg-side. He hit a five and fifteen 4's but he was very slow during the latter part of his innings.[220]

> Among the many successes recorded of late, none has been more remarkable than that credited jointly to Hayward and Hobbs. Four times last week they opened the Surrey innings together and on each occasion made over a hundred for the first wicket ... This fact, I scarcely need add, is without parallel in the whole history of first-class cricket.[221]

An outstanding unbeaten innings of 146 for the Players followed:

> No finer innings has been seen in London this season than Hayward's 146 not out for the Players at Lord's on Monday. It was worthy of the occasion and the man, being a faultless display and the result of attractive cricket. Alone among the professional batsmen he has now made as many as seven three-figure scores in Gentlemen v Players matches – four at Lord's ... and three at the Oval.[222]

Although Tom had a poor Test series that summer, between the first and second Tests, a couple of half centuries contributed to Surrey's victory over the tourists:

To Surrey has fallen the distinction of being the first side to lower the colours of the South Africans, and that they thoroughly deserved their success everyone who saw the match would readily admit. Hayward's superb batting in each innings, Knox's bowling, Crawford's all-round cricket and Strudwick's wicket-keeping were the outstanding features of the match.[223]

A week later his undefeated second innings century against Lancashire proved to be the difference between the sides:

Hayward's not out innings of 114 against Lancashire, whilst not so good as his 146 in the Gentlemen v Players match at Lord's, is nevertheless entitled to rank as one of the best seen in London this year. He went in first and carried out his bat, and obtained his runs at a time when all his companions except Holland, appeared quite unable to make anything of the bowling. Although not scoring as freely as he did a year ago, he is as reliable as ever when a great effort is required of him.[224]

The 1907 England cricket team, in which Tom was a senior player:
Back: C Blythe, EG Arnold, GL Jessop, JN Crawford, LC Braund.
Middle: AFA Lilley, CB Fry, RE Foster (capt), TW Hayward.
Front: GH Hirst, JT Tyldesley.

Another Australian tour was looming. It would have been his fourth, but along with a number of others, he declined to make himself available. FS Ashley-Cooper deplored the decision, though conceded Hayward had a more valid reason than some of the others:

> Everyone, both in this country and the colonies must deplore the difficulty which the MCC are experiencing in getting together the team for their trip to Australia in the autumn. The decision of Hayward, Tyldesley, Lilley and Hirst not to undertake the journey makes it an assured fact that whatever the constitution of the side which goes out, it will be one far from representative of the full strength of England. An exception might, however, be made in the case of Hayward, for the health of his father is causing some anxiety.[225]

And so it proved. The non-availabilities, coupled with the non-selection of CB Fry, provided opportunities for Surrey colleagues – the two Jacks, Hobbs and Crawford – but the series was lost by the not unfamiliar margin of 4-1.

Before all that, however, Hayward and Hobbs continued their prolific combination with their eighteenth century partnership – a double-century one in fact – against Worcestershire:

> Everything on the opening day was dwarfed by the partnership of 219 by Hayward and Hobbs for the first wicket of Surrey. Hayward was second out at 280 for a faultless 127 made in 205 minutes.[226]

In more difficult batting conditions in the North v South match at the Scarborough Festival they were the only batsmen to provide any serious resistance to Wilfred Rhodes' bowling:

> Rhodes who took six wickets for 19 runs, found the conditions quite to his liking and had all the batsmen in difficulties. It is worthy of remark that Hayward and Hobbs made 56 between them, and the other nine players on the side only 45.[227]

Surrey's and Hayward's seasons were appropriately summarised:

Surrey could never quite adapt to the soft wickets, especially in their out-matches and they experienced defeat at Nottingham, Manchester, Blackheath and Bristol. Hayward, without indulging in such bursts of scoring as in 1906, again proved the most reliable batsman on the side, and gave evidence that his powers were still unimpaired.[228]

Despite his ill health and rumours of retirement, Tom saw out the season by supporting the benefit of a fellow professional, this time with the Rodney Club at Ely:

> The curtain has at last been rung down on the cricket season, and winter pastimes now hold undisputed sway. The concluding cricket fixture of note in this district was at Ely on Saturday, when Tom Hayward, ever ready to assist a brother professional, took a team over from Cambridge to play a match for the benefit of Curgenven, the Ely City pro. There was some appropriateness in Tom rendering this service as Curgenven can claim some connection with both Cambridge and first class cricket, having been up at Clare College and played for Derbyshire as an amateur. During the past season he has rendered yeoman service for Ely, and that his splendid work has been appreciated was shown by the large crowd which assembled in the Paradise Ground on Saturday.
>
> Tom Hayward's team was composed entirely of members of the Rodney club with the exception of young Hitch, the latest Surrey recruit from Cambridgeshire. The outstanding feature of the game was, of course, Hayward's batting. It was the first time Tom had played at Ely, and many of those present had never previously seen him at the wickets. He was only batting three quarters of an hour but in that short period he charmed everyone with a stylish display which was in every way characteristic of England's greatest batsman. His brilliant strokes were only excelled by the marvellous catch with which Captain Mander dismissed him, and although the crowd were not slow to appreciate the Isle of Ely Chief Constable's feat, they were very loth to see the last of the Surrey 'crack'.[229]

That contribution, however, did not prevent his honouring his annual commitment to bring a Surrey team to Cambridge, this time for the benefit of Addenbrooke's Hospital. Once again, there was a whole-hearted family commitment:

The final meeting of the General Committee in connection with the recent Hayward Charity match was held at the Prince Regent on Friday evening, when it was reported that there was a balance of £60 for Addenbrooke's Hospital.

The chairman said that their thanks were due to Mr Tom Hayward for his extreme liberality and kindness in bringing down a team to play in the match. Thanks were also due to Mr Dan Hayward Sen. for his hospitality to the team and other members of the committee, to Mr Dan Hayward for his services as umpire, and to Mr Frank Hayward for his work in connection with the erection of the tents, and to other members of the Hayward family.

Mr Tom Hayward in reply said that it was a great pleasure for him to bring down these teams to dear old Parker's Piece and it was also a great pleasure to make them welcome when they came.[230]

As senior professional, he presided at the presentation to Lord Dalmeny to mark his Lordship's relinquishing of the captaincy:

During the luncheon interval at the Oval yesterday the Surrey professionals presented Lord Dalmeny with a handsomely illuminated testimonial in view of his forthcoming retirement from the captaincy. Hayward made the presentation and also handed his Lordship the ball with which he took two Worcestershire wickets for 16.[231]

Parliamentary duties compelled Lord Dalmeny who, to the surprise of many (including himself) had been elected as an MP in the Liberal landslide of 1906, to relinquish the captaincy. In 1908, HDG Leveson Gower took over for three seasons. Surrey were to finish in the top half of the table, but not until 1914 were they to repeat the success of the late nineteenth century. In the meantime, the Championship was shared around with Kent being the most successful in the years between Surrey's triumphs. It was respectable, but not earth-shattering. The three aspirates of Hobbs, Hayward and Hayes held the batting together now Abel had retired but with Richardson off the scene, the bowling was inevitably weaker and there was no way Hayward himself could resurrect earlier bowling skills.

The end-of season 'Hayward' match in Cambridge, in which all his Surrey colleagues seemed willing to participate, was this year for the benefit of George Watts who had rendered sterling service to the sport in Cambridgeshire over a number of years.

The 1909 season started with a few low scores for Tom, then a double century against Warwickshire, but fitness issues, the end of his Test career and controversy in the Committee Room meant it was a pretty erratic passage from April to September.

Tom captained the team against the touring Australians, a rare tribute by the Committee to a professional cricketer (though he had done so previously, for instance, against Middlesex at Lord's in 1905). It also has to be said that Surrey had run out of amateurs, Jack Crawford having declined to captain a team consciously weakened by the omission of key professionals for quite trivial disciplinary reasons.

It was an age of deference and Jack Crawford did not do deference or, if he did, it was based on an opinion that deference should be earned, rather than assumed via an accident of birth or background. It cost Crawford a successful career as Surrey (and probably England) captain and provided another opportunity for Tom Hayward to captain the county side. As in 1896, he recognised that deference, however reluctant, was at the time a prerequisite for progression, indeed to holding on to the job.[232] As it happened, what Crawford described as a 'second eleven sort of team', acquitted itself none too badly and emerged with a creditable draw.[233]

As a result of his declining to captain Surrey against the Australians, the powerful triumvirate of Lord Alverstone, HDG Leveson Gower and William Findlay, supported by the Surrey committee, imposed a lifetime ban on Crawford. It was an unequal struggle which the precocious all-rounder was never going to win. The politics of envy and jealousy had kicked in. He had some support from members and the media, but on the whole was generally cold-shouldered by his county. He cut his losses and took himself off to Australia to make a name for himself there. Tom Hayward, perhaps still smarting from 1896, empathised with the young amateur and was one of the few to wish him well. One was a professional because he couldn't afford to be anything else, the other a professional in attitude. The two had a mutual respect which was not always the case in relation to other members of the team.

Now approaching the end of his fourth decade, Tom's outstanding batting continued, but his health and fitness were showing signs of decline: 'Hayward was in his best form, though unable to take part in many matches owing to rheumatism.'[234] Water on the knee affected both his availability and his mobility and he played only one Test match, the Lord's one, that summer. He was run out for six in what turned out to be his final Test innings, falling a tantalising single short of 2,000 Test runs.

The writing which signalled the end of his international career had perhaps been on the wall when he elected not to go on a fourth tour of Australia in 1907/08, allowing his Surrey colleagues Jack Hobbs and Jack Crawford to move ahead of him in the selection stakes. England had surrendered the Ashes on that tour and failed to regain them in the 1909 season. But Hayward was no longer part of that scene. He had played his part in the past and could look back and say that he was the future once, a future well fulfilled, but now the torch had to be passed on to younger, fitter players. In the context of his career, an average of 34.46 was perhaps slightly disappointing when compared with the overall figure of 41.79, but he made thirty-five appearances for his country. Not many can say that.

Tom's house purchase and court case had used up his benefit money and more. As early as 1906 he raised the possibility of a testimonial match, eventually granted and handed over to him after minimal negotiation. The Committee had made and would continue to make a number of financial decisions, mostly favouring Hayward. Few of his contemporaries would have benefited from such generous treatment. He was still a valuable asset, as the following extracts from the minutes indicate:

'An application of T Hayward for a benefit in 1902 was granted.' (15 August 1901)

'An application from T Hayward that he might have the Yorkshire match on July 31 and two following days was granted.' (20 March 1902)

'A grant of £50 was made to Hayward's benefit.' (1 May 1902)

'It was decided to pay winter wages to Hayward and Strudwick during their trip to Australia.' (3 September 1903)

'It was decided to give Hayward sixty pounds for the coming winter.' (12 September 1904)

'T Hayward attended relative to his winter pay. Hayward was informed that the Committee were prepared to give him, as an exceptional case, Eighty pounds for winter pay instead of Sixty Pounds as heretofore.' (15 February 1906)

'The following recommendations of Match Committee were approved: 1. That Hayward be engaged for three years on the terms of his last engagement, with the understanding that the Committee would endeavour to arrange either a testimonial or a complimentary match for him in 1909.' (15 November 1906)

'A letter from T Hayward, asking the Committee to give him a Complimentary Match in 1909 and to allow him to choose the Match was read. The Secretary was instructed to inform Hayward that the Committee would arrange a Testimonial for him during the Season 1909, or later should he prefer it.' (16 July 1908)

'T Hayward's Testimonial – A letter from T Hayward asking the Committee to re-consider their previous decision, and give him a benefit match in 1909, instead of a Testimonial, was read. It was resolved that the President and Mr Leveson Gower be requested to see Hayward, on the understanding that should the Committee decide to give him a Benefit Match, such Match should not take place until the time of Hayward's retirement from First-Class Cricket.' (15 October 1908)

'A letter from T Hayward accepting a Testimonial was read. It was resolved, that Hayward be asked to place his services at the disposal of the Committee for the purposes of County Cricket if required, for five years after receiving such Testimonial, and that all monies accruing from the Testimonial be invested to the satisfaction of the Trustees.' (12 November 1908)

'Letter from T Hayward – A letter from Hayward was read agreeing to place his services at the disposal of the Committee for the purposes of County Cricket (if required) for five years after receiving his Testimonial, and to leave the investment of all monies accruing from the Testimonial in the hands of the Trustees.' (17 December 1908)

'Hayward's Testimonial – The President gave notice that he would move at the next Committee Meeting that a grant of £200 be made to the Hayward Testimonial Fund.' (21 January 1909)

'Hayward's Testimonial – Mr HDG Leveson-Gower's Motion, that a grant of £200 to the Hayward Testimonial Fund, was carried. It was resolved that notice of this grant should appear on the Annual Report.' (18 February 1909)

'Hayward's Testimonial – It was decided: (a) That a Subscription Card should be placed in the Pavilion. (b) That Subscription Cards should not be sent to the Counties. (c) That collecting boxes should be sent round the Ground during one Surrey match; the choice of such match to be left to Hayward.' (15 April 1909)

'Accounts to be Paid – T Hayward's Testimonial – Grant £200.' (16 September 1909)

'Testimonial to T Hayward – The Secretary reported that the Testimonial to T Hayward amounted to £382.8.6. It was decided to hand over the money to Hayward in accordance with his request.' (21 October 1909)

It was just seven years after his benefit that Surrey awarded Tom this testimonial, a rare tribute to a solid professional to whom they owed much of their success. Surrey headed the subscription list with £200.[235]

His outstanding innings of his testimonial year was the undefeated double-century against Warwickshire which enabled Surrey to declare at 400 for four in their second innings and win by a comfortable 171 runs. On the way he had an opening partnership of 342 with Hobbs, the highest of the forty they shared:

Hayward played a more vigorous game than is customary with him … When hitting freely he was missed by Baker at slip but made no other mistake. He hit twenty-two 4's and eight 3's and always appeared to be master of the bowling.[236]

Much of the credit for Surrey's earlier victory over the Australians has been given to Jack Crawford for his astute captaincy, but the young amateur was probably grateful to the old pro for his advice, but more especially for yet another outstanding contribution with the bat:

> The Australians sustained their first defeat at The Oval yesterday when Surrey won a splendidly contested game by five runs. There have been many opinions concerning the wicket upon which the game was played, but on the authority of some of those who took part in it, I can state that all through it gave some assistance to the bowlers and that it was at its worst during the second afternoon when Surrey were batting. The feature of the game was the superb second innings of Hayward, who alone played the Australian bowling with much success. It is doubtful if he has ever been seen to greater advantage, and it is to him that the chief credit for the victory must be given.[237]

Tom was in a squad of fifteen for the first Test at Edgbaston, but omitted from the final eleven because, said *Cricket*, 'Hayward's knee was not sound enough to justify his participation in the match.' This was a series in which the selectors failed to find a settled team and used twenty-five players. Meanwhile, the knee was apparently strong enough to stand up to a three-day Championship match against Nottinghamshire where Surrey sustained a defeat by an innings and 170 runs which, but for Hayward would have been heavier still:

> Losing the toss had a very great deal to do with the reverse sustained by Surrey at Trent Bridge, though it seems probable that the game might have been saved but for several blunders in the field early on the first day. Hayward played a really great innings when everything was against Surrey and was unfortunate to be on the losing side. In the follow-on Hayward was seen at his best, but although he had the personal satisfaction of making a hundred, he could not save his side from a crushing defeat.[238]

Similarly against Lancashire in another heavy innings defeat, he had 22, the only double-figure score, out of 56 and 25 out of 96. It seemed that Hayward on one leg was more effective than most of his teammates on two. Surrey had a good start to the season, but fell away towards the end and finished in fifth place, their lowest since the wilderness years of 1903 and 1904. Injury to the captain had an unsettling effect, the knee of the senior pro deprived them of runs and who knows what effect the Crawford affair had on the dressing room:[239]

> At the moment Surrey cricket is under a cloud. When, early in May, Hayes, Hobbs and Hayward each made over 200 runs in an innings, and the bowlers obtained their wickets at a reasonable cost, it appeared probable that the side would experience a successful season. At the present time, Hayward, Hobbs and Leveson-Gower are unable to play, the two first-named owing to injuries and the latter on account of a family bereavement, whilst Crawford is showing a preference for club cricket and Marshal has been dropped owing to a temporary loss of form. Hayward and Hobbs have done so well on the limited number of occasions on which they have played that their inability to assist the side is little less than tragic.[240]

The paragraph does not tell the whole truth. Marshal had been omitted for disciplinary reasons and Crawford was opting for club cricket because, after his declining to captain the side against the Australians, the Committee had imposed a life ban.

There was only one more century for Hayward that year, against Leicestershire in late August. That concluded his season. His knee meant he was unavailable for the Rest of England v Champion County (Kent) match. Injury had restricted his appearances and consequently his aggregate of runs for the season, 1,359, of which fewer than 1,000 were in the Championship, was way below the standard of recent seasons when the other side of 2,000 had been the benchmark. However, an average of over 40 was testimony to the fact that, when fit, he still had a crucial role to play. He had carried his bat through an innings twice, scored a double century and brought the number of his Surrey opening partnerships with Hobbs to 26. The pain in his knee was perhaps alleviated a little by his testimonial.

36

CENTURY OF CENTURIES

1910-1913

Tom missed much of the early part of the 1910 season because of his father's terminal illness and death at the end of May. His century in his first match of the season, against Warwickshire, included a hundred before lunch and laid the foundation for an innings victory in two days after the first day had been lost to the weather. It flattered to deceive, however, and despite later hundreds against Sussex and Nottinghamshire, Tom ended the season with just over a thousand runs, as opposed to his regular 2,000 and occasional 3,000. Surrey though had a much better season, finishing second to Kent, on results the strongest county at the time. This, despite the fact that a disgruntled Rushby had taken himself off to the Lancashire League and Crawford was banned for life (though the decision was subsequently rescinded) and was plying his trade in the southern hemisphere.

Tom was now very much the *éminence grise*, approaching the end of his fourth decade, an autocrat and figure of awe to the junior players, including Jack Hobbs and fast bowler Bill Hitch, both of whom had joined Surrey at his instigation. He had ways of demonstrating his seniority. Hitch recalls such an occasion and illustrates the hierarchy with a cautionary tale of Hayward, Hobbs and Hitch at a hotel in Horsham (a good exercise for Professor Higgins and

Eliza Doolittle). Hayward had earned and demanded the respect of junior players and had ways of ensuring he got it:

> During an away match against Sussex, when the Surrey team were staying at a hotel in Horsham, Hayward had retired to bed early feeling unwell. But his attempts to drift off to sleep were ruined by the antics of Hobbs and some other junior professionals. 'The lads started running round the corridors making an awful row and I joined in,' recalled Bill Hitch, the young fast bowler who had been complaining earlier in the day of a sore leg. Suddenly Hayward's bedroom door opened and the veteran appeared in his nightshirt. Hobbs and the others fled but Hitch was caught. 'So that's your game. I thought you had a bad leg. I'll see your leg is better tomorrow. You'll bowl all day,' growled Hayward, through his moustache. 'And I did. I could hardly walk that night,' concluded Hitch. For all his devotion to his fellow Cambridge batsman, Hobbs recognised that Hayward was a bit of an autocrat, the last of the Surrey professionals to be 'the boss'. His word was law with the other professionals and we had to be careful what we said and did. Cricket was a serious business with him.[241]

The tale is exaggerated for maximum effect. Hitch bowled twenty-one overs in the Sussex first innings, Lees forty-one and Smith fifty-four. And in any event, Morice Bird was captain, not Hayward. There were limits to even his influence.

Not inconsistent with that anecdote is that related by Herbert Strudwick about an incident during his early days at The Oval when he had inadvertently wandered into the senior professionals' area:

> Within the professional ranks distinctions were far more rigid than among the amateurs, just as the gulf between the regimental sergeant-major and the private is infinitely greater than that between the colonel and the subaltern. The senior professional expected and received profound respect from the recruit. Herbert Strudwick has related (*Wisden 1959*) how, as a new-comer to Surrey, he strayed up the stairs of the professionals' quarters at The Oval and encountered Tom Hayward, who demanded to know his name. When told, Hayward remarked coldly: 'You have the advantage of me and your place is downstairs.'[242]

Demarcation lines at The Oval persisted long after that, though the reasons for the demarcation differed. Here it is between senior and junior professionals. Before the 1960s it was between amateurs and professionals and not until the 1990s were dressing rooms for capped and uncapped players amalgamated.

Not until the 1950s did Surrey emulate their successes of the 1890s and, although they did not plumb the depths of 1903 and 1904, by their standards and expectations the years between the end of the century and the First World War were disappointing ones:

> The dry season was favourable to long scoring, but with the exception of Hayward who has probably never played better ... the batting at times broke down badly.[243]

> Hayward was quite himself. The hot weather and hard wickets suited him.[244]

Surrey were back to fifth in the table in 1911 and five centuries, including a double century against Derbyshire and 177 against Yorkshire, brought Tom's career hundreds to ninety-six. A hundred hundreds, a landmark previously reached only by WG Grace, was now within reach, though it was to take a while yet. Warwickshire broke the monopoly of the 'big six' by taking the Championship for the first time.

Tom captained the Players again, but the season marked his last appearance in the traditional fixture. It was in this year, however, that Andy Sandham was to play his first matches for Surrey. Tom was now forty-one and about to be replaced as Jack Hobbs' opening partner. He had the highest season's aggregate for the tenth time and the highest average for the seventh.

Yet, despite concerns about his weight and fitness, he had one of his most successful seasons, once again scoring over two thousand runs at well over 40 (just over 50 in the Championship). Rev RS Holmes, always an admirer, defended his by now below-average fielding, was optimistic about Surrey's prospects for the season and even pressed his claims for the 1910/11 tour of Australia.

The omens were favourable when, back in their home town of Cambridge following a large win at The Oval against Warwickshire, Hobbs and Hayward helped themselves to yet another century opening partnership:

> On their native heath, Hayward and Hobbs passed the University's total [of 123] without being parted in 87 minutes.[245]

A week later, Rev Holmes followed up with:

> Nearly all their men are young. Hayward is the one exception, but a batsman of his physique and temperate habits should last several seasons yet. Cricketers have no business to be old at forty, although their joints are sure to be a bit stiff after a winter's rest. I fully expect Hayward to be in the Surrey eleven for at least five more years, and now that the youngsters are shaping well and so great a responsibility does not rest on him, I hope that he will play his natural free game, although, owing to his perfect style, his cricket always gives pleasure to an old fogey even when he is not scoring rapidly.[246]

Ashley-Cooper had his reservations, stating that 'Hayward looks like having a good season – good even for him – but much will depend on his ability to keep down his weight.'[247] But it seemed not to hamper him in his 170 not out against Essex, nor in his next innings, a century against Gloucestershire and another century opening partnership with Hobbs:

> On a perfect wicket on Monday, Surrey scored 448, Hayward and Ducat sharing the honours. The former made 112 in 80 minutes with Hobbs for the first wicket, and scored his 121 out of 195 in 135 minutes without a mistake.[248]

Again Rev Holmes followed up, this time with a comparison of Hayward and his contemporary and occasional opening partner, CB Fry. It was midsummer and already there was speculation about the party to tour Australia the following winter:

Two famous cricketers must be mentioned in Fry and Hayward. A pity the former had to decline the invitation: as for the Surrey man – just glance at last Monday's averages: he saved his county from defeat at the hands of Essex and he won the match against Sussex. Where would Surrey have been without him? It is an exciting race between him and Fry in the matter of county centuries, Hayward having compiled 67, Fry 65. Hayward's first century came in 1893, Fry's first a year later: and last week each added one more to their respective piles.[249]

It triggered media interest in who might be first to reach a thousand first-class runs. Would it be Tom for a fifth time?

At the time of writing, Tom Hayward looks safe, bar accidents, for the distinction of being the first batsman to reach a four-figure total in big cricket this season This will be no new experience for the Surrey crack, who won the race in a canter in 1900 (when he scored his thousandth run on May 31st) by a short head in 1901 and quite easily in 1906 and 1908.[250]

As it happened, he did not make it on this occasion, making only 33 runs in his next three innings to be overtaken by the lesser-known and long-odds Joe Vine. Nevertheless the hero worship from Rev Holmes continued:

I am amused to see Hayward described as 'the Surrey veteran', when he is in his prime. At forty, no cricketer, provided he has observed the laws of health, should dream of retiring. I have no patience with men getting old before their time. WG at forty-seven was still the greatest batsman in the world.[251]

Hardly a sustainable point of view nowadays when all forms of the game demand athleticism and fitness, strength and conditioning unheard of a century ago, but a valid point in the context of its time. After all, Jack Hobbs had more centuries after his fortieth birthday than before. Nowadays it is only a handful of players who continue beyond that age.

Further heavy scoring, in particular Tom's against Derbyshire, stimulated speculation on the possibility of another winter tour:

Hayward played confidently for four hours, hitting twenty-six fours and offering only one chance – when 158. He added 144 with Hayes and 155 (in 75 minutes) with Bush.[252]

Rev Holmes again:

Hayward's 202 was in striking contrast to his 170 not out against Essex in May. The latter was the most perfect innings I have seen this year. He has two styles: when much depends on him he plays every ball as it should be played by a master, and scores at the rate of about 30 runs per hour. But when, as against Derbyshire last week, other batsmen are in form, his runs come at the rate of 50 an hour, and he is evidently bent on enjoying himself; having done so he gets out, as if he had had enough for the time and longed for a rest. His first-class centuries now number 95; surely the century of centuries is now in sight.[253]

In the same issue, speculation in 'Pavilion Gossip' was that:

It is hardly likely that John Tyldesley or Sharp would leave his business. An agitation has been set afoot for Tom Hayward's inclusion. If asked, he would go. He certainly would not strengthen the fielding, though, like those chosen, he must not be written down a duffer in the field – merely a man past his best there.[254]

Rev Holmes would not let it go:

In the absence of Fry, should not Hayward have been invited? He has a splendid record in Australia; in each of his three visits he has played right up to his reputation, and at the present time he is out and away our greatest professional batsman. If you were at the Oval last Friday you would have endorsed this judgment; a more masterly innings than his against Yorkshire I never wish to see. He's the very man to go in first and wear down the bowling. 'Oh, but he's slow in the field.' No, not slow, but leisurely, true, he's not like a cat on hot bricks, but he manages to stop any ball that comes his way, although he does not hurry when no run is attempted.[255]

It was all in vain. He was not invited and did not go.

In the wet summer of 1912 which ruined the only triangular Test tournament ever held, Hayward had a modest season. He must have thought his international career had ended at Lord's in 1909. His call up for The Rest against England in a Test trial at The Oval – caught Rhodes bowled Barnes 0 and run out 4 – ensured that it had.

He made his only 'pair' this season, run out for 0 in the second innings against Kent, at Blackheath. Maybe it was rheumatism, maybe water on the knee, or maybe the avuncular genes had filtered through. However, one of Tom's finest achievements was to come the following year, in 1913, despite it being a relatively unexceptional season:

> Hayward did not, in such a dry summer, have for him a remarkable record, but for a man of forty-two, who was in his twenty-first season for Surrey, an average of 34 with an aggregate of 1,326 runs, must be considered very good indeed. As was only natural, he failed more often than he used to, but on his great days he was the real Hayward. During the season he and Hobbs beat the record in the number of first wicket partnerships of over a hundred runs.[256]

Notwithstanding his unremarkable record during the season, Tom reached a remarkable point in his overall career when he joined WG Grace as the only batsman at the time to reach a hundred centuries in first-class cricket when he scored 125 against Lancashire, having recorded his ninety-ninth in the equivalent fixture just over twelve months previously. It was not his best ever innings, but was certainly one of his most memorable.

The tributes were numerous, as the Surrey Yearbook noted, 'Hayward ... received many congratulations on securing his 100th century in First-Class Cricket.'[257] His long-term friend and former county captain, Digby Jephson, supplied the poetry:

> So now, instead of one, we gather two,
> That from the smiling face of willow wood
> Have drawn a hundred hundreds – sportsmen true
> In every sense, in every varying mood,
> The GOM and Tom!

Tom's former Test captain and opening partner, AC MacLaren, supplied the prose. MacLaren was the captain for whom Tom had the most respect. He had led in fourteen of the thirty-five Tests in which Tom had played and the two were regular opening partners for England on the 1901/02 tour and 1905 series, so the Harrow-educated Lancastrian was well equipped to make a judgment. MacLaren would join JN Pentelow as joint-editor of *World of Cricket*, which had superseded Charles Alcock's *Cricket: A Weekly Record of the Game,* established in 1882 and thus covering the whole of Tom Hayward's career. MacLaren would have had access to its pages and made full use of that privilege to eulogise Hayward's not-quite-unique achievement:

> Hayward's great achievement in scoring his hundredth century is the outcome of self-denial and hard work, and it is a fitting reward for all the time and trouble he has taken over our game. I doubt if any professional has ever been more careful in his living or more painstaking in his methods to attain success for the captains for whom and the sides for which he has played. A more popular player alike with spectators and with those who have had the pleasure of playing with him there has never been. Experiences in the past have told one that he is the type of player who reduces the worries and anxieties of a captain to a minimum. No batsman has ever filled me with such supreme confidence, and not a few of my own successes with the bat have been due in no small measure to the fact that I have had such a gloriously sound partner at the other end. Only those who have taken part in big games know what a difference there is between partnering Tom Hayward and partnering a nervy batsman who sandwiches wind-and-water strokes between fine cricketing shots. I wonder how many bowlers Tom has worn down for his comrades to lay out absolutely flat?
>
> For absolute soundness Tom Hayward has always occupied, in my mind, a very easy first place. He possesses, too, the ideal temperament for a cricketer, and I never recollect seeing him put out over any circumstance connected with the game. One of my most valued pictures is one of Tom and myself going in together at Sydney in a Test match – it brings back, as Willie Bard would say, 'Happy days, happy days'. So easily, one might say lazily, Tom batted on big occasions, at times I

have caught myself wondering if he realised he was batting for England v Australia! One such occasion was during my last Test at Adelaide when we had 100 up and no-one out. I had cut Trumble hard and clean to Trumper at third man, but in reply to a very strong 'No', Tom came thundering down the wicket. So off I went, knowing he could not get back, and that I might scrape home if the ball was fumbled. But our opponents did not miss many opportunities in those days, and I saw my wicket sent flying with another six yards to go. I have always felt that Tom was bordering on the comatose stage on that occasion![258]

Tom has his other side, as Prince Ranji (as he then was) will tell you. They had gone up one of the big rivers on a steam launch, and with the prospects of wild duck the Prince had taken his gun. After many fruitless attempts to get within range, they at last, with Ranji's skilful manoeuvring, actually got to the tickling the trigger stage, when Tom pulled the cord attached to the launch's whistle! The scene that followed I leave to my readers' imagination. Unfortunately, I was not there; but Prince Ranji tells me there was no word to fit the occasion.

In concluding these few paragraphs, let me beg all young players to note the use of the left shoulder, and how the left leg is brought across for Hayward's off drive. Note too that he never gets back on to his wicket and then plays forward, as some have got in the way of doing. My readers will join me in the wish that Tom will add more centuries to his list.

ACM.[259]

Tom's activity on the duck shoot had clearly passed into folklore in the aristocratic and quasi-aristocratic circles of which MacLaren and 'Prince Ranji' formed part and Tom clearly did not. Maybe with his family roots in gardening and groundsmanship, his sympathies were with the ducks rather than the hunting-shooting-fishing mentality of his companions.

Two more centuries followed to bring his tally for the season to three and his career record to 102. Against Leicestershire:

> It was a great triumph for two Surrey men, Hitch and Hayward. Though the latter and Hobbs scored 114 for the first wicket (their 35th stand of over 100 for Surrey and their second 100-partnership of the week) in 85 minutes, they were so ill supported that the total was under 250.

Then, in the second innings:

Yet another good start by Hayward and Hobbs realised 63 in 45 minutes, the veteran (166 in the match) scoring his 101st century in big cricket. His three hours' display was absolutely faultless and he hit thirteen 4's.[260]

While against Worcestershire:

Hayward and Hobbs were associated in a remarkable partnership, scoring 313 runs in three hours and ten minutes for the first wicket. Hayward made his runs by a variety of well-timed strokes, his command over the bowling being so complete that he did not make a mistake until his score stood at 114. He hit eighteen 4's.[261]

37

MATILDA

Having avoided matrimony definitely once and possibly twice, Tom did eventually marry, aged forty-two, on 19 January 1914 at Wandsworth Registrar's Office. It was all very respectable, but the ceremony attracted little publicity and only one newspaper photograph has been traced. The bride, Miss Matilda Mitchell, the thirty-eight-year-old daughter of Mr Sydney Mitchell of Putney, is described as 'a tall striking blonde with commanding figure and steady blue eyes'. The wedding photograph sees her striding from the Registrar's Office ahead of her new husband, wearing a fashionable two-piece costume with a fox fur slung around her shoulders and dainty high-heeled boots. Her head is bowed but there is a smile playing on her lips. The happy couple honeymooned in Paris. 'Tom and I go to Paris today and we are going to be very happy.' she told a journalist:

Marriage of Tom Hayward to famous Lady Detective. Big, ruddy-cheeked and bashful – but beaming happily – Tom Hayward, the great Surrey batsman, was yesterday married to Miss Matilda Emma Mitchell, one of the most famous women detectives, and, in her own way, as remarkable a personality as her husband. They had made elaborate preparations to keep the marriage a secret but Miss Mitchell is not only sympathetic to those who find out things but also has a keen sense of humour, and she made the best of being discovered. 'How did you find out?' she asked.

She also explained how she had come to know the cricketer:

The only known photograph of Tom and Tilly's wedding, taken on 19 January 1914, as printed in the Daily Sketch.

Am I happy? Oh yes, ever so much. You see, I have known Tom for eighteen years – that is, we first met eighteen years ago but lost sight of each other for a long time, but I never forgot him, and in 1911, when, quite by chance, we met again, I agreed to marry him.[262]

Asked how he liked married life Tom Hayward blushed – that is if a blush could possibly superimpose itself on the freshness of his cheeks. Modest, frank and manly, the bridegroom is one of the most charming personalities in the world of sport. He talks little and then chiefly in the similes of his beloved game.[263]

She made a pronouncement that Tom would retire from cricket at the end of the 1914 season ('Mrs Hayward says so' reported the *Daily Mirror*, a bit of a giveaway as to where the decision-making powers in the partnership were to reside).

In an interview for the *People* newspaper, which was also reproduced in papers in Australia, Tilly explained how she had become a detective:

How did I become a lady detective? That is a question which I have often been asked. It was my early experience on the stage that suggested the idea to me. I started my career at the Royal Opera House, Covent Garden, at the age of 15, taking part in several operas. Afterwards, as Ethel Chester I went through several pantomimes at Drury Lane, then under the management of Sir Anthony Harris. It was during this period that I frequently attended fancy dress balls at Covent Garden in all sorts and conditions of disguises' winning many first prizes. These successes, I may say, led to my first engagement as a lady detective.

She started work for the South Western Railway Company when she used to dress sometimes as a man, and later entered the service of the Royal College of Veterinary Surgeons, riding about the country to detect unlicensed vets. Afterwards she became head of the secret service staff at Selfridge's store in Oxford Street. Her work as a store detective had sometimes been recorded in the newspapers when shoplifters were brought to court:

Kathleen Dorothy Nicholson (32) a governess, was alleged to have stolen a silk blouse, 14 handkerchiefs and a bottle of scent from Selfridges. The prisoner was seen by Miss Matilda Mitchell, a private detective in the employ of the firm, to take a blouse from the counter on the ground floor and put it under her jacket. She then went to the book department and stole several small books which she concealed under a cape. She was taken to the Manager's office and when spoken to she replied 'Yes I am extremely sorry. Let me pay.' When searched the prisoner was found to have a pocket pinned under her skirt which contained a bottle of scent and other articles.[264]

Her specialism, though, was divorce and she told many colourful stories of her solved cases:

In my first case I managed to locate the suspected couple at a big West End hotel after a long and anxious search. I at once telegraphed to the husband who came to town with hesitating and faltering footsteps. He was not too keen, but I had to make good and by the happiest chance I managed to secure the room next to that in which the erring wife – she weighed some 15 stone – and her lover were doing their billing and cooing.

She went on to explain how she sprang into action when she heard the chambermaid coming along in the early morning with a breakfast for two. She snatched the maid's cap off her head and put it on:

> She was somewhat remonstrative but I put my hand over her mouth and pushing her aside and the unfortunate husband in the room in front of me, I followed in with the hard-boiled eggs, tea etc. They were both sitting up in bed, reading, like a pair of soiled turtle doves, from the same newspaper, but I'll bet odds they had the surprise of their lives. The poor hubby won his case hands down.

She also took on a commission, for a substantial reward, when 'a smart well-known man of means and foreign extraction' abducted a very young and supposedly innocent girl. Tilly managed to trace them to a place near Caversham:

> Somehow I could get no substantial evidence of the misbehaviour till a happy thought struck me. This was to locate their rooms which, as usual in most of these adventures, adjoined, and secrete myself. This I did, hiding under the bed all night.

This case ended profitably for Tilly but she recalled that she would never forget the scream of the servant of the hotel when she saw her appear, as it seemed, magically from somewhere in the room, and also the threats of the landlord to have her arrested as a lady burglar.

While working on another case for a popular actress she gained access to the home of her client's sportsman fiancé by persuading the painters who were working there to give her a job. The actress knew there was a possible rival and Tilly was engaged to track her down:

> I first approached the foreman painter and inquired whether I could enter his employ as a painter in the guise of a man. He stared at first, then laughed good-day. I duly turned up as a bright, red-haired young painter and commenced to solemnly paint the window frames. He nearly had a fit but I soon found the greenfly in my lady employer's ointment of happiness and when 'the person', the suspicious lady, entered clad very sparsely in a bright green emerald and badly-fitting corset and bade

the bright young house-painter (it was me, poised on a ladder, with a pot of green paint held somewhat gingerly in one hand) a cheerful good morning she did not know that it forefended the end of one of her romantic episodes. At any rate, the popular actress and sportsman are now married and enjoy a real good time together.

Speaking of her experiences as a detective employed by Messrs. Selfridge's, she claimed that one of her cleverest captures was when a French waiter stole a bronze ornament and hid it under his waist-coat. The man had a colleague who managed to escape but Tilly had to hold on to the waiter until other staff came to assist her: 'To my surprise, I had to hold on to him quite a long time before assistance came.'

She did not often have trouble making the arrests, though she recalled:

Only once did I meet a professional shop-lifter who showed fight. She tore my hat and grey coat all to pieces, and I had the greatest difficulty in keeping my temper whilst in the shop, but once she was alone with me in the searching room I soon let her know who was master.[265]

Tom and Tilly set up their home together in Glisson Road. His financial negotiations with Surrey County Cricket Club, the inheritance from his father in 1910, a wedding gift of £500 from his father-in-law in 1914, plus his earnings from playing, winter pay and later coaching meant they were comfortably off in the latter part of his playing career and beyond. They had no family and consequently there are no direct descendants.

38

CLOSE OF PLAY

Early in the season Tom Hayward was not himself, and there can be no harm now in saying that at the end of June his place in the eleven had become rather insecure. However, he re-established himself by means of a fine innings on a slow wicket at Manchester, and later there came a wonderful fortnight in which he renewed his youth and played as finely as at any time in his career. In the space of exactly fourteen days he scored 122 against Kent, at Blackheath, and 91 against Kent and 116 against Yorkshire at Lord's. Fortune was kind to him in the second Kent match, but not for many seasons had he played such an innings on a bad wicket as his 91.[266]

As The Oval was required for military purposes, a couple of 'home' matches in August were played at Lord's where Hayward scored his last first-class century, against Yorkshire. Surrey returned to The Oval for what turned out to be the last match there before the First World War and Hayward's 712th and last first-class match of all. Gloucestershire could raise only ten players, Surrey won by an innings and 36 runs, Hayward taking just a single and taking the last catch (attributed to Hayes on the match scorecard, but subsequently corrected). There were still two matches to play but the programme was abandoned and Surrey, still needing a handful of points to clinch the title, were declared county champions. It would in all likelihood have been Tom Hayward's last season anyway. The Kaiser ensured that it was.

For the twentieth consecutive season, Tom had exceeded a thousand first-class runs. On most occasions it had been far more than that, more than double on ten occasions, including three thousand on two of those.

He had played in 593 matches for his county over twenty-two seasons, a figure at the time approached only by Abel with 514 in twenty-four. Hobbs has since gone top of the list with a record 598 matches between 1905 and 1934 (minus a few years with no county cricket when he took himself off to the Bradford League). With only fourteen Championship matches a season – and maybe fewer in years to come – that pecking order is likely to remain unchallenged. It would now take more than forty years to play enough matches.

Too old for military service, Tom took a coaching appointment at The Leys School in Cambridge during the war and, after that, a similar appointment at the University of Oxford. From the evidence available his approach seems to have been far from conscientious, leisurely in fact. RC Robertson-Glasgow, who was in the Oxford team at the time, commented:

> Tom was our trainer-coach. Good easy man. Tom was not cut out for work. In the nets he bowled off-breaks from 16 or 17 yards. His verbal instructions were limited to three comments: 'How's that?', 'Hit 'em 'ard' and 'Oh, what a shot, sir!' … But he was best of all as a specta-tor, with his face balanced like a luminous walrus over the wall by the dressing room steps.[267]

Robertson-Glasgow also throws light on other post-playing ac-tivities, consistent with his apparent lassitude:

> After his playing days, he returned to his beloved Cambridge, where he was employed as the coach of the university cricket club at Fenner's. Rather bizarrely, for such a gruff, masculine figure, his favourite activity was to give massages to the students. 'He had a weakness for this emol-lient art and regarded it as a more integral part of the day than bowling off-breaks in the nets,' recalled Raymond Robertson-Glasgow.[268]

If this is true it is perhaps best not to go there, but the fact that Leo McKinstry locates the activity in Cambridge, not Oxford, in-troduces an element of doubt. No further evidence has come to light and while the rest of the family remained in Cambridge, Tom was certainly in Oxford. It was there that Robertson-Glasgow was an undergraduate.

Other evidence, however, is that while Tom may have taken it easy physically, he was a harsh critic of those he coached with perhaps the unrealistic expectation that they were all capable of aspiring to and reaching the high standards he had set himself. Philip Trevor, having watched part of a match when Hayward brought his students to his former happy hunting ground, commented:

> When his active career was over he did some coaching. He was coaching Oxford University at the time, and they came up to play Surrey at the Oval. To be quite candid, their early batsmen played rather tamely on a perfect wicket against some distinctly moderate bowling. They scored very slowly and several of them got out. I sat with Tom and watched the performance. One of them was caught in the slips from a poor stroke. Tom was disappointed. He said to me, 'I have been trying for weeks to get them to not peck at that ball. They don't seem to take any notice of me,' or words to that effect. I defended them and said: 'Don't be hard on them, Tom; they have been doing their best to be obedient. This morning I have counted about twenty-five long hops on the off which have not been played at.' You could not bowl Tom Hayward a long hop on the off without being reminded that you had done so. It is desperately hard to teach others what you have taught yourself.[269]

However, while Tom would have been a well-known figure in Cambridge, there was no guarantee that he would enjoy the same recognition on the banks of the Isis. The following anecdote, told in *Wisden Cricket Monthly* by Richard Usborne, a pupil at the Dragon School at the time, might not be accurate in every detail but demonstrates the transient nature of fame and is a sad reflection on post-playing days pathos:

> When we arrived in Summertown at the Summerfield Road bus stop, we scampered for the stairs. A rather fat man with a fair-sized moustache, sitting near the back on top, signalled to me as I was passing him, and gave me a piece of paper on which he had, in pencil, written his name: Tom Hayward. It meant nothing to me, nor to any of the boys

crowding and clattering down the stairs. As we were shepherded on the pavement, I gave the paper to the master. He recognised the signature on it, but scratched his head, wondering how I could have met the great Tom Hayward and got his autograph. I saw him, Tom Hayward, looking down over the rail at us as the bus moved off northwards. I didn't wave to him.

At a time when qualifications were not a requirement for first-class umpiring, except perhaps for some experience of playing the game at a reasonable level (a situation which was to obtain for another eighty years or so), Tom is recorded as umpiring a university trial match and a first-class match against Essex, both in The Parks in 1919 and 1920 respectively.

He was, however, able to use his Oxford and Cambridge connections to arrange a match on Parker's Piece to supersede the ever-popular charity matches played there before the war when he would bring a full-strength Surrey XI to play a local side for a player's benefit or for charity. It was not of course a substitute for or challenge to the traditional Varsity match, a first-class fixture then played at Lord's and dating from 1827, but it nevertheless aroused local interest.

> Considerable interest is being taken in the match between Cambridge and Oxford on Parker's Piece on Tuesday next, for which a special pitch is being prepared. The match will take the place of the County Charity Matches which Tom Hayward used to arrange in the old days and which were always very popular. Tom Hayward has consented to lead the Cambridge side, a decision which will give general satisfaction and, if only the day is fine, will draw a large crowd.[270]

It was also something of a family reunion, with brother Daniel Martin being coach of the Cambridge University side. Meanwhile, both the licensed trade and the sporting equipment side of the business continued to thrive:

> A splendid selection of well-seasoned cricket bats now in stock. All bats personally selected by Tom Hayward, holder of the world's record

*Daniel Martin and Tom
pictured in 1920, when
they were coaching in
the university towns of
Cambridge and Oxford.*

aggregate score of 3,518 runs made in the season of 1906. Slazenger's
Lawn Tennis Racquets and Balls. Marquees of every description kept in
stock for Agricultural and Horticultural shows, Wedding Receptions,
Garden Parties, Camping etc etc. HAYWARD BROS. 91 Regent St.[271]

Now something of an elder statesman, his opinion was sought
and given (though not always heeded) on matters such as the composition of the party to tour Australia:

My team for Australia by Tom Hayward. Selection that should uphold
country's proud record.
    The selection of a representative cricket team for Australia should be
a matter of concern to all lovers of the Mother Country. The war made
many of us realise for the first time what a big part the annual fixtures
between this country and Australia played in both our national and international life. We missed the international struggle with bat and ball
very much indeed, and the popular pastime of choosing an ideal eleven

for the antipodes is at once a testimony to the delight with which we anticipate a return to pre-war cricket conditions and our keen desire to send out the best possible combination worthy to uphold the glorious traditions of cricket history.

I would like to express the hope that the selectors will remember that the war occupied five years. We must not send out men who were great cricketers either with the ball or the bat before the war, and who have not demonstrated equal form since the Armistice. That consideration naturally restricts our choice, for no one can believe that county cricket has yet got back to its zenith. There is a gap between the man of tradition and the young player of promise. It will take two or three years to bridge the gulf, but every true lover of cricket will rejoice, as he looks over the young men at our universities and Public Schools, and the younger players of our county teams, for he will see there abundant promise for the future. In a few years time we will weld together an eleven capable of winning fresh glory for our much-loved pastime.[272]

After Oxford, his final home was 6 Glisson Road, a large, double-fronted, brick, detached house, very convenient for Fenner's and the Prince Regent. Over two generations there had been a major upmarket surge among the Haywards, from a large family in a very small house to two, plus maybe a servant or two, in a very large one. The rest of the family was not far away. Frank was managing the Prince Regent (renumbered from 55 to 91 at some point between the 1901 and 1911 censuses) with his sister Alice acting as his housekeeper.[273] Alice is listed in local directories, suggesting she was involved in the business, and Daniel is listed at Fenner's Ground.[274] Family continued to be extremely important to the Haywards.

They faced heartbreak and tragedy in 1915 when young Tom, Arthur's son and Tom's nephew, died as a result of a motorcycle accident. The local newspaper reported fully on the inquest:

Motor Cycle Fatality. Inquest at Addenbrooke's on Mr Tom Hayward, junior. Verdict of 'Accidental Death'.

An inquest was held by the Borough Coroner on Wednesday morning on the body of Tom Hayward, nephew of the great Surrey cricketer, who died in Addenbrooke's Hospital on Sunday after being picked up unconscious at the bottom of Newton Hill.

Reginald Arthur Hayward, brother of the deceased, stated that he last saw his brother on Sunday afternoon between 2 and 3. He was in his usual state of health. He was partially paralysed, but was not subject to fits. He had ridden a motorcycle for four or five years and was a careful and experienced driver.

Dr JH Owen, surgeon at the hospital said that Thomas Hayward was admitted on Sunday afternoon between 4 and 5 pm. He was unconscious. Witness examined him and found that he was bleeding from the right ear, his head was cut and his hands and his right knee were bruised. Witness made a post-mortem examination and found that the back of his skull was fractured on the right side and some bones were displaced. Death was caused by injuries received from the fall.

Florence Greenwood, laundrymaid, at Newton Hall, said that at 3.45 on Sunday afternoon she was walking up Newton Hill with a friend when a motorcyclist passed her. Shortly after he passed she heard the engine stop. She looked round and saw the rider on the ground near his machine. Her friend went to him and she went to a cottage to get help..

PC Martin said that as a result of a message he went to Newton Hill where he found Hayward being tended by Dr Young. Shortly afterwards Dr Rumsey's car came up and Dr Rumsey offered to take Hayward to Addenbrooke's. Later the witness went back and examined the road. There had been some rain, and the wheel marks were quite plain. About 40 yards from where the accident occurred there was a mark showing where the left rest had scraped. Further on there was a mark where the right rest had scraped the ground, and further on still there was, on one side, a broad mark as though the tyre were being pushed along horizontally and on the other side the mark of where deceased was pulled along. The stains of blood began here.[275]

Among the many floral tributes was one 'In loving memory from Uncle Tom and Aunt Tilly'.

At a happier family occasion in February 1918, Tom, now retired from the game, and able to rest on his laurels, was master of ceremonies at the wedding of his niece, Hilda:

A quiet wedding, which attracted considerable interest took place at St Barnabas Church today, the bridegroom being Mr Stanley A Rose, of the HAC, only child of the late Mr A Rose and Mrs Rose of Markethill, and the bride, Miss Hilda Mary Martin, only child of Mr Dan Hayward, the well-known cricketer and custodian of Fenner's. The ceremony was performed by the Rev JH Grey. The bride was given away by her father, and her uncle Mr Tom Hayward, the old Surrey cricketer acted as Master of Ceremonies. After the service a reception was held at Fenner's.[276]

In later years, Digby Jephson, who in 1900 succeeded Kingsmill Key as Surrey captain, formed a strong trans-class barrier friendship with both Dan and Tom:

During these years he formed a very strong friendship with the Haywards. Daniel Hayward, Tom's brother, the Fenner's groundsman, lived in an adjacent road and became a boon companion, while Tom was frequently at home nearby. Theirs had been a mutually beneficial friendship. Tom's advice had helped Digby's cricket and Digby had helped Tom exploit his great success. Several of Tom's letters, for example, negotiating with Surrey about financial matters, seem written in Digby's polished prose.[277]

Tom and his wife attended Jephson's funeral in 1926. Among the wreaths was one from Surrey and one simply inscribed 'From Mr and Mrs Dan from Fenner's'.[278]

In 1923, Jack Hobbs became the third player to score a hundred first-class centuries, after WG Grace and Tom Hayward. He received a 'purse' of 100 guineas for the achievement. Tom had received no such recognition and felt that should be remedied. After some initial reluctance, the Surrey Committee eventually agreed. The Haywards were now even more comfortably off.

He liked to keep an eye open for the main chance, when a bargain was on offer. When planes dropped vouchers on Parker's Piece enabling those able to retrieve them to purchase 15/6 War Savings Certificates for 10/6, he was there, determined to cash in:

Many scrambles for vouchers occurred on Parker's Piece, where several were dropped. One of the successful was Mr Tom Hayward, the famous cricketer, who, though not as young as he used to be, sprinted fifty yards in record time against another well-known Cambridge gentleman.[279]

Tom was licensee of the Prince Regent until 1919 when he handed it over to his brother Frank, continuing a family connection of half a century's duration. Unfortunately the handover did not go smoothly and there was a bit of bother over the price of beer and the display of prices, but magistrates took the view that contraventions of the law had occurred through negligence, rather than conscious fraud:

> Licensee of 'Prince Regent' fined on two summonses. The Prince Regent figured in three cases at the Borough Police Court on Tuesday afternoon. Jessie Back (26) a barmaid was summoned for selling in the public bar at the Prince Regent half-a-pint of Hudson's India Pale Ale at a price exceeding 4d to wit 7d, contrary to the Beer (Prices and Description) Order 1919. Frank Hayward (36) the Licensee was summoned for aiding and abetting Jessie Back to commit the offence, and further, for not causing to be conspicuously exhibited in the premises a notice stating the price at which such beer was sold.
>
> Mr SJ Miller, on behalf of the defendants, pleaded guilty to all three summonses. Mr Miller addressing the magistrates said that although he had pleaded guilty there were mitigating circumstances. There was no intention of committing an offence. The price of Bass and Worthington was 7d for half a pint and, not knowing the price of Hudson's Pale Ale (note it was 4d), Miss Back charged the same. As to the notice, the landlord took it down when cleaning and through an oversight, did not put it up again.
>
> Thomas Walter Hayward, brother of the defendant, said he was licensee of the house for nine years and before that his father held the licence for 41 years. Witness himself had been born and bred in the house and he loved his dear old home. The licence had been in the family for 50 years. There had never been any complaint while witness held the licence nor in his father's time. His brother had held the licence for five or six weeks.
>
> The magistrates retired. On their return the Chairman said there was no imputation against the character of the house. The bench did not propose to deal severely with the defendants. Mr Hayward would be fined 40s on the first summons against him; on the second – that for failing to exhibit a list of prices – he would be convicted, but not fined. Miss Back would be fined 10s.[280]

Tom's first-class playing career had ended just before the First World War. His life ended just before the Second. In July 1939 he was ill and knew he was dying, but with no regrets. Though married late in life, he had lived just long enough to enjoy a silver wedding anniversary:

> Famous old-timer of Surrey cricket Tom Hayward is lying critically ill at his home in Cambridge. But he is not depressed. 'I've had a grand life,' he said yesterday.
>
> Mrs Hayward who is nursing him told the Daily Mirror how she first met her husband. 'It was as a girl of twenty-one that I first met Tom on the Gloucester ground when Surrey were playing against the county side captained by WG Grace. I did not see him again until we met in London in 1912 and we were married at the beginning of 1914.'[281]

A week later he died. The local press was fulsome in its appreciation of his local, national and international achievements:

> In Cambridge we think of him specially as a member of a famous local cricketing family. Before his time his father and uncle were notable cricketers and in most recent times many of us local cricketers share happy memories of association with him and his brothers. Arthur, a natural batsman if ever there was one, who would assuredly have gone far if he had adopted the game as a profession. Dan (happily still enjoying life) a splendid bowler who did an excellent service for Cambs. County and Frank (the younger brother) who was a stalwart in the old Rodney CC days.
>
> Let us not forget that it was Tom's naturally generous disposition that inspired him to bring the cream of Surrey cricketers to play on Parker's Piece in so many matches in the cause of charity, with such excellent financial results.[282]

He was buried the following Saturday at Cambridge's Mill Road Cemetery, joining previous generations of the family. He had been born in Cambridge and died in Cambridge, in between travelling the hundred miles between there and the capital innumerable times, as well as touring once in South Africa and three times in Australia. In my end is my beginning.

> Funeral of Tom Hayward. Cricket Fraternity Pays Homage.
>
> Representatives of the local cricket fraternity, as well as of the County Club with which he had such a renowned association, were present at the funeral of Mr Tom Hayward at Mill-road cemetery on Saturday. The service was conducted by the Rev P H Potter (Vicar of St Barnabas).
>
> (There was a wreath from Mr and Mrs Jack Hobbs and one from Surrey CCC.)
>
> The Mourners. The immediate mourners were: Mr Dan Hayward (brother), Mr R Hayward (nephew), Mr Tom and Mr Michael Hayward (grand-nephews), Mrs P Hayward, Mrs S A Rose, Miss May Hayward and Miss M Stubbings (nieces). Mrs T Hayward, the widow, was unable to attend owing to indisposition.
>
> Flowers were received from the following: To my darling old boy from his broken-hearted wife; Affectionate remembrance from brother Dan and Maisie; from Reg, Ethel and Mary; Mr and Mrs W W Burrell; Syd, Clem, Ivy and Daisy (brother in law and nieces); Stanley, Hilda and family; Lord Roseberry, Lord's Cricket Ground, in memory of a very great English cricketer; In memory of Tom Hayward from the President and members of the Council of the Cambridgeshire Cricket Association; Stuart Surridge.
>
> Mrs Hayward thanks friends for the kind letters of sympathy received during her sad bereavement and for the flowers.[283]

It was the end of a man whose family had over a century in three generations participated in and contributed to a sea change in the face of professional cricket. One of the legends of the golden age who benefited from Hayward's pioneering approach to cricket was CB Fry:

> The two great professional batsmen of my period were Tom Hayward and John Tyldesley of Lancashire. Tom Hayward was a different type of batsman but a grand one. He was more phlegmatic but peculiarly certain and sound in all his strokes. He did not astonish one by brilliance, but once he got going on a fast wicket one was astonished if he got out. On a wet wicket he changed his game and went in for hitting, which he

did well. But his specialty was to walk in first against the best bowling on a fast wicket and make the bowling look plainly playable. His best strokes were in front of the wicket; he could drive in all directions along the ground with a nice but slightly studied certainty of timing. Tom Hayward was a tallish fellow with a drooping light brown moustache and a long healthy face. He had a habit of keeping his mouth open when he was particularly on the job, which gave him an inconsequent sort of air; but he was not at all inconsequent. A thoroughly reliable and imperturbable hero.[284]

Tom's contemporaries like Fry were unable to compare him with his uncle. An aging William Caffyn had seen both and was able to do so:

Tom Hayward has proved himself a worthy namesake of his famous uncle. Like him, he possesses a fine free style, though little resembling the old Cambridge batsman. The difference in their respective physique is sufficient to account for this. The uncle was slight and delicate, the nephew is big and strong.[285]

Tom's grave at Mill Road Cemetery in Cambridge. He is buried alongside his brother, Frank, and close to his father, Daniel.

As a mark of respect, play was suspended in Surrey's match at Blackheath and in the matches being played on Parker's Piece. The *London Daily News* commented:

> Tom Hayward by 'Fieldsman'. Each generation lives and dies for its own dream. To the modern youth, rapt in his hero worship of Hutton and Hammond, Tom Hayward, who passed away last week, is just a name. Fathers or elder brothers may have been heard talking of how he once used to make runs with almost clockwork regularity for Surrey, or perchance his picture may have been seen when looking through one of those curious old cricket books of Father's in which the players, many of them, wore fierce whiskers and had queer little caps perched on the top of their heads, but to modern youth a name he was and no more.
>
> To those of us who lived and watched cricket on the other side of the war years, however, Tom Hayward meant far more than that, for he was one of the big figures, and it was with sadness that we read that he had gone from us to join the immortal company of great ones who were waiting for him in the pavilion.[286]

Tom's brother and fellow Oxbridge coach, Daniel Martin, retired from the Fenner's job in 1936 at the age of seventy. He was the last survivor of his generation, living on to 1953, surviving Tom by fourteen years, born a Victorian and dying an Elizabethan:

> The death occurred on February 2 in his 88th year, of DM Hayward, for over 25 years groundsman at Fenners. He was an older brother of Tom Hayward, the famous Surrey and England cricketer, and played many times as a medium-paced bowler for Cambridgeshire. Dan Hayward will be remembered with affection by all Cambridge sides from 1908 to 1936.[287]

Like all of us, Tom and Daniel Hayward were products of their heredity and environment. The environment was that of Cambridge, Parker's Piece, its Colleges, groundsmanship and the licensed trade. The heredity, stretching back at least two generations, was cricket and its development as a professional sport. It was in the genes, part of the family DNA.

Tom would scarcely have known his Uncle Thomas, but writers on the game have commented on the similarity of style. Where his uncle does not seem to have influenced him, however, is in the matter of lifestyle and financial profligacy. He seems to have been of sober habits and taken care of himself, enabling him to play professional cricket until his mid-forties. From his father, Tom inherited a sound business acumen and an awareness of the value of money without actually worshipping it, so that thanks also to his inheritance and marrying into an affluent family, he was able to settle into a comfortable retirement in a large house in Cambridge. Thomas Hayward's cricketing skills and Daniel the Younger's common and business sense – both of which were influenced to some extent by their own father, Tom's grandfather – combined to produce in Tom the right kind of balance in the man. Had it been the other way round, cricket's record books would have been quite different.

ACKNOWLEDGEMENTS

Margaret Burgess and Celia Tyler of the Cambridgeshire Collection for their considerable help in locating information on and photographs of the Haywards in Cambridgeshire;

Our friends Roger Campbell and Helen Hodge for the high quality B&B facilities and hospitality extended to us during our research days in Cambridge;

Vicki Clark for reading and commenting on the first draft of the book;

Brian Cowley for the statistics on Tom Hayward's Surrey career;

Bill Gordon for his help in the Surrey Library;

Roger Mann for his prompt and efficient service in providing images;

Mitcham Green Community and Heritage for granting permission to use the image of the Ruff Stone;

Scott Reeves for his advice and editing;

Alec Stewart for kindly contributing the Foreword;

The staff at the Surrey History Centre, Woking;

Peter Wynne-Thomas for providing access to his unpublished index to *The Cricketer*.

NOTES

Part One: Daniel the Elder

1. *The History and Antiquities of the County of Surrey*.
2. Denison, *Sketches of the Players*, p.32.
3. Census of Population 1841.
4. *Scores and Biographies* Vol 1.
5. *Bell's Life*, 17 August 1828.
6. Not all his grandsons played first-class cricket, though all played to a high standard; 'nearly 600' is correct (it was 593) but until the turn of the century, he usually batted at number three before becoming a regular opener, first with Bobby Abel, then Jack Hobbs.
7. *Bell's Life*, 22 June 1834.
8. A more detailed account of the development of cricket in Cambridge and Cambridgeshire can be found in Willie Sugg's publications and on his website.
9. *Bell's Life*, 9 August 1835. Buckley's *Fresh Light on Pre-Victorian Cricket* gives a more detailed version of the match. West had 105, Hayward 112.
10. *Cambridge Independent Press*, 26 June 1841.
11. *Cambridge Independent Press*, 17 June 1848.
12. *Scores and Biographies* Vol 2.
13. *Cambridge Chronicle and Journal and Huntingdonshire Gazette*, 29 August 1846.
14. *Cambridge Chronicle and Journal*, 26 August 1848.
15. *Cambridge Independent Press*, 8 September 1849.
16. The current Chatteris club, established later in the century, plays at a different venue and has hosted a number of Minor Counties fixtures.
17. *Brighton Gazette*, 14 July 1836.
18. *Bell's Life*, 17 July 1836.
19. Surrey was not established as a county club until 1845, so this does not qualify as the lowest total against them. That came in 1872 by the same opponents and remains the lowest.
20. *Cambridge Independent Press*, 21 August 1847.
21. *Cambridge Chronicle* via Cricket Archive.

22. *Cambridge Independent Press*, 15 July 1848.
23. *Bell's Life*, 27 May 1832.
24. *Bell's Life*, 24 June 1832.
25. *Essex Standard*, 14 July 1832.
26. *Huntingdon, Bedford and Peterborough Gazette*, 8 August 1832.
27. *Scores and Biographies* Vol 3.
28. *Cambridge Independent Press*, 1 September 1849.
29. *The Players*, p.26.
30. Major, *More Than a Game.*
31. *Cambridge Chronicle and Huntingdonshire Gazette*, 15 December 1838.
32. *Cambridge Chronicle and Journal*, 21 November 1846.
33. Sugg, pp.35-37.
34. *Cambridge Independent Press*, 6 November 1847.
35. Sugg pp.44-56, Coda to Town and County Club AGM Report 1848.
36 Sugg, p 52.
37. *Cambridge Chronicle and Journal*, 5 June 1852.

Part Two: Daniel the Younger and Thomas

1. Martin-Jenkins, *Wisden Book of County Cricket*, p.436.
2. *Cambridge Chronicle*, 7 August 1852.
3. *Cambridge Independent Press*, 16 July 1853.
4. *Cambridge Chronicle and Journal*, 2 September 1854.
5. *Cambridge Independent Press*, 23 September 1854.
6. *Cambridge Chronicle and Journal*, 22 May 1852.
7. *Cambridge Chronicle and Journal*, 7 May 1853.
8. *Cambridge Independent Press*, 27 May 1854.
9. *Morning Post*, 4 July 1854.
10. *Morning Post*, 26 June 1854.
11. *Who's Who of Cricketers.*
12. *Yorkshire Gazette*, 28 May 1853.
13. *Cambridge Independent Press*, 17 February 1855.
14. *Scores and Biographies* Vol 5, p.146.
15. Register of births, April to June 1855.
16. *Bell's Life*, 18 May 1856. This may have been Dan, the scorecard gives no initials.
17. *Cambridge Independent Press*, 6 September 1856.
17. *Cambridge Independent Press*, 27 September 1856.
18. *Durham County Advertiser*, 25 September 1857.
20. *The Era*, 9 August 1957.
21. *Cambridge Independent Press*, 13 August 1859.
22. Wild, *The Biography of Colonel His Highness Shri Sir Ranjitsinhji Vibhaji.*
23. Caffyn, *Seventy-One Not Out*, pp.117-8.
24. 'Interview with Rev RS Holmes', *Cricket*, 25 April 1895.

25. Altham, *A History of Cricket.*
26. *Nottinghamshire Guardian*, 17 June 1858.
27. *Durham County Advertiser*, 6 August 1858.
28. *Durham Chronicle*, 30 July 1858.
29. *Durham Chronicle*, 1 October 1858.
30. *Scores & Biographies* Vol 6, p.179.
31. Caffyn, *Seventy-One Not Out*, p.141.
32. Caffyn, *Seventy-One Not Out*, p.143.
33. *New York Herald*, 23 September 1859.
34. *New York Herald*, 25 September 1859.
35. Caffyn, *Seventy-One Not Out*, p.144-5.
36. Caffyn, *Seventy-One Not Out*, p.145.
37. *New York Herald*, 11 October 1859.
38. Caffyn, *Seventy-One Not Out*, pp.145-6
39. *New York Herald*, 20 October and other dates.
40. Caffyn, *Seventy-One Not Out*, p.147
41. *Philadelphia Press* and *New York Herald*. Note that Fred Lillywhite, the *New York Times* and Cricket Archive attribute the innings to Jackson. Scott Reeves in *The Champion Band* prefers Hayward as the scorer (p.167).
42. Note on Cricket Archive scorecard, based on information in *New York Times*.
43. Caffyn, *Seventy-One Not Out*, p.149-50.
44. Caffyn, *Seventy-One Not Out*, p.150.
45. *New York Herald*, 23 October 1859.
46. *New York Herald*, 21 October 1859.
47. *New York Herald*, 16 October 1859.
48. *Daily Exchange*, 8 October 1859.
49. Caffyn, *Seventy-One Not Out*, p.186.
50. *Cambridge Independent Press*, 19 November 1859.
51. Ford, *A History of the Cambridge University Cricket Club 1820-1901*, p.241.
52. Daft, *A Cricketer's Yarns*, p.183.
53. *Cricket*, 21 April 1887.
54. *The Era*, 12 August 1860.
55. *Bell's Life*, 14 April 1861.
56. *Irish Times*, 24 May 1861.
57. Caffyn, *Seventy-One Not Out*, p.164.
58. There may have been an earlier instance in 1780.
59. *Illustrated London News*, 6 July 1861.
60. *Cambridge Independent Press*, 8 June 1861.
61. *Sporting Life*, 11 June 1862.
62. *Illustrated Sporting News*, 21 June 1862.
63. *Evening Standard*, 28 June 1862.
64. Caffyn, *Seventy-One Not Out*, p.189.
65. Sissons, *The Players*, p.62.
66. *Sheffield Independent*, 2 March 1863.

67. *Sporting Life*, 22 August 1863.

68. *London Evening Standard*, 16 October 1863.

69. *Sporting Life*, 18 November 1863. Averages at this time were expressed as an integer and a remainder which preceded the practice of using decimal fractions.

70. *The Era*, 12 August 1860.

71. *Sporting Life*, 16 April 1861 & *Bell's Life*, 14 April 1861.

72. Cricket Archive agrees the 44 overs but has eight for 34.

73. *Leeds Times*, 1 June 1861.

74. *Birmingham Daily Post*, 19 June 1861.

75. *Cambridge Independent Press*, 5 October 1861.

76. *Sporting Life*, 7 February 1863.

77. *Bell's Life*, 17 May 1863.

78. Ford, *A History of the Cambridge University Cricket Club 1820-1901*.

79. *Cambridge Chronicle*, 7 September 1872.

80. *The Era*, 24 July 1864.

81. *Cambridge Chronicle and Journal*, 8 June 1867.

82. Altham, *A History of Cricket*.

83. *Manchester Courier and Lancashire Advertiser*, 10 October 1863.

84. Caffyn, *Seventy-One Not Out*, pp. 199-200.

85. *The Argus*, 24 December 1863.

86. *Bendigo Advertiser*, 25 December 1863.

87. Caffyn, *Seventy-One Not Out*, p 201.

88. *Bell's Life in Australia and Sporting Chronicle*, 9 January 1864. Cricket Archive has the third wicket partnership from 16 to 141.

89. Caffyn, *Seventy-One Not Out*, p.202.

90. *The Age*, 11 January 1864.

91. Caffyn, *Seventy-One Not Out*, p.203.

92. *Bell's Life*, 16 January 1864.

93. *Bell's Life in Victoria and Sporting Chronicle*, 23 January 1864.

94. *Taranaki Herald* 16 January 1864.

95. Caffyn, *Seventy-One Not Out*, p.207.

96. Caffyn, *Seventy-One Not Out*, p.209.

97. *Bell's Life in Sydney and Sporting Chronicle*, 13 February 1864.

98. Caffyn, *Seventy-One Not Out*, p.209.

99. *Otago Daily Witness*, 2 February 1864.

100. *Hawke's Bay Herald*, 3 February 1864.

101. *Otago Witness*, 6 February 1864.

102. *Otago Daily Times*, 5 February 1864.

103. *Lyttelton Times*, 6 February 1864.

104. *Otago Witness*, 6 February 1864.

105. *Bell's Life*, 13 February 1864.

106. *Otago Witness*, 30 January 1864.

107. *Nelson Examiner and New Zealand Chronicle*, 13 February 1864.

108. *Daily Southern Cross*, 13 February 1864.

109. *Otago Daily Times*, 19 February 1864.
110. *Otago Daily Times*, 20 February 1864.
111. Caffyn, *Seventy-One Not Out*, p.210.
112. *Bell's Life*, 1 March 1864.
113. Caffyn, *Seventy-One Not Out,* pp.210-211.
114. *The Argus*, 7 March 1864.
115. Caffyn, *Seventy-One Not Out*, p.210.
116. Caffyn, *Seventy-One Not Out*, pp.215-7.
117. *Southern Cross*, 5 March 1864.
118. *Southern Cross*, 25 April 1864.
119. *Wisden 1865*, p.154.
120. *Cambridge Independent Press*, 23 April 1864.
121. *Huddersfield Chronicle*, 25 June 1864.
122. *Cambridge Independent Press*, 20 August 1857.
123. *Cambridge Independent Press*, 19 March 1864.
124. *Sporting Life*, 14 December 1867.
125. *Cambridge Chronicle and University Journal*, 14 August 1869.
126. Census of Population 1861 and marriage certificate.
127. Census of Population 1871, 1881, 1891 & 1901.
128. *Bury and Norwich Post and Suffolk Herald*, 28 February 1871.
129. *Cambridge Independent Press*, 5 October 1878.
130. *Cambridge Daily News*, 18 April 1889.
131. *Cambridge Independent Press*, 16 February 1884.
132. *Cambridge Independent Press*, 11 January 1895.
133. *Cambridge Chronicle*, 2 July 1864.
134. *Morning Advertiser*, 20 July 1864.
135. *Sporting Life*, 24 December 1864.
136. *Sporting Life*, 20 September 1865.
137. *The Sportsman*, 29 August 1865.
138. *The Sportsman*, 12 September 1865.
139. *Nottingham Guardian*, 30 July 1865.
140. *Sporting Life*, 9 August 1865.
141. *Brighton Gazette*, 18 January 1866.
142. *Cambridgeshire Chronicle and Journal*, 12 May 1866.
143. *Pall Mall Gazette*, 18 August 1866.
144. *Cambridge Chronicle and Journal*, 8 June 1867.
145. *The Sportsman*, 11 June 1867.
146. *Cambridge Independent Press*, 25 April 1868.
147. Sissons, *The Players*, p.60.
148. *Sheffield Daily Telegraph*, 11 May 1870.
149. *Kentish Gazette*, 26 April 1870.
150. *The Globe*, 18 July 1870.
151. *The Sportsman*, 9 July 1870.
152. *Sporting Life*, 10 July 1870.

153. *Daily News*, 26 June 1871.

154. *Bolton Chronicle*, 29 July 1871.

155. *Cambridge Chronicle*, 2 September 1871. Not unusually for the period, the bowling figures and total runs in the innings do not coincide. Furthermore, the Cricket Archive record suggests that eight, not seven, bowlers were used.

156. *Surrey Comet*, 13 August 1864.

157. *Cambridge Independent Press*, 1 October 1864.

158. *Sheffield and Rotherham Independent*, 30 September 1865.

159. 'Talks with Old English Cricketers'. The match was played at Chickenley but Cricket Archive gives the opposing team as Earlsheaton.

160. Letter to *Sporting Times*, 25 March 1865.

161. *Sheffield Independent*, 13 July 1870. Dinner, in Sheffield and much of the north of England, would be lunch elsewhere.

162. Daft, *A Cricketer's Yarns*, p.5.

163. *Sheffield Daily Telegraph*, 18 July 1874.

164. *Illustrated London News*, 3 August 1861.

165. Caffyn, *Seventy-One Not Out*, p.157. Caffyn has reversed the venues. The first match Three v Two was played at Sheffield, the return at Stockton. Furthermore *Sporting Life*, probably a more reliable source than the *Illustrated London News* in sporting matters, reports the stake in the initial match as £400.

166. *Nottinghamshire Guardian*, 26 September 1861.

167. *Sporting Life*, 2 October 1861.

168. *Cambridge Independent Press*, 5 October 1861.

169. *Sporting Life*, 1 October 1862.

170. *Cambridge Chronicle*, 19 October 1861.

171. Daft, *A Cricketer's Yarns*.

172. *Bell's Life in Victoria and Sporting Chronicle*, 30 April 1864.

173. *Cambridge Chronicle*, 26 January 1867.

174. *Norwich Mercury*, 19 February 1870.

175. *Cambridge Independent Press*, 19 February 1870.

176. Ford, *A History of the Cambridge University Cricket Club 1820-1901*.

177. *Cricket*, 18 July 1895.

178. *Cambridge Chronicle*, 24 September 1870.

179. *Norwich Mercury*, 30 November 1872.

180. Bob Carpenter's brother, so maybe a bit of insider dealing going on.

181. *Cambridge Independent Press*, 25 December 1875.

182. *Tamworth Herald*, 29 July 1876.

183. *Cambridge Independent Press*, 29 July 1876. There is a mismatch between the press report and the Mill Road Cemetery website which says that Thomas (and indeed his father) are not buried there.

184. The move to Clarendon Street at the north-east corner of Parker's Piece was a recent one. At the time of the 1871 Census, the family was in still in Burleigh Street.

185. *London Gazette*, 30 January 1877.

186. *Bury Free Press*, 9 June 1877.

187. *Cambridge Independent Press*, 16 June 1877.
188. *Leeds Times*, 5 August 1876.
189. Incorrect. Thomas was his younger brother. He had died in 1876.
190. *Cambridge Independent Press*, 3 June 1910.
191. *Sevenoaks Chronicle and Kentish Advertiser*, 12 August 1910.
192. Altham, *A History of Cricket*.

Part Three: Tom

1. *Cricket*, 10 May 1882.
2. *Cambridge Independent Press*, 31 May 1890.
3. *Cambridge Independent Press*, 5 July 1890.
4. *Cambridge Independent Press*, 19 July 1890.
5. *Cambridge Independent Press*, 30 August 1895.
6. *The Cricketer*, 26 January 1905.
7. Wilde, *Ranji: The Strange Genius of Ranjitsinhji*.
8. Morrah, *The Golden Age of Cricket*.
9. *Cricket*, 25 February 1897.
10. *Gloucestershire Echo*, 20 February 1908.
11. *Cambridge Independent Press*, 4 July 1902.
12. *Cambridge Independent Press*, 20 September 1901.
13. *Cambridge Independent Press*, 6 September 1901.
14. *Cambridge Independent Press*, 20 March 1903.
15. *Cambridge Independent Press*, 25 August 1905.
16. *Cambridge Independent Press*, 19 July 1890.
17. *Cambridge Independent Press*, 3 October 1902.
17. *Cambridge Independent Press*, 18 July 1891.
19. *Cambridge Independent Press*, 22 November 1888.
20. *Cricket*, 19 September 1889.
21. *Cricket*, 9 July 1891.
22. *Cricket*, 16 & 23 July & 3 September 1891.
23. *Cambridge Independent Press*, 9 May 1891.
24. *Cricket*, 30 June & 1 September 1892.
25. *Cambridge Independent Press*, 27 May 1892.
26. 'Annual Report', *Surrey CCC Yearbook 1893*, p.132.
27. *Cricket*, 20 April 1893.
28. *Cricket*, 23 February 1893.
29. *Cricket*, 18 May 1893.
30. *Wisden 1894*, p.85.
31. *Cricket*, 23 May 1893.
32. *Cricket*, 3 August 1893.
33. *Cricket*, 10 August 1893.
34. *Cricket*, 31 August 1893.
35. *Wisden 1894*, p.96.

36. *Wisden 1894*, p.91.
37. *Wisden 1895*, p.5.
38. *Wisden 1895*, p.20 (it was actually his third first-class century).
39. *Cambridge Independent Press*, 3 August 1894.
40. *Cricket*, 23 May 1895.
41. *Cricket*, 30 May 1895.
42. *Cricket*, 30 May 1895.
43. *Cricket*, 13 June 1895.
44. *Wisden 1896*, p.14.
45. *Cricket*, 20 June 1895.
46. *Cricket*, 20 June 1895.
47. *Cricket*, 4 July 1895.
48. *Cricket*, 12 September 1895.
49. *Cricket*, 12 September 1895 & *Wisden* 1896, p.5.
50. *St James's Gazette*, 3 August 1895.
51. *Cricket*, 28 November 1895.
52. *Cricket*, 30 January 1896.
53. Wallace, *A Short Autobiography*, pp.90-91.
54. Allen, *Empire, War and Cricket in South Africa*, pp.183-184.
55. Haigh, *Stroke of Genius*, p.8.
56. More details of the causes, negotiations and resolution of the strike including opinions of the media and the public can be found in Booth, *The Father of Modern Sport*.
57. *Sheffield Daily Telegraph*, 11 August 1896.
58. 'Annual Report', *Surrey CCC Yearbook 1897*.
59. *Wisden 1897*, p.59.
60. *Wisden 1898*, p.25.
61. *Wisden 1898*, p.288.
62. *Cricket*, 10 June 1897.
63. *Wisden 1898*, p.209.
64. *Cricket*, 17 June 1897.
65. *Cricket*, 24 June 1897.
66. *London Daily News*, 23 August 1897.
67. *Cricket*, 15 July 1897.
68. *Sheffield Independent*, 14 July 1897.
69. *The Cricketer*, issue 9, 1921.
70. *Cricket*, 19 August 1897.
71. *Cricket*, 8 July 1897.
72. *Cricket*, 6 May 1897.
73. *Wisden 1898*, p.31.
74. *Cricket*, 6 May 1897.
75. *Cricket*, 13 May 1897.
76. *Cricket*, 19 August 1897.
77. *Wisden 1898*, p.23.

78. *Cricket*, 9 September 1897.
79. *Wisden 1899*, p.382-3.
80. *Express and Telegraph* (Adelaide), 26 October 1897.
81. *Evening News* (Sydney), 28 October 1897.
82. *Evening News* (Sydney), 11 November 1897.
83. *Express and Telegraph*, 27 November 1897.
84. *Queensland Register*, 1 December 1897.
85. *Toowoomba Chronicle*, 2 December 1897.
86. *Australian Star*, 14 December 1897.
87. *The Age*, 3 March 1898.
88. *Wisden 1899*, p.60.
89. *Wisden 1899*, p.62.
90. *Wisden 1899*, p.76.
91. *Sheffield Independent*, 27 July 1898.
92. Surrey CCC minutes, 1 September 1898.
93. *St James's Gazette*, 1 June 1898.
94. *Sheffield Independent*, 27 July 1898.
95. *Cambridge Daily News*, 3 February 1899.
96. *Cricket*, 11 May 1899.
97. *Lancashire Evening Post*, 2 June 1899.
98. *Cricket*, 8 June 1899.
99. *Cambridge Daily News*, 5 June 1899.
100. *Wisden 1900*, p.279.
101. *Wisden 1900*, p.283.
102. *Cricket*, 6 July 1899.
103. *Wisden 1900*, p.289.
104. *Cricket*, 20 July 1899.
105. *Sheffield Evening Telegraph*, 14 August 1899.
106. *Wisden 1900*, p.298.
107. *Aberdeen Press and Journal*, 15 August 1899.
108. *Cambridge Daily News*, 15 August 1899.
109. *Cricket*, 6 July 1899.
110. *Wisden 1900*, p.374.
111. *Cambridge Daily News*, 8 July 1899.
112. Kevin Pietersen came within two in 2015.
113. Alec Stewart's 271 not out in 1997 has been the closest to it.
114. *Wisden 1900*, p.19. The Yorkshire scorebook records the fall of the third wicket as 59, not 58, in which case the partnership was 447, not 448. Cricket Archive has 448 and a footnote, *Wisden* 448, Yorkshire CCC Yearbooks 447.
115. *Cricket*, 17 August 1899.
116. *Wisden 1900*, p 224.
117. *Wisden 1900*, p 370.
118. *Cricket*, 6 July 1899.
119. *Cricket*, 6 July 1899.

120. *Cricket*, 3 August 1899.
121. *Cricket*, 24 August 1899.
122. *Daily Express*, 12 April 1919.
123. *Cricket*, 27 July 1899.
124. *Cricket*, 7 September 1899.
125. *St James Gazette*, 14 March 1900.
126. *Gloucester Echo*, 4 April 1900.
127. *Cambridge Independent Press*, 1 June 1900.
128. *Bexhill-on-Sea Observer*, 6 October 1900.
129. *Cricket*, 23 May 1901.
130. *Cricket*, 13 June 1901.
131. *Cricket*, 28 July 1901.
132. *Cricket*, 13 June 1901.
133. *Cricket*, 31 October 1901.
134. *Cambridge Independent Press*, 27 September 1901.
135. Surrey CCC minutes, 6 June 1901.
136. *Australian Star*, 19 August 1901.
137. *West Australian Sunday Times*, 6 October 1901.
138. *Western Mail*, 9 November 1901.
139. *Wisden 1903*, p.495.
140. *The Leader* (Melbourne), 21 December 1901.
141. *The Arrow* (Sydney), 18 January 1902.
142. *The Examiner* (Launceston), 4 February 1902.
143. *Cambridge Independent Press*, 21 February 1902.
144. *The Australasian*, 22 March 1902.
145. *Cambridge Independent Press*, 25 April 1902.
146. *Wisden 1903*, p.61.
147. Surrey CCC minutes, 15 August 1901 & 20 March 1902.
148. *Dundee Courier*, 1 August 1902.
149. *Lancashire Daily Post*, 2 August 1902.
150. Surrey CCC minutes, 16 October 1902.
151. *Cambridge Daily News*, 17 September 1902.
152. *Portsmouth Evening News*, 7 October 1902.
153. *Cambridge Independent Press*, 10 October 1902.
154. *Cambridge Independent Press*, 13 March 1903.
155. *Cricket*, 29 January 1903.
156. *Cricket*, 16 April 1903.
157. *Wisden 1904*, p.172.
158. *Cricket*, 17 September 1903.
159. Sissons, *The Players*, p.98.
160. Surrey CCC minutes, 3 September 1903.
161. *Cambridge Independent Press*, 25 September 1903.
162. *Wisden 1905*, p.477.
163. *Daily Express*, 12 April 1919.

164. *Wisden 1905*, p.479.
165. *Cricket*, 26 November 1903
166. *The Register* (Adelaide), 10 November 1903.
167. *The Critic*, 14 November 1903.
168. *Cricket*, 31 December 1903.
169. *Cricket*, 31 December 1903.
170. Warner, *My Cricketing Life*, pp.134 & 137.
171. *Lancashire Evening Post*, 27 April 1904.
172. *Cambridge Independent Press*, 29 April 1904.
173. *Portsmouth Evening News*, 21 May 1904.
174. *Wisden 1905*, pp.175/6.
175. *Yorkshire Evening Post*, 8 March 1905.
176. *Sydney Mail and New South Wales Advertiser*, 29 May 1905.
177. *Wellington Times* (New South Wales), 6 April 2005.
178. *Cricket*, 27 April 1905.
179. *Cricket*, 25 May 1905.
180. *Cricket*, 1 June 1905.
181. *Cricket*, 1 June 1905.
182. *Cricket*, 22 June 1905.
183. *Cricket*, 29 June 1905.
184. *Cambridge Independent Press*, 7 July 1905.
185. *Cricket*, 6 July 1905.
186. *Cricket*, 13 July 1905.
187. *Cricket*, 27 July 1905.
188. *Cricket*, 3 August 1905.
189. *Cricket*, 17 August 1905.
190. *Cricket*, 7 September 1905.
191. *Cricket*, 21 September 1905.
192. *Cambridge Independent Press*, 20 January 1905.
193. 'Obituary', *Wisden 1964*.
194. McKinstry, *Jack Hobbs*, p.36.
195. McKinstry, *Jack Hobbs*, p.36.
196. McKinstry, *Jack Hobbs*, p.42.
197. McKinstry, *Jack Hobbs*, p.64.
198. McKinstry, *Jack Hobbs*, p.67.
199. *Portsmouth Evening News*, 27 September 1906.
200. *Lancashire Daily Post*, 14 May 1906.
201. *Lancashire Evening Post*, 18 May 1906.
202. Hobbs was to score four consecutive hundreds on two occasions in 1920 and 1925, but neither were in the same week. Ian Ward had four consecutive in 2002. In 2017, Kumar Sangakkara went one better with five, missing out on a world-record equalling sixth by just 16 runs.
203. *Wisden 1907*, p.47.
204. *Surrey CCC Yearbook*, 1907.

205. Laughton, *Captain of the Crowd*, p.251-2.
206. Burns, *A Flick of the Fingers*, p.76.
207. *London Daily News*, 12 September 1906.
208. *London Daily News*, 21 September 1906.
209. *Cambridge Independent Press*, 28 September 1906.
210. *Portsmouth Evening News*, 30 May 1907.
211. *Leeds Mercury*, 27 August 1907.
212. *Cricket*, 9 May 1907.
213. *Cricket*, 16 May 1907.
214. *Cricket*, 16 May 1907.
215. *Cricket*, 6 June 1907.
216. Meredith, *The Demon and the Lobster*, p.169.
217. *Cricket*, 6 June 1907.
218. *Cricket*, 6 June 1907.
219. *Cricket*, 20 June 1907.
220. *Cricket*, 20 June 1907.
221. *Cricket*, 27 June 1907.
222. *Cricket*, 11 July 1907.
223. *Cricket*, 18 July 1907.
224. *Cricket*, 25 July 1907.
225. *Cricket*, 15 August 1907.
226. *Cricket*, 29 August 1907.
227. *Cricket*, 12 September 1907.
228. *Cricket*, 5 September 1907.
229. *Cambridge Independent Press*, 4 October 1907.
230. *Cambridge Independent Press*, 29 October 1907.
231. *Nottingham Evening Post*, 5 September 1907.
232. Fuller details of the rift between Crawford and the Surrey committee can be found in Booth, *Rebel with a Cause*.
233. Jack Crawford's letter to Lord Alverstone of 17 July 1909.
234. 'Annual report', *Surrey CCC Yearbook 1910*.
235. *Cricket*, 15 April 1909.
236. *Cricket*, 13 May 1909.
237. *Cricket*, 20 May 1909.
238. *Cricket*, 3 June 1909.
239. *Cricket*, 3 June 1909.
240. *Cricket*, 29 July 1909
241. McKinstry, *Jack Hobbs*, p.62.
242. Morrah, *The Golden Age of Cricket*, p.233.
243. *Surrey CCC Yearbook*, 1912.
244. *Wisden 1912*, p.80.
245. *Cricket*, 13 May 1911.
246. *Cricket*, 20 May 1911.
247. *Cricket*, 20 May 1911.

248. *Cricket*, 3 June 1911.
249. *Cricket*, 10 June 1911.
250. *Cricket*, 17 June 1911.
251. *Cricket*, 15 July 1911.
252. *Cricket*, 29 July 1911.
253. *Cricket*, 5 August 1911.
254. *Cricket*, 5 August 1911.
255. *Cricket*, 26 August 1911.
256. *Wisden 1914*, p.49.
257. *Surrey CCC Yearbook 1914*.
258. Almost certainly correct. Tom himself was run out later in the same innings.
259. *Cricket*, 5 July 1913.
260. *Cricket*, 13 August 1913.
261. *Wisden 1914*, p.49.
262. *Sheffield Independent*, 21 January 1914.
263. *Daily Mirror*, 21 January 1914.
264. *Sheffield Evening Telegraph*, 29 September 1910.
265. *The Sun* (Kalgoorlie), 8 March 1914.
266. *Wisden 1915*, p.5.
267. Robertson-Glasgow, *Forty-Six Not Out*.
268. McKinstry, *Jack Hobbs*, p.36.
269. Trevor, *Cricket and Cricketers*.
270. *Cambridge Daily News*, 29 August 1919.
271. Advertisement in *Cambridge Daily News*, 29 April 1920.
272. *Sunday Post*, 11 July 1920.
273. It is still there, still numbered 91, still a busy city centre pub. It was, however, recently destroyed by fire and none of the original remains.
274. *Spalding's* in the 1920s.
275. *Cambridge Independent Press*, 30 July 1915.
276. *Cambridge Daily News*, 14 February 1918.
277. Meredith, *The Demon and the Lobster*, p.168.
278. Meredith, *The Demon and the Lobster*, p.175.
279. *Cambridge Daily News*, 9 March 1918.
280. *Cambridge Independent Press*, 5 December 1919.
281. *Daily Mirror*, 12 July 1939.
282. *Cambridge Daily News*, 20 July 1939.
283. *Cambridge Independent Press*, 28 July 1939.
284. Fry, *Life Worth Living*, p.225.
285. Caffyn, *Seventy-One Not Out*, p.243.
286. *London Daily News*, 29 July 1939.
287. *Cricketer Spring Annual 1953*.

BIBLIOGRAPHY

Books

Allen, Dean, *Empire, War and Cricket in South Africa: Logan of Matjiesfontein* (Zebra Press, 2015)

Altham, HS, *A History of Cricket* (George Allen and Unwin, 1926)

Alverstone, Lord & Alcock CW, *Surrey Cricket Its History and Associations* (Longmans Green and Co, 1902)

Amey, Geoff, *Julius Caesar: The Ill-Fated Cricketer and the Players of His Time* (Bodyline Books, 2000)

Bailey, Philip, Thorne, Philip & Wynne-Thomas, Peter [eds.], *Who's Who of Cricketers* (Guild Publishing, 1984)

Birley, Derek, *A Social History of English Cricket* (Aurum Press, 1999)

Booth, Keith, *His Own Enemy: The Rise and Fall of Edward Pooley* (Belmont Books, 2000)

–, *The Father of Modern Sport: The Life and Times of Charles W Alcock* (Parrs Wood Press, 2002)

–, *George Lohmann: Pioneer Professional* (Sportsbooks, 2007)

–, *Ernest Hayes: Brass in the Golden Age* (ACS, 2008)

–, *Walter Read: A Class Act* (ACS, 2011)

–, *Tom Richardson: A Bowler Pure and Simple* (ACS, 2012)

–, *Rebel with a Cause: The Life and Times of Jack Crawford* (Chequered Flag Publishing, 2016)

Buckley, GB, *Fresh Light on Pre-Victorian Cricket* (Cotterell, 1937)

Burns, Michael, *A Flick of the Fingers: The Chequered Life and Career of Jack Crawford* (Pitch, 2015)

Chatteris Town Guide (Rotary International, 2009)

Callaghan, Helen, *Cambridge University in Old Photographs* (Sutton Publishing, 1998)

Caffyn, William, *Seventy-One Not Out: The Reminiscences of William Caffyn* (Blackwood and Sons, 1899)

Cowley, Brian (ed.), *Surrey County Cricket Club First Class Records 1846-2000* (Surrey County Cricket Club, 2001)

Daft, Richard, *A Cricketer's Yarns* (Chapman & Hall, 1926)

Denison, William, *Sketches of the Players* (William Stevens, 1846)

Ford, WJ, *A History of the Cambridge University Cricket Club 1820-1901* (William Blackwood, 1902)

Frindall, Bill (ed.), *The Wisden Book of Test Cricket 1876-77 to 1977-78* (Macdonald and Jane's, 1978)

Fry, CB, *Life Worth Living* (Eyre and Spottiswood, 1939)

Gault, Adrian, Gault, Julia & Green, Ewan, *Outstanding: Lives of the Sixteen Mitcham Commemorated on the Ruff Memorial Stone* (Mitcham Cricket Club, 2013)

Goodger, Rita & Spooner, Andrew, *The Archive Photograph Series: Chatteris* (Tempus, 1997)

Haigh, Gideon, *Stroke of Genius: Victor Trumper and the Shot that Changed Cricket* (Simon and Schuster, 2016)

Hayward, Tom, *Cricket Guide and How to Play Cricket* (British Sports Publishing Co, 1907)

Higgs, Tom, *300 Years of Mitcham Cricket* (The Club, Mitcham Surrey 1985)

Jenkinson, Neil, *Richard Daft: On a Pedestal* (ACS, 2008)

Laughton, Tony, *Captain of the Crowd: Albert Craig, Cricket and Football Rhymester 1849-1909* (Boundary Books, 2008)

Lillywhite, Fred, *The English Cricketers' Trip to Canada and the United States 1859* (Lillywhite, 1860)

–, *Guide to Cricketers* (Lillywhite, 1848-66)

Lodge, Jerry, *Jack Hobbs: His Record Innings-by-Innings* ((ACS, 2001)

–, *100 Surrey Greats* (Tempus Publishing, 2003)

Low, Robert, *W.G.* (Richard Cohen Books, 1997)

Manning, Rev Owen & Bray, William, *The History and Antiquities of the County of Surrey* Vol 2 (1809)

Major, John, *More than a Game: The Story of Cricket's Early Years* (Harper Press, 2007)

McKinstry, Leo, *Jack Hobbs: England's Greatest Cricketer* (Yellow Jersey Press, 2011)

Martin-Jenkins, Christopher, *Wisden Book of County Cricket* (Queen Anne Press, 1981)

Meredith, Anthony, *The Demon and the Lobster: Charles Kortright and Digby Jephson* (Kingswood Press, 1987)

Morrah, Patrick, *The Golden Age of Cricket* (Eyre & Spottiswoode, 1967)

Percival, Tony, *Cambridgeshire Cricketers 1819-2006* (ACS 2007)

Plumptre, George, *The Golden Age of Cricket* (Queen Anne Press, 1990)

Reeve FA, *Victorian and Edwardian Cambridgeshire from Old Photographs* (BT Batsford, 1976)

Reeves, Scott, *The Champion Band: The First English Cricket Tour* (Chequered Flag Publishing, 2014)

Robertson-Glasgow, RC, *Forty-Six Not Out* (Hollis & Carter, 1948)

Scores and Biographies Vols 1-14 (Lillywhites then MCC, 1862-1895)

Sheen, Steven & Bartlett, Kit, *Tom Hayward* (ACS, 1997)

Sissons, Ric, *The Players: A Social History of the Professional Cricketer* (Kingswood Press, 1988)

Spalding's Directory of Cambridge 1920s

Sugg, Willie, *A Tradition Unshared: A History of Cambridge Town and County Cricket, Part One 1700-1890* (Real Work Publishing, 2002)

Sugg, Willie, *Fenner's Men: A History of Cambridge Town and County Cricket, Part Three 1822-1848* (Real Work Publishing, 2009)

Surrey County Cricket Club Yearbooks

Trevor, Col Philip, *Cricket and Cricketers* (Chapman and Hall, 1921)

Victoria County History for Surrey

Wallace, Edgar, *A Short Autobiography* (Hodder and Stoughton, 1929)

Warner, Pelham, *My Cricketing Life* (Hodder and Stoughton, 1921)

Wild, Roland, *The Biography of Colonel His Highness Shri Sir Ranjitsinhji Vibhaji* (Rich & Cowan/Griffin Press, 1934)

Wilde, Simon, *Ranji: The Strange Genius of Ranjitshinji* (Aurum Press, 1999)

Wisden Cricketers' Almanack

Yorkshire County Cricket Club Yearbooks

Articles

Cowley, Brian, 'Bobby Abel "steals" four runs from Tom Hayward', *Cricket Statistician* (Winter 2000)

Sugg, Willie, 'Preparing the wicket: my first researches into Cambridge Cricket', *Cricket Statistician* (Winter 2002)

–, 'Parker's Piece and the New Ground', *Cricket Statistician* (Summer 2004)

Newspapers

Aberdeen Press and Journal, Australian Star, The Age, The Argus, The Arrow (Sydney), *Bell's Life in Australia and Sporting Chronicle, Bell's Life in London and Sporting Chronicle, Bell's Life in Sydney and Sporting Chronicle, Bell's Life in Victoria and Sporting Chronicle, Bendigo Advertiser, Bexhill-on-Sea Observer, Birmingham Daily Post, Bolton Chronicle, Brighton Gazette, Bury and Norwich Post and Suffolk Herald, Bury Free Press, Cambridge Chronicle and Journal and Huntingdonshire Gazette, Cambridge Daily News, Cambridge Independent Press, Cape Argus, Cricket: A Weekly Record of the Game, The Cricketer, The Critic, Daily Exchange, Daily Express, Daily Mirror, Daily News, Daily Southern Cross, Dundee Courier, Durham Chronicle, Durham County Advertiser, The Era, The Examiner* (Launceston), *Evening News* (Sydney), *Evening Standard, Express and Telegraph* (Adelaide), *Gloucestershire Echo, Hawke's Bay Herald, Huddersfield Chronicle, Huntingdon, Bedford and Peterborough Gazette, Illustrated London News, Illustrated Sporting and Dramatic News, Irish Times, Kentish Gazette, Lancashire Daily Post, Lancashire Evening Post, Leeds Mercury, Leeds Times, Leicester Journal, London Daily News, London Gazette, Manchester Courier and Lancashire Advertiser, Morning Advertiser, Morning Post, Nelson Examiner and New Zealand Chronicle, New York Herald, New York Times, Norwich Mercury, Nottingham Daily Guardian, Nottingham Evening Post, Otago Daily Times, Otago Daily Witness, Pall Mall Gazette, The People, Philadelphia Press, Portsmouth Evening News, Queensland Register, The Register* (Adelaide), *St James's Gazette, Sevenoaks Chronicle and Kentish Advertiser, Sheffield Daily Telegraph, Sheffield Evening Telegraph, Sheffield Independent, Sporting Life, Sportsman, Sydney Mail and New South Wales Advertiser, The Sun* (Kalgoorlie), *Sunday Post, Surrey Comet, Tamworth Herald, Taranaki Herald, Toowoomba Chronicle, Wellington Times* (New South Wales), *West Australian Sunday Times, Western Morning News, Yorkshire Evening Post, Yorkshire Gazette.*

Websites

Cricket Archive, ESPNcricinfo, Measuring Worth.

STATISTICS

Daniel the Elder
Batting and fielding, major matches

Year	M	Inn	NO	HS	Runs	Avg	50s	Ct	St
1832	2	3	-	24	55	18.33	-	-	1
1833	1	1	-	0	0	0.00	-	1	-
1834	2	4	-	8	13	3.25	-	1	2
1836	2	4	-	3	7	1.75	-	1	1
1838	1	2	-	17	17	8.50	-	-	-
1839	1	1	-	43	43	43.00	-	-	2
1841	2	4	-	39	69	17.25	-	1	1
1845	2	4	1	5	14	4.66	-	1	-
1846	2	4	2	21	49	24.50	-	-	-
1847	5	9	1	53	124	15.50	1	3	2
1848	1	2	-	5	7	3.50	-	-	-
1849	2	3	-	14	22	7.33	-	1	-
1851	1	1	-	0	0	0.00	-	-	-
TOT	24	42	4	53	420	11.05	1	9	9

Bowling, major matches (detailed figures not available)

Year	Overs	M	Runs	Wkts	Avg	Best	5wI	10wM
1832-51				5				
TOT				5				

Daniel the Younger
Batting and fielding, major matches

Year	M	Inn	NO	HS	Runs	Avg	100s	50s	Ct
1852	1	1	-	8	8	8.00	-	-	-
1853	1	2	-	22	41	20.50	-	-	1
1854	2	2	-	59	60	30.00	-	1	1
1855	1	2	-	12	23	11.50	-	-	-
1856	1	2	-	4	5	2.50	-	-	-
1859	1	1	-	4	4	4.00	-	-	-
1860	1	2	-	7	12	6.00	-	-	-
1861	4	8	1	20*	69	9.85	-	-	3
1862	5	9	1	22	64	8.00	-	-	-
1863	2	4	-	22	32	8.00	-	-	1
1864	4	7	-	37	83	11.85	-	-	1
1865	4	7	1	19	59	9.83	-	-	2
1866	7	12	2	12*	53	5.30	-	-	6
1867	5	10	3	58*	155	22.14	-	1	3
1868	3	6	-	7	18	3.00	-	-	-
1869	1	2	-	4	4	2.00	-	-	-
TOT	**43**	**77**	**8**	**58***	**690**	**10.00**	**0**	**2**	**18**

There is no record of Daniel bowling in major matches

Thomas
Batting and fielding, major matches

Year	M	Inn	NO	HS	Runs	Avg	100s	50s	Ct
1854	1	1	-	1	1	1.00	-	-	-
1856	1	2	-	10	14	7.00	-	-	-
1857	2	3	-	35	42	14.00	-	-	1
1858	2	3	-	51	55	18.33	-	1	-
1859	8	15	-	68	297	19.80	-	2	6
1860	14	23	2	132	557	26.52	1	2	10
1861	17	30	1	112	838	28.89	2	3	11
1862	14	22	1	117	661	31.47	1	5	8
1863	9	15	1	112*	341	24.35	1	-	5
63/64 Aus	1	2	-	17	18	9.00	-	-	1
1864	8	14	-	66	355	29.58	-	2	7
1865	8	14	1	112	394	30.30	1	1	4
1866	7	12	-	78	312	26.00	-	2	2
1867	7	13	3	55*	300	30.00	-	2	4
1868	4	8	1	84	270	38.57	-	1	1
1869	2	3	-	43	50	16.66	-	-	1
1870	5	8	-	42	67	8.37	-	-	1
1871	6	10	1	45*	205	22.77	-	-	1
1872	2	4	-	9	12	3.00	-	-	-
TOT	**118**	**202**	**11**	**132**	**4789**	**25.33**	**6**	**21**	**63**

Thomas
Bowling, major matches (some scorecards incomplete)

Year	Overs (4 ball)	M	Runs	Wkts	Avg	Best	5wI	10wM
1859				7		5-	1	
1860	313.2	115	423	50	9.40	9-30	5	1
1861	545	157	944	58	16.27	6-47	4	1
1862	387.2	131	644	33	19.51	5-86	1	-
1863	186	69	330	19	22.00	5-32	1	-
63/64 (Aus)	53	22	77	4	19.25	3-38	-	-
1864	92	32	163	14	11.64	6-72	1	-
1865	141	48	264	24	14.66	7-73	3	-
1866	252	98	372	25	14.88	5-35	3	-
1867	155	63	221	14	15.78	4-51	-	-
1868	97	46	159	8	19.87	3-78	-	-
1869	71	31	99	2	49.50	2-99	-	-
1870	21.3	7	60	4	15.00	4-14	-	-
1871	99	37	181	5	36.20	2-61	-	-
TOT	**2413.3**	**856**	**3937**	**267**	**15.14**	**9-30**	**19**	**2**

Tom
Batting and fielding, Test matches

Year	M	Inn	NO	HS	Runs	Avg	100s	50s	Ct
95/96 (SA)	3	4	-	122	189	47.25	1	-	4
1896	2	4	1	13	38	12.66	-	-	2
97/98 (Aus)	5	9	-	72	336	37.33	-	2	2
1899	5	7	1	137	413	68.83	2	1	4
01/02 (Aus)	5	9	-	90	305	33.88	-	2	2
1902	1	2	-	7	7	3.50	-	-	-
03/04 (Aus)	5	9	-	91	321	35.66	-	4	1
1905	5	9	-	82	305	33.88	-	3	3
1907	3	5	-	24	63	12.60	-	-	1
1909	1	2	-	16	22	11.00	-	-	-
TOT	**35**	**60**	**2**	**137**	**1999**	**34.46**	**3**	**12**	**19**

Tom
Bowling, Test matches

Year	Overs	M	Runs	Wkts	Avg	Best	5wI	10wM
95/96 (SA)	9*	4	28	2	14.00	1-0	-	-
1896	13*	3	61	-	-	-	-	-
97/98 (Aus)	53	15	164	4	41.00	2-24	-	-
1899	39*	7	148	3	49.33	2-45	-	-
01/02 (Aus)	45	13	113	5	22.60	4-22	-	-
TOT	**159**	**42**	**514**	**14**	**36.71**	**4-22**	**-**	**-**

(* = five-ball overs)

Tom
Batting and fielding, all first-class matches

Year	M	Inn	NO	HS	Runs	Avg	100s	50s	Ct
1893	13	24	2	112	400	18.18	1	1	11
1894	26	37	4	142	884	26.78	2	-	9
1895	30	43	3	123	1169	29.22	3	6	15
95/96 (SA)	4	6	-	122	277	46.16	1	1	4
1896	34	54	8	229*	1951	34.58	5	4	23
1897	28	39	3	130	1368	38.00	1	8	28
97/98 (Aus)	12	21	3	96	695	38.61	-	5	4
1898	26	38	2	315*	1523	42.30	3	6	13
1899	35	49	4	273	2647	58.82	7	13	27
1900	38	57	7	193	2693	53.86	10	11	33
1901	36	58	8	181	2535	50.70	2	21	47
01/02 (Aus)	11	19	1	174	701	38.94	1	4	5
1902	37	56	3	177	1737	32.77	3	9	21
1903	38	64	3	156*	2177	35.68	3	12	35
03/04 (Aus)	11	17	-	157	785	46.17	2	5	4
1904	36	63	5	203	3170	54.65	11	11	33
1905	36	64	6	129*	2592	44.68	5	18	30
1906	36	61	8	219	3518	66.37	13	17	30
1907	34	58	6	161	2353	45.25	7	12	23
1908	37	52	1	175	2337	45.82	5	16	27
1909	20	37	4	204*	1359	41.18	3	7	13
1910	27	42	1	120	1134	27.65	3	4	12
1911	30	51	6	202	2149	47.75	5	10	14
1912	30	49	5	182	1303	29.61	3	4	10
1913	23	41	2	146	1326	34.00	3	8	9
1914	24	38	1	122	1124	30.37	2	5	13
TOT	**712**	**1138**	**96**	**315***	**43547**	**41.79**	**104**	**218**	**493**

Tom
Bowling, all first-class matches

Year	Overs	M	Runs	Wkts	Avg	Best	5wI	10wM
1893	134*	38	322	10	32.20	2-39	-	-
1894	79*	24	206	11	18.72	3-31	-	-
1895	281.2*	83	663	41	16.17	5-39	1	-
95/96 (SA)	9*	4	28	2	14.00	1-0	-	-
1896	645*	202	1541	91	16.93	7-83	6	-
1897	832.3*	244	2073	114	18.18	7-33	6	1
97/98 (Aus)	195	40	645	15	43.00	5-66	1	-
1898	363.2*	92	1028	30	34.26	4-53	-	-
1899	540.4*	133	1534	67	22.89	7-20	2	1
1900	207.3**	46	687	21	32.71	3-37	-	-
1901	195.5	39	613	30	20.43	8-89	2	-
01/02 (Aus)	74.1	18	208	10	20.80	4-22	-	-
1902	255	39	844	20	42.20	3-35	-	-
1903	48.2	9	172	7	24.57	4-11	-	-
03/04 (Aus)	14	5	27	-	-	-	-	-
1904	102.1	12	421	11	35.27	3-76	-	-
1905	8	1	26	1	26.00	1-21	-	-
1907	1	-	2	-	-	-	-	-
1908	1	-	2	-	-	-	-	-
TOT	3987.1	1029	11042	481	22.95	8-89	18	2

(* = five-ball overs, ** 7 five-ball & 200.3 six-ball overs)

INDEX

Index

Index

INDEX

ALSO FROM CHEQUERED FLAG PUBLISHING

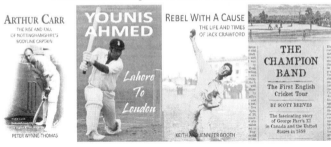

Rebel With A Cause: The Life and Times of Jack Crawford
by Keith and Jennifer Booth

Jack Crawford, described as the greatest ever schoolboy cricketer, blazed into the
Surrey team at the age of seventeen and broke a host of records: the youngest Surrey
centurion and double centurion, the youngest player to achieve the double of 100
wickets and 1,000 runs in a season. He became the youngest cricketer to play for
England and a Wisden Cricketer of the Year.

Yet, not long after his twenty-first birthday, he played the last of his twelve Test
matches. He fell out with the Surrey committee, then with the South Australian
Cricket Association and Otago Cricket Association after moving to play in the
Southern Hemisphere. What went wrong?

Crawford's career raises many questions which have only been partially answered.
Why did he stand up to the Surrey committee? What happened in Australia and New
Zealand? Did he try to dodge the Great War? Was he a bigamist? Now, thanks to
Keith and Jennifer Booth's meticulous research, the truth is fully known.

Arthur Carr: The Rise and Fall of Nottinghamshire's Bodyline Captain
by Peter Wynne-Thomas

When Arthur Carr played his last first-class cricket match in 1934, it was the end
of an impressive career which saw him play for Nottinghamshire for 25 years, lead
England as captain and score 45 centuries.

Yet Carr graced Trent Bridge little in the years after his retirement. The reason? He
was tainted by Bodyline – it was Carr who pioneered Bodyline bowling as the captain
of Nottinghamshire and defended its use after the infamous tour of Australia.

Winner of the County Championship, soldier in the Great War, Wisden Cricketer of
the Year, inspiration for novelist Alec Waugh – Carr was far more than the instigator
of a bowling tactic. Based on years of research, Peter Wynne-Thomas is bringing
this forgotten captain – who could be both inspiring and alienating – back into the
spotlight.

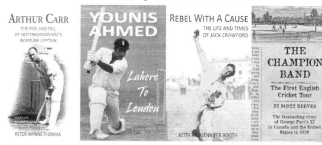

The Champion Band: The First English Cricket Tour
by Scott Reeves

In 1859, twelve cricketers left Liverpool to embark on the first overseas tour by a representative England side. Their destination was the place where cricket looked most likely to flourish: Canada and the United States.

It was not an easy trip - the English players experienced death on the high seas, were threatened at gunpoint and sensed unrest in the pre-Civil War USA.

Led by George Parr, the English tourists came up against the best of the New World cricketers. Some of the locals would go on to pioneer the sport that ultimately caused the death of North American cricket: baseball.

A gripping account featuring original research, THE CHAMPION BAND tells the fascinating story of the first English cricket tour.

Lahore To London
by Younis Ahmed

Younis Ahmed was a talented middle-order batsman who left his native Pakistan to forge a successful career in cricket around the globe. But he is not remembered for his vibrant batting. Instead it is for moments of controversy: an international ban for touring apartheid-era South Africa, taking Surrey to a tribunal, leaving Worcestershire under a cloud. Now Younis tells his side of the story.

Younis also describes winning the County Championship and Quaid-e-Azam Trophy, replacing Garry Sobers at South Australia at the invitation of Don Bradman, pioneering professionalism and sponsorship in cricket, taking the sport to the Middle East and playing alongside legends including Javed Miandad and Imran Khan.

This is the colourful and chequered story of how one cricketer's journey from Lahore to London took him to the top of the game, but also to the depths rejection and despair.

HOWZAT FOR A GREAT CRICKET BOOK?

Chequered Flag
PUBLISHING

www.chequeredflagpublishing.co.uk